Ministry Matters

Ministry Matters

Pastors, Their Life and Work Today

MICHAEL PLEKON

foreword by Tim Vivian

CASCADE *Books* · Eugene, Oregon

MINISTRY MATTERS
Pastors, Their Life and Work Today

Cascade Books
An Imprint of Wipf and Stock Publishers
199 W. 8th Ave., Suite 3
Eugene, OR 97401

www.wipfandstock.com

PAPERBACK ISBN: 978-1-6667-8995-9
HARDCOVER ISBN: 978-1-6667-8996-6
EBOOK ISBN: 978-1-6667-8997-3

Cataloguing-in-Publication data:

Names: Plekon, Michael, 1948–, author. | Vivian, Tim, foreword.

Title: Ministry Matters : pastors, their life and work today / Michael Plekon ; foreword by Tim Vivian.

Description: Eugene, OR : Cascade Books, 2024 | Includes bibliographical references.

Identifiers: ISBN 978-1-6667-8995-9 (paperback) | ISBN 978-1-6667-8996-6 (hardcover) | ISBN 978-1-6667-8997-3 (ebook)

Subjects: LCSH: Pastoral theology.

Classification: BV4164.5 P58 2024 (paperback) | BV4164.5 P58 (ebook)

06/17/24

Contents

Foreword by Tim Vivian | vii

Acknowledgments | xi

Introduction: An Icon of Ministry | xiii

1   Why Examine the Ordained and Their Ministry? | 1

2   George Keith: What Is a Priest/Pastor? | 15

3   Nicholas Afanasiev: The Ministry of All
and the Ministry of Some | 24

4   Cathie Caimano: "Free Range" Priests | 35

5   C. Andrew Doyle, David Barnhart, Andrew Root:
Rethinking the Place and Ministry of the Ordained | 46

6   Sam Wells: Ministry with the Church, Abundant Life | 63

7   Barbara Brown Taylor: Ministry Difficulties and Failures | 72

8   Nadia Bolz-Weber: Pastor on the Edge | 84

9   Sarah Coakley and Rowan Williams: Priests as People
of Prayer and Place-Keepers | 95

10   Henri Nouwen: Ministry in the Name and Model of Jesus | 109

11   Pope Francis: Shepherds "With the Smell of the Sheep" | 120

12   Will Willimon: Pastors from Many Angles | 136

13   The Parish Pastor: The Experience of Ministry, Rites,
and Passages | 154

Bibliography | 167

Foreword

by Tim Vivian

THE REV. DR. MICHAEL PLEKON has served forty years in ordained ministry. He has written numerous articles and books on prayer, spirituality, and theology. In 2021 he did an interview for *Faith and Leadership* on how stories tell us about church,[1] the ugly, the bad, and the good; that year he also published *Community as Church, Church as Community*. He co-edited *The Church Has Left the Building: Faith, Parish, and Ministry in the Twenty-First Century*, published in 2016. In other words, he is one of our foremost thinkers across denominations on church and ministry in these fraught times for the church as a whole. Here, with the work of the late Loren Mead in hand, he re-emphasizes his major earlier theme: "a community of faith cannot be measured in terms of bodies and bucks, status in the community, or stability in operation and management, all accepted goals in the corporate world. Rather, the purpose of a congregation emerges in its traditional scriptural names, such as the 'body of Christ,' the 'people of God,' the fellowship or community of faith (*koinonia*)."

I'm a retired parish priest and served with a resurrecting congregation for ten years. I'm also a scholar whose field is early, not contemporary, Christianity, yet I've profited greatly from Michael's varied works and deeply appreciate this one. Many of the people whom the author presents will be well-known to readers, as they are to me: Barbara Brown Taylor, Nadia Bolz-Weber, Sarah Coakley, Rowan Williams, Henri Nouwen, and others. Many of those here whose work and contributions Michael studies may not be familiar, as they were unfamiliar to me, so I'm grateful to Michael for alerting his audience to these folk (however eminent, they are still folk), who can, if they wish, follow up with their works. Early in the book, he clearly presents his intention and method: "Here, I propose to listen to

---

1. Hicks, "Michael Plekon."

a group of gifted pastor-theologians. . . . Using a method I previously have employed effectively, I want you to listen to these master pastors with me and learn from them. I will act as host and commentator, sharing what I think will be worthwhile responses and connections to their narratives." For me the key sentence here is "I want you to listen to these master pastors *with* me and learn from them" (my emphasis). Rather than dry exegesis or lecture, we have conversation. As he says later, "This is not a prescriptive book. Rather, it is a gathering of reflections from the wealth of experience had by the authors to whom we will listen with my commentary."

I value the double entendre in the book's title, *Ministry Matters*. Yes, ministry does matter—a lot, and not just ordained—and, yes, ministry's matters are and will be of vital importance to those of us who still value church and its community, its many communities. With this conversation I appreciate also the book's thirteen relatively brief chapters; they stay with you more readily than long, complex discussions—they will draw you in, as they did me. One can use a brief chapter as a form of daily lectio, contemplative reading. One of the books I'm reading now is *The Unjust Steward: Wealth, Poverty, and the Church today* (which I highly recommend), by Miguel Escobar, a priest in the Episcopal Church. I use the book as quiet lectio to begin my afternoon reading. This book will also do that.

Each of the chapters here is worthy of reading and re-reading, reflecting on, with further reflection. Then, and very important, application, for yourself and for the church community you benefit and benefit from. To finish, I've chosen one chapter to reflect on with you, chapter 8, "Nadia Bolz-Weber: Pastor on the Edge." I do so because there was a not-so-great schism where I live: the conservatives left the Episcopal Church because they were opposed to full inclusion of LGBTQ+ human beings, and they took all three properties in town with them. Resurrecting the Episcopal Church here, those of us who ministered together for ten years at Grace-St. Paul's ministered on the edge: in greater Bakersfield with its 300,000 people, we were one of only *four* fully inclusive churches, where *all* were welcome. We opened our doors also to the poor and very quickly started a food pantry.

As Michael succinctly puts it, we, like Nadia's, were not "your average middle-class parish"; the community that she was part of "included all those not often welcome in mainstream congregations and even condemned in some church bodies."[2] An intentional ecclesiastical troublemaker, in a rant

---

2. In an honest footnote, and elsewhere in the chapter, Michael expresses some of his reservations about Bolz-Weber.

against folks not like her and her congregation, she learns a lesson vital (as in *vita*, "life") to us all: "She then reflects on how a pastor friend confirms for her that her rage is misplaced and wrong. Why should her congregation of self-styled 'misfits' be privileged over white bread, middle-class folks who come to visit?" Amen. Say it again, sister—and keep saying it, within first, then without. Forever and ever, amen. Scenes like this dramatize the themes of the book and give it additional power. As I used to joke to a clergy friend, now retired, when I sent him my publications, "Sermon material!"

Each chapter in this fine book has numerous passages where we stop, listen, listen again, and learn. I strongly recommend *Ministry Matters* not only to those considering ordained ministry and to seminarians but also to members of church councils, and to parishes and churches doing searches for a new priest, minister, or pastor. In fact, I recommend it to churchgoers who want to better understand the role of their clergy and the clergy's relationship(s) with members of the congregation. And who want to better understand their own ministry. "Repeatedly in her writings," Michael points out, "Bolz-Weber specifies that her work has focused on grace and compassion, a message she offers because she herself continuously needs to hear it." If I were still a parish priest I'd ask our community to make the following our statement of welcome: "We in this community of faith focus on grace and compassion, a message we offer because we ourselves continuously need to hear it."

Tim Vivian is professor emeritus of religious studies at California State University, Bakersfield and a retired priest in the Episcopal Church. In 2018, he received an honorary doctorate of divinity from the Church Divinity School of the Pacific (CDSP, Episcopal) for his scholarship and work for social justice. He has published numerous books, articles, and book reviews on early Christian monasticism, including, with Cistercian Publications, *The Life of Antony, Words to Live By, The Holy Workshop of Virtue, Becoming Fire,* and the two volumes of *The Sayings and Stories of the Desert Fathers and Mothers.*

Acknowledgments

A BOOK IS ONLY POSSIBLE because quite a few people help bring it about. Having been ordained for over forty years, there are a great many people I would like to acknowledge and thank. They helped me to serve all that time. To be exhaustive is not possible, as in sketching out a list, I kept coming up with yet another name. First, my mother and father encouraged me. Jeanne, my wife, has always supported me with her love and strength. Our children likewise endured being pastor's kids and were a blessing.

All the writers, the pastor-theologians to whom we will listen, have also sustained me in ministry. This is why I chose to share their visions here. The first group of people I thank comes from my early experience when I decided to enter the Carmelite Order, striving to be a brother or friar as well as a priest. Of those who were especially important at that time were teachers at the high school preparatory seminary, St. Albert's, in Middletown, New York. Albert Daly stands out for his wisdom and patience. Later, a priest I have written about earlier, Vincent McDonald, opened a window to joy as the heart of serving God and the people of God. Two former fellow friars are still great friends and colleagues in ministry, Jim Hess and Tom Connolly.

I'd also like to recognize the rectors or senior pastors under whom I served for most of my time in ministry, who I have mentioned in other writings, including H. Henry Maertens from my years at Trinity in Brewster, New York, and Alexis Vinogradov from St. Gregory's in Wappingers Falls, New York. In addition, Bishop Seraphim Sigrist, Peter Rustico, and Ken Jetto have been colleagues and friends for many years. I am in debt and grateful to so many other members of these two parishes and the others I have served, especially St. Barnabas.

Another important friend and colleague has been Chris Mietlowski, a parishioner and former student of mine who is now assistant to the bishop of the ELCA Metro NY Synod. Other former interns of mine have influenced me as much or more than I them, particularly Justin Mathews and John Frazier. Nicholas Densysenko has also been a special friend and colleague, as have Laura Brecht, George Keith, David Madsen, and David Frost. Finally, I have been a friend of the New Skete communities for as long as I have been ordained and am grateful to the sisters and brothers there for their hospitality and prayer.

So many other people from the parishes I have served have left their mark with me. I can only mention a few, but behind them are dozens more—Wendy Healy, Gary and Lisa McCarthy, Jeremy Ingpen, John Hotrovich, Joanne Chacolov, Margaret Liggett, Chuck Bennett, Patrick Grannan, Llouise Jee, Diane Johnson, Jan Naragon, Cary Page, Tom and Angela Cassidy, Sherry Harapat, Richard Helvig, and Cathy Gay.

I'd also like to recognize Anastacia Wooden and Tagore Vojnovic; Wooden shared with me her expertise in Afanasiev's work and Vojnovic his gifts in graphic design. Adam DeVille and John Jillions are additional friends and fellow scholars. Peter L. Berger was my doctoral mentor and shaped my vision of church and society as always connected. He was happy when he saw me ordained after completing my degree with him. Charlie Collier and Matt Wimer at Cascade I want to thank for their attention to this book. I am most grateful to Julie Lind for her wonderful gifts of helping the writing here to be the best it can be.

To these and all the rest whose names are too numerous to list, I give my thanks and love.

Michael Plekon
Feast of Saints Peter and Paul 2023

Introduction

An Icon of Ministry

Congregations are shrinking and in decline in the United States and elsewhere. Fewer people are part of communities of faith. Put differently, increasing numbers of people have no congregation or faith tradition, and, as a result, do not regularly attend services. Increasingly, people are "done" with religion in any organized form. Jessica Grose has recently investigated religious "nones" and "dones" in her newsletter in the *New York Times*.[1]

For me, one project of research and writing always leads to another. My previous book, *Community as Church, Church as Community*, traced the factors behind the decline in church attendance, detailing the disappearance of parishioners and closing of parishes as well as the diverse ways that parishes have resurrected and reimagined themselves in response. These stunning efforts have coincided with a revisioning of the connections between church and the wider community, manifest in the repurposing of parish buildings and the replanting of congregations in their larger neighborhoods. None of this could happen through the efforts of pastors alone. It is truly the result of the work of all the people of God, the women and men who gather to pray, learn, enjoy each other's company, and serve their neighbors along with their pastors.

While *Community as Church* describes numerous examples of the essential role that pastors played in the reimagination of church, *Ministry Matters* is a sustained meditation on the vocation, lives, and work of pastors today. It features an ecumenical group of exceptional pastor-theologians who describe how pastors live and serve in our present church and world, in this time of division, suspicion, anger, hate, misinformation, and loss of both faith and community.

1. Grose, "Lots of Americans"; Grose, "Christianity's Got a Branding Problem"; Grose, "Why Do People Lose"; Grose, "Largest and Fastest"; Grose, "What Churches Offer."

The icon on the cover of this book captures much of what is contained within it. By their color and design, icons do not just depict a figure or a scene but have us look at Christ, one of the saints, or a biblical passage in a most elemental way. As a result, some have called icons windows for the sacred to shine in on us. Others call them doorways to the kingdom, maps of how it looks to live the gospel, the good news Jesus brought.

Unlike those of Byzantine and Slavic origin, Ethiopian icons have a very simple, almost primitive quality. One is immediately drawn to the faces in the imagery, especially the eyes. The vivid colors convey that the scene they depict is from our world and yet, at the same time, it takes us somewhere else. The icon on the cover, by an anonymous Ethiopian iconographer, surely fits these descriptions. It brings us into the Last Supper in the Gospel of John (13:1–35) This final gathering, a fellowship meal of Jesus with the disciples, is distinctive in John's narrative. There is no familiar breaking of the bread and sharing it and the cup by Jesus as he utters, "This is my body . . . this is my blood." Rather, after an unusual foot-washing event, which appears only once in the Gospels, a long farewell discourse occupies four chapters.

In the foot-washing scene, Jesus's action is itself an icon, an image of what he is doing and of what his friends, his disciples, will also need to do. It is a radical act of inversion, of turning things upside down. As the rabbi or teacher, Jesus takes on the role of a servant, or, in the ancient world, a slave. He removes his outer robe and puts a towel around his waist. Pouring water into a basin, he then proceeds to wash his disciples' feet. In the Middle East, foot washing was an important act of hospitality, a manifestation of welcome and love. But it would be done by servants, never the head of the house. By performing the action, Rabbi Jesus becomes a servant to his disciples. Almost immediately, Simon Peter, the head of the disciples, protests; it is not as it should be, the teacher lowering himself to the role of servant, slave. He says he will not allow Jesus to do this for him. Jesus responds by saying that Peter clearly does not understand what is happening, but he will later. He adds that if Peter will not allow his feet to be washed, then he will fracture his relationship with Jesus. Jesus then emphasizes what he is doing by saying that if he, the teacher and Lord, has waited upon the disciples, lovingly serving them, then so they also must do for each other and for everyone.

In the passage, it becomes clear that servants are not greater than their masters nor are messengers greater than the one who sends them. A little later, during the last moments he spends with the disciples while alive, Jesus underscores the meaning of the washing of the feet. He stresses that it is an icon of the new commandment that he gave them throughout their time together by healing, teaching, eating with them, and traveling around the countryside: love one another, just as I have loved you, and this is how others will know who you are, my disciples—that you love one another.

In icons of the washing of the feet, the convention is to show the twelve apostles with Peter at the center, receiving the washing. This is not an idealized vision of the apostles or the larger community of disciples who followed Jesus. Most likely, more than just these twelve would have been present at the Last Supper. Other disciples would have been there too. Some may have prepared the meal, but like all of their nightly fellowship suppers, the table would have been open to everyone.

The presence of Judas makes the icon an accurate representation of the way that the church always contains a mixed group of sinners and saints, the exemplary and the weak. The icons of the Ascension and Pentecost likewise depict the disciples together to see Jesus depart and to receive the wind and fire of the Spirit descending on them and the whole world. Always, at the washing of the feet and in other moments, Jesus abides and works through an all-too-human community.

In the book before you, many aspects of the life and work of pastors visible in this icon receive attention. The ministry of the ordained is never theirs by an inherent right that accompanied their selection and the laying on of hands upon them in prayer. They are servants. Their ministry is that of their teacher and master, Jesus. It is a gift for new life in the community and the larger world. It is not primarily about good order in the church nor about the administration of church structures and enforcement of canons or rules. Rather, the work of the ordained remains to love and care for those around them, not just the sheep of their flock but beyond that.

In this respect, pastors are always to be seen in the likeness of the Good Shepherd. They should be like the sheep; they should "smell like them," as Pope Francis says.[2] They will need many gifts and tools—learning, discernment, patience, compassion, humility, and generosity. In the end, though, it will all come down to that new commandment, which is echoed in all the Johannine writings. Pastors are among us to bring God to the people and the people to God. This is what love for God and for the community look like.

---

2. Pope Francis, *With the Smell*, 6–7.

Soon after the foot washing, Jesus is taken into custody while praying in the garden of Gethsemane. The few disciples who he asks to join him cannot stay awake but sleep there until the soldiers come to arrest him. Then, almost all the disciples, minus Judas and John, who is there by the cross, disappear. Out of terror, they hide in Jerusalem. Only after Jesus's terrible death by crucifixion and burial, followed by the moment when the women disciples find an empty tomb, will these fear-paralyzed disciples find the risen Jesus in their midst. They encounter him not because they went out to find him, but because he passed through locked doors and windows to be with them. Neither their fear and absence from Jesus's suffering and death nor their inability to grasp his resurrection, however, mattered. It is their nature to be human beings gripped by fear and inaction.

In this context, the foot washing remains a sign of the ministry of love the disciples were given to serve the world. It was also their initiation into their teacher's work of death and resurrection. As a result, it evokes many aspects of ministry. It shows, for instance, how Christ chooses his ministers. Their desire to follow and serve is preceded by this primary divine action. It also conveys that no one is worthy or equipped for this ministry, no matter their learning, skills, or experience. All those who become Christ's ministers will make mistakes, lose their nerve, and fail because they are the human messengers, witnesses, and servants of Christ.

As teacher, Jesus turns everything upside down, inside out. The kingdom will be brought, he shows, not by the authority of an elite but by the power of love. Despite the ease with which a church institution will be constructed and a hierarchy established, he insists that no servant is greater than the master. The messengers are there to wait on the tables and wash the feet of those invited, not to occupy the best places and first service at the feast. He reminds us that just as he suffered so will all who serve in his example. Those following Jesus in ministry should bring his gifts—forgiveness, healing, and new life—rather than condemnation and punishment.

So much about the church and pastors manifests at the Last Supper, where feet were washed and the bread and cup shared. In his farewell talk, Jesus assured his disciples, along with all pastors who would follow them, that he would always be with them. The Spirit would constantly be present and at work in them. The pastor-theologians to whom we will listen will touch on all these aspects of the foot washing and more, helping us to reflect on who pastors are, how they should live, and what they should be doing for the rest of the people of God and for the world.

I

Why Examine the Ordained and Their Ministry?

Being ordained is not about serving God perfectly, but about serving God visibly, allowing other people to learn whatever they can from watching you fall and rise.

—BARBARA BROWN TAYLOR[1]

LOOKING AT THE ORDAINED IN THE CONGREGATIONS OF TODAY

What you have before you is a book about the ordained and their ministry. Why? Gifted theologian and priest Sarah Coakley has wondered herself about the point of such inquiry, given all we know and the state of things in the world as well as in the church.[2] There was a good bit of material about the ordained and their ministry in my previous book on community as church.[3] There had to be. You cannot seriously look at congregations, at community as church and church as community, without considering pastors. But that study simply did not have the space for extended attention to pastors. Contrary to what members of a parish often think, the church is not all about the clergy. Pastors do not exhaust the meaning of church. The canons and other ecclesiastical codes recognize this, usually requiring

1. Taylor, *Leaving Church*, 37.
2. Coakley, "Prayer, Place and the Poor," 1.
3. Plekon, *Community as Church*. Also see Plekon, *Church Has Left*.

1

the presence of at least one layperson for valid eucharistic liturgy. There are also standards for candidacy to ordination, including membership in the church in which ordination is sought. Further, it is obvious that no matter how one describes a congregation, it is fundamentally a community of faith. Reaffirming this was the aim of my previous book.

In the Christian tradition, ordained ministry is the service of God and the people of God by women and men who have trained for and been discerned to be appropriate as pastors. As the bishop or other ordaining minister lays his hands on the new pastor, he or she is set apart by prayer and by the descent of the Holy Spirit, who is called down for the occasion. Their ministry is essential to the life of a community of faith, which is what the church is, at least as has been claimed through Christian history. In my earlier book, I gathered many examples of congregations in which community showed itself to be the heart of church. These congregations also gave evidence of ordained ministry or service as a source of inspiration and leadership to the local church. Some were seriously threatened by decline, shrinkage, and decaying or underutilized facilities. This is widely the case today, across the many church bodies or denominations in America. It is a truly ecumenical reality.

In my earlier book, I strove to show both how and why this was happening, as others have too, most notably Andrew Root, in a remarkable series of books.[4] But it was not just a diagnosis of closure and loss that I was trying to demonstrate. Since the paschal mystery of Christ's death and resurrection is at the center of the faith and the church, it is not surprising that the book contained numerous cases of parishes rising from death. How this happened varied widely, and the volume offers many different cases to inspect. I also considered the effects of shrinkage and decline on ordained ministry. In this study, however, I will be listening to more constructive, upbuilding understandings of the ordained and the meaning of their work, particularly in a time of decline and change for communities of faith. This is based on the necessary place of pastors in the community of faith in the greater Christian tradition.

A few reviewers of *Community as Church* found the emergence of yoga, art classes, and after-school and daycare programs in underused congregation space to be underwhelming instances of resurrection. Even more, the transformation of entire parishes into commercial or residential

---

4. Root, *Faith Formation*; Root, *Church after Innovation*; Root, *Churches after the Crisis*; Root and Bertrand, *When Church Stops Working*.

spaces were not recognized as happy instances of the enactment of the paschal mystery. On the other hand, most of the examples of parishes I offered looked rather different than commercial or residential takeovers. In some congregations, educational and office rooms that were not used during the week became locations for medical and mental health clinics or spaces for food banks and soup kitchens to feed the hungry. Excess parking space was designated for local gatherings on Sunday afternoons or play spots for young people during the week. Some urban churches rented their space to other not-for-profits and arts groups and events.[5]

Sam Wells, vicar or pastor of St Martin-in-the-Fields in Trafalgar Square, close to the National Gallery in downtown London, who has worked in inner-city ministry and spent years as dean and professor at Duke Divinity School, has written about the repurposing of medieval village churches in the UK. He describes the conversion of church space that had been otherwise vacant all week into after-school and daycare programs, sometimes even cafes. In addition to these newer childcare and café functions, along with the continuation of religious services, at least one building, St. Peter's, one of several churches in a parish in the aptly named English village of Peterchurch, has become the site of a kind of village bazaar where local craftspeople, artists, and others present their work. Each of these new roles that Wells describes connects with the church's earlier historical place at the center of town or city life. As Wells argues, the phenomenon signals a return to a real tradition of the local church's mission. This example links with the argument that Wells has maintained in several publications, that the church exists to give people access to the abundant life that is communion with God and each other. He bucks against the idea of preserving a sort of "spiritual niche," or oasis, for liturgy, sacred images, and space. Rather, as we will hear further on, he pushes for a robust public presence for the local church.

Likewise, late Episcopal priest Loren Mead, who was a specialist in parish life efforts, emphatically argues that the local church of the parish cannot live for itself. After years of working on the instauration and renewal of parishes, he challenged people to come to terms with and accept this essential truth, which differs from the various "church growth" strategies that well-meaning laity and clergy have pursued for decades. For instance, Bill Hybels's Willow Creek and Rick Warren's Saddleback Churches—along with numerous others, some now defunct, like Mars Hill, the troubled

5. Post, "Churches Become Art Hubs." Also see Neuman, "Faithful See."

Hillsong Churches, as well as the Calvary Chapels—were involved in such growth enterprises, where consultants were paid to coach congregations in their own pattern of expansion and success. For Mead, a community of faith cannot be measured in terms of bodies and bucks, status in the community, or stability in operation and management, all accepted goals in the corporate world. Rather, the purpose of a congregation emerges in its traditional scriptural names, such as the "body of Christ," the "people of God," the fellowship or community of faith (*koinonia*). Of the many elements that figure in defining "church" noted by Kara Faris and Tim Shapiro, they cycle back to this emphasis on community.[6]

THE MINISTRY OF ALL, LAITY AND CLERGY

The local church of the parish is a community of the baptized. In baptism, people are consecrated as priests, prophets, and the royalty of the kingdom of God. As the household, the family of God, they continue the life of those who followed Jesus around in his years of preaching and healing. Since, as the Scriptures make clear—for example, the Acts of the Apostles describes the setting apart of deacons to care for widows and orphans while others preach and teach, preside and lead—there is a diversity of ministries, the community acts accordingly. Not all are trained to or capable of preaching, teaching, and administering or caring for those in need. Some are accordingly selected to minister in specific ways; they are set apart by prayer, the laying on of hands, and the gift of the Spirit. Some of those set apart preside and lead. Others preach and teach. Still others reach out and offer material assistance as well as care for those in need.

As described in the first letter of Peter, the church is a house of "living stones," not a building.[7] The people are gathered by the Spirit to Christ and the Father. They hear the Scriptures and listen to them preached by those who have been set apart. With the guidance of these pastors, they share the bread and cup of the Eucharist. Led by a deacon or another trained member, the community lifts up people from their town and neighborhoods in the course of the service; they pray for family and friends by name. They also pray for situations beyond their immediate area, including lands afflicted by war, like Ukraine; situations of drought and famine; and climate change and the exploitation of the environment.

6. Shapiro and Faris, *Divergent Church*.

7. 1 Pet 2:4–6.

Together, the church is more than a conglomeration of reciters of sacred texts and rites; it is more than a gathering to celebrate and pray on Sundays and other days. Congregants take the liturgy they celebrate with them as they leave; it becomes the "liturgy after the liturgy" in their daily lives. They continue the sacrament of the word and table in the "sacrament of the neighbor," the sister and brother in need around them. Their faith may be summarized in the creed they confess at the Eucharist as well as in the Scriptures, however it is brought to life in their love for each other and for those who are their neighbors. Pastors offer further teaching of the Scriptures and how we live out what we believe in daily life. Those same ministers visit the sick, counsel those in turmoil, and serve as witnesses to the gospel in their larger community, along with the rest of the community of faith. This, though safe and traditional, has always been the life of the church, both in the past and today, amid the divisions in our country.

CALLED AND ORDAINED TO SPECIAL MINISTRY

Nicholas Afanasiev was an important figure in the community of Russian émigré scholars in Paris between World War I and II. He was a true polymath, at one and the same time a church historian, New Testament exegete, canon law specialist, and innovative ecclesiologist (or theologian of the church). In addition to all these gifts, he was an experienced pastor. Following his vision of the eucharistic ecclesiology of the early church, evidenced both in the New Testament and in the many authors he looks at as well as the liturgical texts themselves,[8] I have deliberately not split the church into clergy and laity.[9] However, neither is it the case that there is just a congregation with no distinctions. This is clear even in the Gospels, which show the original church as the community of the Teacher, Rabbi Jesus, and his disciples, who would later be his messengers, living out his teachings and spreading them to the whole world. Contrary to fanciful interpretations, Jesus does not set apart and ordain the twelve apostles, who did set apart and ordain others as ministers. Yet in letters that predate the Gospels, Paul speaks of

8. In *The Church of the Holy Spirit*, Afanasiev looks very carefully at what the Acts of the Apostles say of the earliest church communities and ordained ministries within them. Beyond the New Testament, he pays special attention to Hippolytus's *Apostolic Tradition*, Justin Marty's *First Apology*, Irenaeus of Lyon's *Against the Heresies*, Cyril of Jerusalem's *Mystagogical Catecheses*, Dionysius Areopagite's *Ecclesiastical Hierarchy*, and Ignatius of Antioch's *Letter to the Smyrnaeans*, among numerous writers.

9. Afanasiev, *Church of the Holy Spirit*.

his five "coworkers" in ministry, naming married couples Andronicus and Junia,[10] Priscilla and Aquila,[11] along with Phoebe and almost thirty others including Mary, Tryphena, Tryphosa, Persis, Rufus's mother, Julia.[12] Some, like Phoebe, are explicitly called "minister" (*diakonos*), while Andronicus and Junia are "prominent among the apostles" and Priscilla and Aquila are two "who worked with me in Christ Jesus." Timothy is his "coworker" and, in another letter, a "servant," actually "slave" of Christ. Likewise, the Acts of the Apostles describes the setting apart of some to serve as deacons by prayers and the laying on of hands.[13] While the church at Ephesus had an "overseer" (*episkopos*), and while "minister" (*diakonos*) is used frequently, so are beloved sisters/brothers (*adelphoi*). The titles are fluid and vary in the early years of the churches. Nevertheless, some women and men were set apart as leaders, preachers, and teachers of small communities, many of them meeting in someone's home, as in the case of Priscilla and Aquila in Ephesus and Phoebe at Cenchrae near Corinth.

Later, Ignatius of Antioch would begin talking about the bishop as the head of the church in the way that Christ is the ultimate leader. Raymond Brown, one of our era's great New Testament scholars, describes the different arrangements of local church leaders in the earliest days of the church.[14] Only later did the threefold ministries of bishop, presbyter/elder/priest, and deacon emerge. Episcopal bishop C. Andrew Doyle is but one among others wondering how this trio of ministries might better be employed going forward in our century.[15]

ORDAINED MINISTRY TAKES NEW FORMS

Methodist pastor and theologian David Barnhart likewise goes from planting "white steeple" congregations to nurturing a network of house churches named after Paul's coworker, Junia, who was married to another, Andronicus.[16] What David Barnhart describes in St. Junia's Parish is neither a romantic return to the "primitive" church of the earliest days nor a

10. Rom 16:7.

11. Acts 18:2–3, 18, 26; Rom 16:3; 1 Cor 16:19; 2 Tim 4:19.

12. Rom 16:1–2.

13. Acts 6:1–7.

14. Brown, *Churches the Apostles Left*.

15. Doyle, *Vocātio*.

16. Barnhart, "Methodist House Churches"; Worthy, "Pastor Dave Barnhart."

hearkening back to periods of revival now past. As a Methodist, he is in the tradition of the ministry of John Wesley, who, much to the scandal of his fellow priests in the Church of England, preached outdoors to a parish spread over the countryside through which he rode. Both thinking back to the early church and looking forward, he encouraged his clergy to be itinerant, "circuit-riding" ministers. Likewise, he urged the organization of small groups to study the Scriptures, pray, provide mutual encouragement, and to celebrate the sacraments when a minister was available.

Similarly, Episcopal priest Cathie Caimano calls herself a "free range priest."[17] In her blog, from which we will hear more, she describes how, going forward, pastors can function more faithfully when they care for congregations to which they are not financially dependent, which enables them to do other work. As described in my earlier book, whether one classifies such "tent-making" ministry in the model of Paul or considers it "ministry alongside" another profession or the role of "worker priests," the dissolution of a financial relationship between the ordained minister and a congregation seems to be a more normal feature of parish life as we move into the twenty-first century. The variations on this include clergy who serve in a team, "covering" several particular churches. This is a widespread model in the UK, as the weekly posting of parish positions in the *Church Times* indicates. It is also a model among US denominations, often in rural areas. For instance, a contemporary "circuit-riding" clergy team who happen to be married to each other, Pastors Jason and Jess Felici, cares for five congregations in the Lutheran Mountain Parish in West Virginia.[18] In yet another example of adaptation, Justin Mathews, a priest of the Orthodox Church in America (OCA), is both canonically attached to a local Kansas City parish and director of Reconciliation Services, a collection of outreach services and activities that began as a ministry.[19] When the parish went its own way, Reconciliation Services continued to be a twenty-first-century version of a community of faith in action. While not canonically or formally a parish—Father Justin is not appointed as priest there—there is nevertheless prayer; the feeding of people; and counseling, medical care, and more. In spite of his lack of a formal title, it is clear that Father Justin *is* the priest, the pastor of Reconciliation Services.

17. See https://freerangepriest.org/#blog.

18. Plekon, *Community as Church*, 178–79.

19. Plekon, *Community as Church*, 171–76. See also Plekon, "Holy Tables"; Hicks, "Michael Plekon."

The seemingly new "version" of church exemplified through ministers such as Father Justin is actually quite ancient. St. Basil the Great had a multipurpose facility in Caesarea, which is located in Cappadocia in Asia Minor, now Turkey. Called the Basiliad, the conglomeration consisted of a hospital, hospice, orphanage, shelter, and soup kitchen, along with the church where services were held. Basil would often be found serving people in the dining rooms. There were also diaconal centers in Rome, locations that provided similar ministry to those in need alongside regular liturgical services. Clearly, the dedication of religious communities to care for those suffering and in need has been a staple of Christian life both in the East and the West. Even today, many hospitals retain in their names their original church or religious roots.

No matter what variations are present today, the ministry of the ordained is simultaneously in continuity with the beginnings of the church and constantly evolving. Purists may abhor the latter characterization, but the historical record witnesses the development of different forms over the centuries as the core of ministry remains constant. It is a tradition that is both unchanging and ever-changing, as is the movement of the Holy Spirit and the presence of Christ, gathering us to the Father.

THE ORDAINED AND LAITY MINISTER TOGETHER

At the outset, I want to make clear that the point of view here is that ministry is the calling of the entire church, of every baptized member of the people of God. If it can be said that in the last century or more there has been a "rediscovery" of the meaning of "church," it is precisely that we are all sent out to "proclaim the Gospel, using words if necessary," in the saying attributed to Francis of Assisi. The actions and words of Jesus and his disciples in the Scriptures make clear that following him creates a community, making church a communal reality, as argued in my previous book. In that context, this book aims to understand the decline and shrinkage of actual communities of faith, congregations. If there is any way in which to interpret what is happening to congregations in our time, and for that matter, in earlier periods, however, it has to be considered in the context of the very core of the faith: the paschal mystery of Jesus's death and resurrection, the saving acts that are reflected in baptism and the Eucharist.

This book is the product of research I gathered over several years of accounts of parishes confronting their current existence. Some had gone past the point of reviving. Some simply closed and ceased to exist. Others, however, found ways of reinventing themselves, of repurposing their buildings, replanting themselves in their neighborhoods, and renewing their purpose by becoming the home of a more contemporary congregation or the location of new ministry with fresh ways of serving sisters and brothers in need, as I have indicated. To provide another example, Redeemer Lutheran Church in North Minneapolis acquired an almost adjacent block of buildings with commercial space downstairs and residential space on the second floor. Opening these spaces to commercial and residential tenants revived the neighborhood, as did the use of parking lots for food trucks so that the neighborhood could enjoy meals together. Meanwhile, Bethesda United Methodist Church in Haw Creek, North Carolina, repurposed educational and office space that had been unused during the week to create the Haw Creek Commons, which held art and yoga classes and clinics.[20] Likewise, Oakland's First Christian Church offered its massive parish center, which had been vacant much of the time, to numerous not-for-profit groups in the city with the hope that they would facilitate repair and maintenance of the space as it became a vital location for a variety of community services.[21] Another North Carolina parish, Carr United Methodist Church in East Durham, had been in the process of closing when it became the home of a Zimbabwean congregation, Shepherd's House Methodist Church. This new parish began to conduct much of the Sunday service in English, not only helping members with language skills but also welcoming non-Zimbabweans and the former congregation's members, integrating previously non-associated people.[22] The Borrego Ministers Association in Borrego Springs, California, and the Welcome Ministry of El Cajon, California, are two other cases I know of where otherwise unconnected people—including Anglos and Latinos, refugees and local residents, and laity and clergy of different faith traditions—encounter each other and benefit from new relationships.

CHALLENGES AND CHANGE FOR PASTORS

In spite of the diversity of examples I have gathered of resurrected congregations, the trend in decline, shrinkage, and closing continues, exacerbated

20. Plekon, *Community as Church*, 68–69.

21. Plekon, *Community as Church*, 75–76.

22. Plekon, *Community as Church*, 52–53.

by the pandemic, which has taken its toll on the lives of many parishes.[23] Estimates are that up to one-third of members have been lost in the aftermath of the pandemic, along with other changes tracked by the Hartford Institute for Religion Research.[24] Likewise, emerging data suggests that as part of the "Great Resignation," there is a steady exodus from ordained ministry. Edie Gross profiles several pastors, women and men, who confronted the stress ministry placed upon them and their different paths toward redefining their callings, including the departure from ordained ministry and subsequent return to lay status.[25] There is also a movement away from parish ministry toward what some church bodies call "special ministry" in hospitals, schools, social service, and education. A Barna Group survey found that 38 percent of clergy were considering leaving.[26]

Given this context, Eileen Campbell-Reid calls the post-pandemic clergy situation "a new era of ministry."[27] Data from the Episcopal Church Pension Group reported that 14 percent of Episcopal clergy are now "specialty ministers," meaning they do not fit the conventional model of a priest hired by and working solely for a particular parish.[28] This connects to the vocation of Cathie Caimano's earlier noted "free range priest."[29] All told, 56 percent of Episcopal clergy are now in what Caimano calls the "emerging model," which comprises part-time parish priests with some employment outside of the congregation. Their work goes beyond the traditional tasks of ordained ministry, including professions like law, social work, education, consultant services, and more. For all of my forty years of ordained ministry, for example, I had a consistent "day job" as a university professor, teaching mostly undergraduates, doing research, writing, publishing, and presenting papers at professional meetings. The corresponding reality is that parishes are increasingly unable to financially support full-time pastoral ministry. Hence the team ministry approach noted, as well as the increase in "free range" or "specialty ministers."

---

23. See Grose, "Christianity's Got a Branding Problem." See also Bullivant, *Nonverts.*

24. Harvard Institute for Religion Research, "Navigating the Pandemic."

25. Gross, "Great Resignation."

26. Barna Group, "38% of U.S. Pastors."

27. Miller and Banks, "#Pandemic Pastoring."

28. Church Pension Group, "Trends in Ministry," 18:23, 21:29; cf. Church Pension Group, Research and Data Team, "Trends in Ministry"; Church Pension Group, *2020 Episcopal Clergy.*

29. Caimano, "Church Stats."

All this said, no one argues that the time of ordained clergy is past or that ministry is priced out of feasibility, perhaps no longer as necessary due to growing lay leadership and service in congregations. This brings us to the point of this book. It is my aim to reflect at length on what ordained ministry is for; echoing Loren Mead, I aim to show that neither pastors nor parishes can exist just for themselves. They have to have reasons for being and doing that are rooted beyond them, beyond a congregation of just one church body, beyond the tasks of a pastor as parish leaders may envision them; they have to be rooted in the Spirit, in the larger community. This appears straightforward, but as far as I can tell, it is not. Not only has the local church of the parish changed significantly, but this pattern of change will continue despite efforts to merely grow a congregation's membership and finances. The trend, which is inevitable, is in completely the opposite direction. As this century progresses, congregations will continue to shrink and church bodies will continue to decline despite the anomalies of some large non-denominational churches. The essential functions or purpose of ordained ministry, in my view, remain the same.

Still, the meaning and enactment of ordained ministry are worth serious examination, going back to the origins and subsequent development. Ordained service is also a subject for real debate and discussion. To do so, it is necessary to see what ordained ministry looks like, which will entail looking at what the ordained do and what, perhaps, they no longer need to do. In turn, this leads to how pastors relate to their congregations. Are they leaders as well as companions, part of the whole people of God? How do pastors relate to the larger community beyond their congregation, to the world? And, what about the pastor her/himself? What is necessary in caring for oneself as a pastor?

LISTENING TO PASTOR-THEOLOGIANS

During such reflection, it will be useful to listen to clergy who have written eloquently about their often extremely difficult and painful experience in ministry. Some of this has already been done in a collection I edited, *The Church Has Left the Building*, in my previous book, *Community as Church, Church as Community*, as well as in other projects I have put together. Here, I propose to listen to a group of gifted pastor-theologians, several of whom I have already mentioned. Using a method I previously have employed effectively, I want you to listen to these master pastors with me and learn from them. I will act as host and commentator, sharing what I think will be worthwhile responses and connections to their narratives.

We will hear from George Keith, Nicholas Afanasiev, Cathie Caimano, C. Andrew Doyle, David Barnhart, Andrew Root, Sam Wells, Barbara Brown Taylor, Nadia Bolz-Weber, Sarah Coakley, Rowan Williams, Henri Nouwen, Pope Francis, and Will Willimon. This is an ecumenical, diverse group of figures who represent many traditions: Roman Catholic, Eastern Orthodox, Episcopal, and Methodist, among others. All are themselves ordained and have served in congregations or in other venues. Of course, there are many others to whom we could listen, but the Mies van der Rohe adage is, I think, wise: "Less is more." Not only that, but given the breadth (and depth) of the women and men just mentioned, their experience in ministry and discernment, the result will be rewarding. I will also draw on my own forty years of experience in ordained ministry, bringing the lessons I have been taught by friends and colleagues in pastoral service.

This is not a prescriptive book. Rather, it is a gathering of reflections from the wealth of experience had by the authors to whom we will listen with my commentary. Neither is this a "recipe" or "how to pastor" guide. I am not aiming to detail what pastors should do, though from what is said, there will be implications for that, as well as for what they should not do. If I had to say what you, as a reader, will receive, it would be this: a set of rich reflections on who a pastor is, which will necessarily entail what a pastor does. What this book offers can be summarized in a wonderful statement I heard in a sermon by George Keith and will examine more fully in the next chapter: "What is a priest? Someone who takes God to the people and the people to God."[30]

AN ECUMENICAL LISTENING AND REFLECTION

There are a number of names or titles for the ordained. The already referred to New Testament letters speak of those involved in *diakonia*, which is "ministry" or "service." Hence the term "ministers." There are also references to specific ministries, such as those of teacher, evangelists, and those caring for the everyday needs of widows and the poor. There is also the *episkopos*, an overseer or superintendent, the frequent version of which has historically been the bishop. Elders or presbyters (*presbyteroi*) are mentioned in addition. From this as well as from other titles, like the rarely

30. See chapter 2, "George Keith: What Is a Priest?"

used *hierus*, comes "priest." In the history of the Christian churches, all of these titles—as well as others like archbishop, metropolitan (bishop), dean, archdeacon, among others—have been used. During the Reformation, however, some churches distanced themselves, as some do today, from titles like bishop and priest, considering pastor and deacon to be more biblical. Anti-Catholic sentiment also came into play, plus the theological rejection of anything resembling "sacrifice" in the Eucharist. Sacrifice, however, has been offered by priests both in Judaism and other traditions. Priesthood was mandated in the Torah, where the details of vestments, purification and ordination rites, and liturgical responsibilities are laid out in detail. The Anglican, Methodist, Scandinavian, some other Lutheran Churches, and, of course, the Catholic and Orthodox Churches never stopped using the titles of bishop and priest.

Here, several of these titles will be employed without theological interpretation or preference. That is, minister/pastor/priest will be used as functionally synonymous. Less will be said about the particular roles of bishop and deacon. Bishops are, regardless of denominational differences, for the most part regional pastors without congregations. Though in some church bodies they do serve congregations, they often have other clergy perform day-to-day pastoral activities. While deacons do largely serve congregations, they do so under and with pastors.

This look at ordained ministry is deliberately ecumenical, not restricted to a particular church body. The intention is to follow what is called the "Catholic" or universal tradition. Of course, from the very beginnings of the church, there have always been local differences. For all the theological differences, there remains, however, a still recognizable common tradition about what ordained ministry looks like. Also, despite differing theological and church perspectives, here it is assumed that both women and men can be set apart and ordained. Ministry is, by definition, personal. It is a call heard by a person. It must be acknowledged and extended by the community to a person, with the Spirit's descent through the laying on of hands. It will be assumed here that there are no obstacles to such ministry on the basis of sexual identity, race or ethnicity, which, along with gender, have been historical impediments to ordination, along with other factors such as illegitimacy and age.

WHAT YOU WILL LEARN

Who will benefit from what follows in this book? I must confess that some of the difficult, painful experiences I have had as a priest, which have been based on how the institutional church dealt with me and others I have known, made me pause for some time in starting to work on this book. One particularly challenging confrontation came from being marginalized upon retirement. At first, this felt like a kind of punishment for past actions and positions not favored by ecclesiastical authority. It is one thing to be retired from regular active ministry. It is another to be deprived of the ability to preach, preside, and offer pastoral care. This situation thankfully changed. I was welcomed elsewhere and invited to continue to contribute as a priest, an unexpected gift of graciousness and hospitality.

However, what most urged me to do the work here was the listening, as in *lectio divina*, to voices I had heard and heeded before. These are what I offer to you above all else. By revisiting these true teachers of pastoral service in writing, I again learned much. I again saw that despite, or even perhaps because of, the division in our society and the challenge of shrinkage and decline in our congregations, pastoral leadership is all the more important.

Finally, pastors need pastors themselves. That is what this volume provides from exemplary mothers and fathers in the practice of pastoral ministry. I think that those serving in ministry will find much that is valuable from them, as will those in formation for ordination, and, for that matter, the rest of the people of God living out the gospel in their everyday existence, walking the path of dying and rising. If *Community as Church* offered something of worth, it is my hope that the same will be the case for this reflection on ministry matters and that ministry matters.

2

George Keith

What Is a Priest/Pastor?

What is a priest? Someone who takes God to the people
and the people to God.

—GEORGE KEITH[1]

LISTENING TO GEORGE KEITH

As the above epigraph indicates, George Keith, a good friend of mine
who was a priest for almost forty years and also studied and taught drama
and acting, is not only a discerning preacher, but he is also exceedingly
compassionate. Over the years, I have seen him listening to troubled folk
and greeting everyone both as they come into and as they leave church. He
knows what it is to be a priest not because he is a professional theologian,
but because he realizes what he preaches in his works. He exemplifies what
it means to bring God to the people and the people to God.

Alongside his vocation as a priest, George has nurtured his relationship with people in his work in theater. He has been an actor in and director
of numerous stage productions. He also worked for the national church
in the 1980s with the task of presenting the new hymnal to congregations. Anyone who has experienced a new prayerbook or hymnal knows
the often-hostile reaction to anything new when it comes to worship and

1. Quote is taken from a sermon given at St. Barnabas Church, Borrego Springs, CA,
March 27, 2022.

singing. Yet George was perfect for this thankless task. He also excelled in team ministry in two historic churches yoked as a parish in New York City and as principal, and later parish rector, of a large parish school on the West Coast.

Of all of the bishops and pastors I have encountered in the forty years I have been gifted of ordained service, George stands out among the extraordinary servants of both God and the people of God. In more autobiographical passages I have written, I have brought forward several others who have taught me, shaped my ministry, and even ministered to me. Two such mentors were my first rector, H. Henry Maertens, and my longest rector, Alexis Vinogradov. In addition to them, I can go all the way back to my time as a student friar in the Carmelites and recall exemplary priests like Vincent McDonald and Albert Daly, among others.[2]

One line does not a great sermon make, though, and in the sermon I cited above, George Keith goes on to note several other elements of ordained ministry. I start this project with him because, in ways, his above description of ordained ministry is the most fundamental I know. He recalls how at the start of his priestly work, he, and most newly ordained, were sure they knew what the church needed and that they could deliver it. Is that the thrill of receiving the Spirit, the energy of being ordained, or the foolishness of the newbie?

PASTORS AND THE MESS THAT IS THE CHURCH

As Keith later explains, however, time and humility taught him—and all the rest of us—otherwise. Only in time, he shows, do those set apart by the laying on of hands and the Spirit come to see that Christ is the real head and that the church is Christ's body. Put another way, this means coming to realize that the pastor serves best by being aware that she or he is not the savior. Christ is. In effect, celebrity pastors like Carl Lentz of Hillsong have shown just how human, weak, and failing they are, despite their high-profile connections with entertainment notables. In addition, Lentz and others came to admit their own misdeeds, long hidden behind the hype of being extraordinary leaders.[3] Even those in leadership positions, such as

2. Plekon, *Saints as They Really Are*, 105–50. Also see Plekon, *World as Sacrament*, 1–13, 233–52; Plekon, *Uncommon Prayer*, 95–119, 168–221.

3. Becker, "Hillsong Was Extraordinary."

bishops and church administrative staff, do not know better than the ragtag motley crew of local pastors and their people.

There is truth, however, in that the church is not an organization obliged to maintain itself and enhance its growth. Church is a sacrament. We encounter life and strength in the ordinary activity of being church. All the elements are there—the bread, the cup, the water and prayer, the presider and the preacher, the word of God speaking, and the assembly that celebrates together with them and the Father, who is praised and thanked through the Son, Christ, and in and through the power of the Spirit. It is most inaccurate to either underestimate or ignore any of the elements, the parts, of the body. Nonetheless, whether the local church of the parish or that of a regional grouping such as a diocese, conference, presbytery, or, for that matter, an organization at the national or denominational level, the church is never wholly right or wise in its thinking or action. Nor is it ever just a well-structured and governed social institution. Rather, as George Keith reminds us, the church has always been a glorious, wonderful mess that comprises both the divine and the human. The human component makes it interesting, beautiful, complicated, distorted, as well as trouble-some. Though rooted in the Scriptures and tradition, church is thereby chaotic, often changing. In this beautiful mess, we count on priests and pastors for guidance as well as comfort. They are a bridge between us and God, expressing both our need and God's generosity.

The needs of the people of God that the pastor comes to know and communicate with God are massive. What is more, the ordained also are needful, as is the world beyond the congregation. All of us are in need, all the time. The needs of everyone that come together in the church are diverse and reflect a world in which disagreement and argument are rife. It seems a miracle that they all come together on Sunday, but this has always been the case in the church. There is nothing recent or new about it.

There it is. In the church, there is something "totally other" in God's essence. It is a miracle that God chooses to abide or "pitch his tent" among us, or, as Eugene Peterson says in his translation of the Scriptures, *The Message*, "to move into the neighborhood."[4] This allows us to draw near to, or become intimate with, God. In so doing, we miraculously become closer to each other.

Focusing on the role of the priest to bring God to us and us to God, in his sermon George Keith suggests that Archbishop Desmond Tutu remains

4. Peterson, *Message*, John 1:14 (p. 1455).

a model of faithful ministry, of what a pastor looks like, says, and does. There are also many others, as Andrew Root and Samuel Wells have pointed out.[5] All the way from Paul the apostle to Augustine, Thomas Becket, Martin Luther King Jr., and Pauli Murray, the procession of remarkable holy pastors is long. Some who could not be ordained in their days also belong here, like Hildegard of Bingen, Teresa of Avila, and Julian of Norwich.

MINISTRY IS NECESSARY, PERSONAL, AND COMMUNAL

In his focus on the priest as a bridge between God and the people, Keith emphasizes that for all the weaknesses and failures of the ordained, they are necessary for the people of God and the whole of the church. The image of the shepherd here comes to mind, a trope that predates its memorable usage by Jesus. The sheep need the shepherd and the herding dogs to keep them safe, to get them to food and water. In turn, the shepherd also needs them, an aspect to which we seldom pay attention. The flock are the shepherd's livelihood, the reason for being a shepherd in the first place. The reciprocal relationship between them reveals the core of both ministry and church. In this context, as Nicholas Afanasiev argues, the church should not only live by the power of law, status, office, or hierarchy. From the perspective of the Scriptures, the only law, the only rule, he maintains, is that of love.[6] Tragically, we have come to regard church canons and constitutions as the necessary force that must be imposed, the fences that keep us orderly. We have also come to regard church leaders, bishops, other ordained ministers as authority figures who must be obeyed, placated, flattered, and kept happy.

Only by the power of love, rooted in God's own self-emptying capacity that is described throughout the Scriptures, can the church and ministry work. Examples of this love abound in the psalms and in encounters with Abraham and Sarah, David and Elijah, John the Baptist, and the Virgin Mary, reminding us that God is not the monarch to be feared and heeded, nor is God the wrathful judge. Rather than the almighty adversary prominent in the consciousness of many religious folk and pushed by some preachers, God is more the loving parent, spouse, sister, or brother, giving everything necessary, waiting patiently, welcoming back the prodigal daughters and sons, as well as supporting the faithful friends who are always there. If the priest or pastor is rightly called a "man" or a "woman of God," then what

---

5. Root, *Pastor in a Secular Age*, 3–152; Wells, *Incarnational Ministry*.

6. Afanasiev, *Church of the Holy Spirit*, 255–76.

is good for God must be good, applicable, to the one who herds, feeds, and even gives their life for the flock.

In his sermon, George also notes that while there is much in the history and the theology of ministry, all the descriptions and analyses of this life and work only underscore that it is at root *personal*. When a pastor retires or otherwise leaves a congregation, a congregation faces the inevitable challenge of getting used to another pastor who will come to preach, administer the sacraments, teach, counsel, and encourage and support the community. The strengths and gifts of each will be distinctive, as will the failings and defects. The longer they serve, the more pastors realize that what some congregation members love about them will be precisely what others dislike. Comparisons will always be made, whether with pastors of one's childhood and youth or with the predecessor whose place is being filled. However, every pastor will have her or his own way of doing ministry. The sense of humor of one will not be there in another, but there might be more sensitivity and patience. This diversity is necessary. Just as God deals with each of us as a unique and irreplaceable individual, it is no different with every pastor. Each is a unique builder of the bridge between the people and God and between God and the people.

In this sense, the ministry of the ordained is personal, as we will hear over and over, shaped not only by formation but also by the personality, gifts, and weaknesses of the individual. In addition, another human element of ministry is its communal essence. This too will become a familiar refrain. The clergy should not be put above or at distance from the congregation. Priests are not some "other" being. They too are members of the body of Christ. They share the same baptismal priesthood as all the rest. It is *for* the people of God that pastors are discerned by both laity and clergy as appropriate for ministry, trained, mentored, and ordained to perform it. They become part of a community of ministry, a fellowship of pastors.

Though clergy wear vestments to remind us that our worship is no mere business meeting but the liturgy of the kingdom of heaven, so too that vesture, even the street version, makes all clergy appear to be equal, part of the same group. Though in some traditions there is no clerical dress and in others bishops wear different colors than priests and deacons, if the clothes don't make this unifying point, then maybe the similar titles do—reverend, pastor, mother or father. Further, at ordinations, the one ordaining is usually joined by other ordained clergy in the laying on of hands and the celebration of the rest of the service, usually the Eucharist.

As this emphasizes, there is a community of the clergy that, though not better than the laity, is distinctive in the work for which they are ordained.

Although it might seem that a lot has already been said about George's seemingly simple line—the priest is one who brings God to the people and the people to God—a great deal can still be discussed. Even before we have heard from the other writers, George's compact description holds its own. The truth of it will not have been diminished by the time we reach the end of this book. Thus, it is an apt summary of all that will be heard here.

Nevertheless, George certainly did not stop at that great line with which we began this chapter. He directed us to think about the personal, communal, and transcendent aspects of the ordained and their ministry. In particular, the transcendent is often overlooked or taken for granted. I used that term rather than "spiritual," because it evokes the reality that ministry, for all the humanity involved, is also divine, as made clear in the prayers of the ordination rite. The ordaining bishop or minister asks for the Spirit to come down to the one being ordained to give the new priest the grace and power to do the work of ministry. In some rites, an ancient hymn, "*Veni Sancte Spiritus*" ("Come Holy Spirit"), is sung just before the prayers of ordination and the laying on of hands. The physical imposing of hands on the head of the ordained, both by the principal ordainer and others, is a human action done with the knowledge that the Spirit is acting in and with the sense of touch. Words and touch are the outward human signs; the Spirit brings the *dynamis* or power of God for the work of ministry, which includes preaching, teaching, presiding at the Eucharist, counseling, comforting, baptizing, blessing marriage, anointing the sick, and burying the dead. These are all human acts, things said and done by the priest. At the same time, God is acting through this ordained person, as John Chrysostom describes as Christ using the hands, voice, eyes, ears, and heart of the priest.[7] In effect, George Keith wanted to make sure in his preaching that those hearing him did not forget the presence and power of the divine, of God, in the priest. Though all of the priest's works are ministry, God is what the ministry of the ordained is mostly about.

While much of ordained ministry can be described in terms of instruction, fostering interpersonal connections, and therapeutic work, it also goes beyond these categories. Over the centuries, the formation process has identified various aspects of pastoral ministry for which training is necessary. At the start, a candidate learned these from a mentor, a pastor

---

7. Chrysostom, *On the Priesthood*, 72–73.

they served as an apprentice. However, it soon became clear that academic preparation was also necessary, at least for some clergy. After the schools of rhetoric and philosophy in the ancient period, cathedral and monastery schools became the locations for the study of languages, the Scriptures, the liturgical texts, the writings of great teachers, as well as allied disciplines such as history, law, politics, and even rudiments of management and healing. The manuals prepared by Gregory the Great and Ambrose emphasize the necessary tools of ministry and areas of study.[8]

MINISTRY IS SACRED, TRANSCENDENT

The transcendent dimension of the ministry of the ordained has been recognized throughout the history of the pastoral education outlined above. Beyond the management of a parish or even the care of members in need, the reason for preaching and studying the Scriptures, as George Keith reminds us, is taking God to the people and the people to God. This is what happens in all of the sacraments and, most especially, in the gathering of the community to give thanks, break the bread, and share the cup as they receive the body and blood of the Lord. As Augustine said, "Be what you see, and receive what you are. That's what the apostle said about the bread."[9]

The ministry of the ordained is thus not just about leading the congregation and consoling the troubled and grieving. It is not just about communicating and interpreting Jesus's teachings or about sustaining and growing a congregation. In the Hebrew Bible as well as in the early chapters of the Christian New Testament, the priest is the one to enter the sacred space, bringing the prayers of all and offering their sacrifices; the priest then brings God with him or her back to the assembly. The blessing of Aaron and the Levitical priesthood with extended arms, the many times the patriarchs blessed their children, the words of blessing at the conclusions of the apostolic letters, and the blessings the celebrant makes over the worshippers at the end of the service are all the choreography of going to the people with God and returning the congregation to God. By bringing the people back into communion with God, the priest also brings them back into communion with each other. In addition to those listed above, many other moments in the Christian tradition enact this core encounter—the washing in baptism, the anointings of the newly baptized and the ill, and

8. Gregory the Great, *Book of Pastoral Rule*; Ambrose of Milan, *On the Duties*.

9. St. Augustine, "Sermon 272," para. 2.

the sharing of the bread and cup. In each, God is brought to the people and the people are brought to God.

Although in certain historical periods, notably the Reformation, there has been a type of allergic reaction to certain sacred objects or gestures, the one who proclaims and then preaches the word, sums up the prayers of the assembly, and repeats the Lord's words at communion has remained a holy figure. This is not a matter of personal sanctity or purity. Rather, the very tasks performed by the priest are holy. In both the Eastern Church and in some Western rites, before communion the following invitation is proclaimed: "Holy things for the holy. . . . The gifts of God for the people of God." Thus, many prayers of ordination acknowledge that the candidate on whom hands are laid will receive the called-for Holy Spirit and be set apart for the ministry of Christ in and with the people of God.[10]

In the chapters that follow, the pastor-theologians I have brought together will discuss this other dimension, the transcendent or divine aspect of ordained ministry. As almost all of them are ordained and have ministered in the church, they know what it is to bring God to those around them and those people to God. Throughout their discussions, we will hear several different experiences and visions of the ministry of the ordained that will help clarify what it is about and what it requires.

In his emphasis on the relationship between God and the people, George Keith insists on the enduring, necessary connection between the clergy and the rest of the congregation. Put another way, he sees the roots of ordained ministry in the community that is the church, a view we will hear echoed in the following pages. We will also hear that the pastor must be a person of prayer, alert and open to the Spirit, while also completing the necessary mundane tasks associated with the congregation.

I once heard at an ordination service that perhaps in addition to vestments, a stole, Bible, and liturgy book, the newly ordained should be given a toilet brush and broom. I suppose a complete pastoral toolbox would also have to contain keys, a computer and cell phone, addresses and phone numbers, and many more very ordinary items essential to leading and communicating with a parish. These items signal that though ministry may begin with sacred communion vessels, it extends to the very ordinary apparatus of everyday life.

Nowadays, the candidate for ordination brings the results of a psychological evaluation, recommendation letters, the reports of discernment

10. See, for example, *The Book of Common Prayer*, 531–34.

panels, a seminary transcript, and a certifying letter from a bishop or other church head. However necessary these are, they also bring something even more important: a heart open to God and to God's people, as well as a willingness to listen and to speak from God's mind and heart. Finally, many bring a family and partner willing to accompany them in the awesome, sometimes terrifying work of being a shepherd in the manner of the Great Shepherd.

3

Nicholas Afanasiev

The Ministry of All and the Ministry of Some

NICHOLAS AFANASIEV, A SCHOLAR, A PRIEST

Of all the voices to which we listen in this book, that of priest and scholar Nicholas Afanasiev (1893–1966) is distinctive. Afanasiev taught at St. Sergius Orthodox Theological Institute in Paris for most of his adult life. During WWII he was asked by his bishop to serve as rector of a small parish in Tunisia, where he became stranded until the war's end. In spite of the war, his time there was a transformative pastoral experience for him, marked by grace. After his death, his wife recalled that he became pastor to everyone in the town, whether they were Christian, Muslim, or nonbeliever.[1] In some ways, the war's isolation of both Afanasiev as a priest and of the parish and town provides a glimpse into the experience of local congregations in the earliest days of the church, which Afanasiev would use as the basis for the important work that he began while there, *The Church of the Holy Spirit*.[2] A remarkable scholar, Afanasiev's influence is still felt in ecclesiology and ecumenical theology today. He was also lovingly known as Father Nicholas, one with the heart of a pastor. It is for both of these aspects of his identity that we listen to him here.

I have written about Afanasiev and his book, a major contribution in recovering the eucharistic ecclesiology of the first centuries of the church,

1. Afanassieff, "Genèse," 12–23.

2. Afanasiev, *Church of the Holy Spirit*.

24

and I have also benefitted greatly from the research and writing of Viktor Alexandrov and Anastacia Wooden, the two leading Afanasiev scholars at present. Having served as advisor of Wooden's doctoral dissertation committee, here I draw on her work.[3] When published, her study on Afanasiev will become the standard; her dissertation is nearly encyclopedic in comprehensiveness.

Afanasiev ended up in Paris after his first exile from the Russian Revolution in Belgrade. In the city's a vibrant community of émigré scholars and church people, he found the opportunity to learn from the scholars and churches of the West, an experience shared by many who had been forced to exile. Working alongside Sergius Bulgakov, Georges Florovsky, Kyprian Kern, Anton Kartashev, Cassian Bezobrazov, and Paul Evdokimov, Afanasiev became an important figure in what some call the "Paris School" at St. Sergius.[4] Paul Valliere sees this group as offering an open, ecumenical, and progressive vision of Orthodox Christianity to Western churches. This was expressed in many publications and in their efforts in the Anglican-Orthodox Fellowship of St. Alban and St. Sergius, still in existence almost a century after its founding. The "Paris School" also participated in the Edinburgh and Lausanne meetings that would lead to the formation of the World Council of Churches after the war. Their perspectives were gathered in the groundbreaking anthology *Living Tradition* (*Zhivoe predanie*) in 1937. Afanasiev in particular offered an important essay on the changeability of the canons in this anthology, some of which is translated in *Tradition Alive*.[5]

Throughout his life, Afanasiev was intensely active in the church at numerous levels. He was part of the Fellowship of St. Alban and St. Sergius and started the summer Liturgical Week of Study at St. Sergius with Kyprian Kern, an event that continues seventy years after its beginning. Photos of early Liturgical Weeks show the array of ecumenical participants, Bernard Botte, Max Thurian, Joachim Jeremias, Charles Dumont, Lambert Beaudoin, and Olivier Rousseau, among others. Afanasiev also took part in ecumenical conferences, especially those at the then Dominican house of studies Le Saulchoir. His work, along with that of other faculty, made

---

3. Wooden, "Limits of the Church"; Wooden, "Eucharistic Ecclesiology"; Wooden, *Church as an Assembly*. Another important study is Nichols, *Theology in the Russian Diaspora*.

4. See Arjakovsky, *Way*, an important work on the émigré theologians of the Paris.

5. Plekon, *Tradition Alive*, 31–46.

St. Sergius a leading center of modern Orthodox theology and ecumenical exchange.

Though interrupted by his wartime parish service in Tunisia, Afanasiev stayed at St. Sergius for his academic and ecclesiastical career, teaching future priests and scholars and investigating the history of the councils and their connections to the state, along with the place and purpose of the canons. He spent much time exploring the universal and local dimensions as well as the structure of the church, the sacraments, and the ministry. He served the local hierarch as a canon law advisor and took part in other administrative tasks at the church and in the poverty-stricken archdiocese, including the thankless duty of overseeing finances. Those who knew and studied under him—particularly his Tunisian flock and fellow faculty and students at St. Sergius—observed that he was a man of extraordinary humility and graciousness, deferring to others almost to a fault, though Vassily Zenkovsky, a priest and faculty colleague of Afanasiev's at St. Sergius, faulted him for his quiet, non-assertive personality in an unpublished personal reminiscence.[6] Among his students was the later leader in liturgical theology, Alexander Schmemann. Though Schmemann rarely cited him or acknowledged his influence, the impact of Afanasiev's vision of the church and the Eucharist on him was significant.

While he specialized in canon law, Afanasiev was a polymath, a Renaissance scholar of the kind seldom seen anymore. He was a church historian, a New Testament exegete, a patristics and liturgical scholar who taught ethics, and, very importantly, a pastor. On the recommendation of Patriarch Athenagoras I, he was invited to the Second Vatican Council's last session as an ecumenical observer, and his theological writing was the only work by an Orthodox scholar cited in conciliar documents.[7] He was able to witness the laying down of the eleventh-century condemnations or anathemas between Rome and Constantinople by Pope Paul VI and Patriarch Athenagoras I on December 8, 1965. One of his last articles argued that while there had been a schism or rupture between the Catholic and Orthodox Churches conventionally but not accurately dated to 1054, many elements of communion remained.[8] He explained that communion

6. I was privately sent unpublished translations of these reminiscences by Fr. Alvian Smirensky.

7. *Acta Synodalia* 1, pt. 4, 87, note 2; *Acta Synodalia* 2, pt. 1, 251, note 27; *Acta Synodalia* 3, pt. 1, 254. Cited in Nichols, *Theology in the Russian Diaspora*, 253, 270.

8. Plekon, *Tradition Alive*, 47–50.

would be restored or resumed not by the discussions or decisions of groups of scholars or bishops but by the celebration of the Eucharist; it was this gathering, the giving thanks for and sharing of the bread and cup, that constituted communion in the holy things, the title of the article. In this he echoes the essay Bulgakov wrote for *The Journal of the Fellowship of St. Alban and St. Sergius*, "By Jacob's Well," where he argued that despite centuries of distance and division, many elements of unity in faith and practice still existed among the churches.[9] The article also resonates with Sergius Bulgakov's call that members of the Fellowship share the Eucharist with the blessing of their bishops and a preliminary act of confession and forgiveness for the division.[10] Although Patriarch Athenagoras I fervently encouraged this, even gifting Pope Paul VI the chalice and paten to do it, it never took place because of the intensity of the opposition between the Catholic and Orthodox Churches.

While Afanasiev's parish experience was important to him, his vision of the church and ministry also draws on his research into the ways in which ministry developed and functioned in the early church. Later theologians would benefit from the integral and communal vision he described, which saw all members as consecrated to ministry by baptism, the foundation of all ministry, and set apart some for special, particularized ministries by a distinctive call and ordination. He insisted that all ministry flows from the community that gathers around the bread and cup of the Eucharist, where the word is proclaimed and preached. In this sense, he went on to proclaim that all Christian life leads to service, in the example of the Lord who said he came to serve and not be served.

THE MINISTRY OF ALL: LAITY AS PRIESTS

While some critics charge that Afanasiev makes too much of the Eucharist as the center of the church, his writings suggest otherwise. As stated in the above paragraph, he argues that baptism is the crucial act of initiation into both the community of faith and into ministry. Thus, church and ministry cannot be separated from each other. Further, the clericalism we know, which namely views the church as completely ruled by bishops and their vicars, the presbyters, did not exist in the first centuries of the church. The division and stratification of the church into the ordained clergy and the

9. Plekon, *Tradition Alive*, 55–66.

10. Gallaher, "Bulgakov and Intercommunion," 9–28.

laity was inconceivable in those early days. Though accepted as normative today, they did not envision bishops appointed solely by other bishops, without the say of the people of God, or priests segregated from a laity that ends up being "second class" citizens of the kingdom, subject to the power and authority of bishops, and vicariously, priests. These are patterns that developed later, only traces of which were apparent in the early centuries, through the movement toward law and the emergence of a juridical church. The last chapter of *Church of the Holy Spirit* details this development, holding up, in contrast to the domination of law in the church's history, the "rule of love" as the only authentic basis of governing in the church (*vlast lyubvi*).[11]

Put another way, it is Afanasiev's great achievement to have recovered not only the eucharistic ecclesiology of the early church but also its inherently communal character. In his emphasis on community, he continually draws attention back to the "common ministry," the priesthood of all the baptized.[12] He insists that every Christian is set apart, ordained in the Spirit, and sent to ministry in the church. He uses the tern "*laic*," or layperson, not to signal a population that is the opposite of clergy, the ordained, but rather to designate the "people of God," emphasizing that lay/laic/laity all derive from *laos* to *theou*. They are not deprived of anything because they are not ordained to special service in the church. In his great vision, baptism provides initiation for particular or special ministries; in baptism and chrismation/confirmation, all women and men are consecrated to service, that is, to ministry.[13]

In this sense, Afanasiev reiterates the biblical sentiment that the whole people of God are a "royal priesthood."[14] After baptism and confirmation, the new Christians exercise the "common ministry" of all in the church, concelebrating and sharing the Eucharist. This they will do every Sunday and feast day for the rest of their lives. Thus, in the eucharistic prayer or anaphora, the plural is always used: "We praise you, give thanks to you, we offer you . . ."[15] While Afanasiev notes that there is one presider at the

11. Afanasiev, *Church of the Holy Spirit*, 255–76.

12. The most accessible statement of Afanasiev's perspectives is in *The Church of the Holy Spirit*. It appears in other of his writings as well, in a particular way in *The Lord's Supper* and in articles and courses he gave at St. Sergius.

13. Afanasiev, *Church of the Holy Spirit*, 3–4, 12.

14. 1 Pet 4:10–11; 1 Cor 12:7; Rom 12:6.

15. At communion, the invitation is "Holy things for the holy," echoed as "The gifts of God, for the people of God" in *The Book of Common Prayer*, 364.

Eucharist, as Christ presided over the Last Supper and all the other meals with his friends, every believer present is a celebrant.[16]

It is only from this common identity and ministry, Afanasiev writes, that some are identified and selected, chosen for special ministry or particular service by the local community. This is the first element of ordination to special ministry. The second is the conferral of special ministry by the Spirit, not by some administrative decision of a bishop or the assembly, which is called down by prayer in the laying on of hands by the ordaining bishop during a eucharistic celebration. The third element is the reception of the one ordained, which is sealed by the agreement of the assembly. It is here where the people of God receive one of their own, now set apart for special service.

Later, the authority of the episcopal office and the contents of canons would become the seemingly obvious means by which candidates would be ordained. To be sure, selection by the assembly and reception or ratification of the candidates are essential elements, but these are nothing without the action of grace, the descent of the Spirit. Nonetheless, in time, through conciliar decisions, the role of the local community was diminished so that only the bishops received, chose, and approved candidates for ordination.[17] The legalistic control of ordination was accompanied by the gradual differentiation of one special ministry into those of bishop, presbyter, and deacon, and then a progression from the lowest to highest. Eventually, an "absolute" character to ordination enabled not just presbyters but even bishops to be reassigned to different locations, something unimaginable in the first centuries.

In *The Church of the Holy Spirit* and his articles, Afanasiev returns repeatedly to the common ministry of the laity or laics. As Wooden notes in terms used by another pioneering student of ministry, Yves Congar, the work becomes the core of a "total" or integral ecclesiology. Because of the historical enlargement of the clerical part of the community of faith, the title of "lay" becomes a kind of default, having meaning only in contrast to ordination. This, however, is completely at odds with the New Testament and the writings and practice of the early church, including those of Justin Martyr, Irenaeus, and Ignatius of Antioch.[18] Despite all the changes over

16. Afanasiev, *Church of the Holy Spirit*, 34.

17. The further historical modifications to ordination are described in Afanasiev, *Ecclesiology*.

18. Afanasiev, *Church of the Holy Spirit*, 237–40.

time that obscured and diminished the ministry of the people of God, Afanasiev continues to note the scriptural foundations and embedding of this vision in the prayers of the rite of baptism as well as the Eucharist.[19] While the presider is necessary to lead both the liturgy and the community, there is nothing monarchical about such a special ministry. This point is what I believe Afanasiev offers us today, as we see congregations shrinking and the full-time ministry of the ordained becoming less capable of financial support, not to mention pastoral need.

THE SPECIAL MINISTRY OF THE ORDAINED

These are, for Afanasiev, the three essential elements of the further ordination to ministry, whether of bishops, presbyters, or deacons.[20] Special ministry is community-generated and affirmed. It is not an entrance to a different or superior category or group within the church. Ministry is, by definition, always reciprocal, mutual. One thinks here of Sam Wells's emphasis on ministry as always "with" others. Ministry is also charismatic, as seen through the prayer and laying on of hands that calls down the Spirit to fill the ordained with the gifts necessary for the work to be done. Finally, special ministry is local. Candidates are identified as appropriate by the community to which they belong. In contrast, in the early church, prophets or preachers were itinerant. Since they moved about, they were not selected and affirmed by the communities to whom they went. There was nothing like an "absolute" ordination.

In time, the communal selection and reception of the ordained would disappear; bishops would take over the popular election and affirmation of candidates. The acclamation by the congregation in Eastern Church ordinations is a mere vestige, for the community has had no role in the process. Even those instances where a diocesan assembly in some church bodies was able to select one name out of several proposed by the bishops for episcopal ordination have disappeared. Now only one name is presented, if at all.

Afanasiev further emphasizes the communal character of both the Eucharist and the church, and hence of ministry, in *The Lord's Supper*. Later historical developments, he writes, would lead to multiple congregations not just spread among towns and villages but even in a single city. At first, he reminds us, there was one bishop, one congregation, and one Eucharist,

19. Afanasiev, *Church of the Holy Spirit*, 12.
20. Afanasiev, *Church of the Holy Spirit*, 94–104; Afanasiev, *Ecclesiology*.

just as there is but one Lord, one faith, and one baptism. Through his distinctive vision of ministry, he stresses the reality of the assembly gathering as church as a way of translating the expression "*epi to auto*" found in Acts of the Apostles.[21] He insists, especially in *The Lord's Supper*, that while all at the Eucharist—not just the ordained—concelebrate, the ministry of the presider (*proestôs*) is to be distinguished from the common ministry of the church. Just as Christ presided at the last supper and the meals with his friends (*havourot*), there can be only one presider. This would originally have been the chief pastor of the local church, the *episkopos* or overseer, the bishop.

Afanasiev devotes two chapters of *The Church of the Holy Spirit* to a meticulous historical examination of the presider and the emergence of this role over time.[22] When congregations began to multiply and the experiment of having "country bishops" (*chorepiskopoi*) cover these parishes did not take hold, presbyters became the presiders at eucharistic assemblies. This eventually became the universal pattern and is the current norm, though it is undergoing change. In time, presbyters would also concelebrate with the bishop-presider, as is done today, something about which Afanasiev has reservations. He objects to what became a clericalized liturgy, in which a non-vested "audience" of lay people passively attend, merely observing what the vested, ordained clergy celebrate. His insistent point is that the entire assembly concelebrate the liturgy. This is his overarching vision of church and ministry: again, all are ordained to ministry in their baptism.

Another significant matter dealt with in *The Lord's Supper* has to do with the reception of communion. At the time Afanasiev was writing this, in 1952, communion among Orthodox Christians was infrequent, only several times a year, a trend that was similar in many other churches including those of the West. Afanasiev shows in detail how frequent communion disappeared and reveals how the explanations created over the centuries to support and defend it were at odds both with the Scriptures and the practice of the early church. His student, Alexander Schmemann, would become the primary voice in the Eastern Orthodox Church urging a return to regular reception of communion at Sunday liturgies.

To go back to Afanasiev's main thrust, he insists that criticism of the common ministry, or priesthood of all the faithful, as some version of a Reformation denial of special ministries in favor of the priesthood of all

---

21. Acts 2:47; Afanasiev, *Church of the Holy Spirit*, 17.

22. Afanasiev, *Church of the Holy Spirit*, 133–216.

believers is not warranted. The priesthood of all the baptized does not make the ordained priesthood unnecessary, as made clear in confessional texts like the Thirty-Nine Articles of the Anglican tradition or the Augsburg Confession of the Lutheran. Afanasiev cannot but echo the Scriptures and apostolic writers in recognizing the development of the special ministries, albeit in different forms in different places. In effect, he acknowledges that the ministries of bishops, presbyters and deacons are integral to the church's identity and to the church's functioning. That these became a clerical caste, with supposedly ontological differences from the nonordained, surrounded by canons that walled these ministers off from the rest of the community are, for Afanasiev, historical mutations. He does not reduce the whole of the church to each local congregation nor does he diminish the place and the role of the bishop in lifting up the priesthood of all the baptized. Although some of his critics say otherwise, Wooden shows that their critique is unfounded. For him, the Scriptures, as well as the writers and practice of the early church, do not see a conflict or a contradiction between the common and special ministries.

In the introduction to *The Church of the Holy Spirit*, Afanasiev says that a church historian should serve the church.[23] This he most certainly does, and he offers a singular vision in our effort of trying to better understand the ordained and their ministry in the twenty-first century. As he shows, returning to the church of the first centuries is not a romantic pilgrimage to some idealized past. He is not in pursuit of recreating the community of faith in the ancient world. Such would be pointless, a denial of the passage of time and of much evolution, though it is a move often made by Christians who desire to get back to their origins, the "pure" church of apostolic times.

COMMON MINISTRIES, SPECIAL MINISTRIES
REDISCOVERED

What Afanasiev underscores as the communal character of the church is something that congregations and pastors have stumbled back into, as several cases shared in *Community as Church* witness. Necessity has made for a "return to the sources" in a way that church leaders and congregation specialists might not have imagined. Perhaps the best explanation is not that there is nothing new in the church—the church is constantly being renewed, which Bulgakov calls a "permanent Pentecost." Authentic

23. Afanasiev, *Church of the Holy Spirit*, 7.

tradition continues to assert itself. Congregations have come to realize that their existence is not dependent upon a distant bishop and staff, no matter how solicitous. Nor is the old pattern functional any longer. Everything does not fall upon the ordained pastor presiding every Sunday, preaching, teaching, and providing pastoral care. While, as Afanasiev admits, a congregation should have a pastor/presider, as the writings and practice indicate, he insists that the whole assembly is the church. All are ordained to ministry. Today, with various pressures exerted on them, congregations have discovered their cooperative nature. People have come to realize not only that there are many traditional pastoral tasks that they can do, but also that they must do them, as many pastors are part-time pastors. They have come to see that they are able to do them very well.

Afanasiev is also among those who "rediscovered the church" in the last century through a "return to the sources"—namely, the Scriptures, liturgical texts, and apostolic and patristic writers. For centuries before his time, "church" had meant canons and other rules, various levels of administration and structure, as well as the hierarchy of the ordained led by the bishops. Along with Afanasiev, others who turned to the Scriptures for images of the community that is God's people include Congar, de Lubac, Tillard, Bulgakov, and Bonhoeffer. In Afanasiev's case it is fair to say that he also rediscovered the ministry of all believers within the sacrament of gathering of the assembly. Because he saw the special ministries of those ordained to preside and lead—the bishops, presbyters, and deacons— alongside this common ministry, he showed the interconnected nature of ministry. In other words, he saw the clergy and laity as different only in function. The sharper division between the two is a later development, he stressed, and not definitive.

In keeping with the early church's vision and practice, Afanasiev offers no handbook on how either the common or the special ministries should be carried out. Neither does he single out those ordained to special service to describe their formation, lifestyle, or spirituality. At this early stage of the church, everyone partook of the same Scriptures, broke the same bread, and shared the same cup. He is clear that the life of the assembly was not merely cultic but was founded in the members of the eucharistic community who went home and to work to put into practice what they heard read and preached. In this manner, they realized what they saw in the fabric of the assembly, moved by the "power of love" that descended through the Spirit and nothing else.

If we fast-forward to our own time, there are many examples of more intensive cooperation between congregation members and pastors in the work of the gospel that I have described in *Community as Church*. One example lies in two parishes that closed and then reappeared as Grace Church in Great Barrington, Massachusetts, which is located in the Berkshires, where they facilitated a joint effort by laity and clergy, exemplifying a community acting as one.[24] Cathie Caimano's agreement with St. Paul's Church in Salisbury, North Carolina, is another instance where the parish does not depend on the pastor to "be" the church but rather behaves as such all week long.[25] I also detailed communal parish efforts to visit members unable to get out, to be responsible for building maintenance, and to gather people for study groups. The members of Redeemer Lutheran Church in North Minneapolis, for example, coordinated to seriously invest in their neighborhood, where they reaffirmed their location. They acquired surrounding properties and offered both residential and commercial space, thus revitalizing the church's surroundings.[26] Another example is found in Reconciliation Services in Kansas City, mentioned earlier.[27]

What does this decidedly communal ministry have to do with Afanasiev's vision and the larger issue of ministry that is the focus of this book? As suggested, I believe such efforts as those just noted, and many others described in my previous book and documented in various venues like *Faith & Leadership*, tell us something about the shape of both congregational life and the role of pastors in the twenty-first century. Despite undeniable shrinkage in numbers and decline of parish units, there is striking growth and remarkable health in what Afanasiev calls the "common ministry" of all the baptized. We also see that the ordained, the pastors, benefit from the cooperation of parish members. They experience them as Paul did those named in his letters as "coworkers": as women and men doing the work of gathering congregations and serving those in need around them. Afanasiev's memorable description rings true here. This is "the power of love" in action.

<hr>

24. Plekon, *Community as Church*, 113–15.

25. Plekon, *Community as Church*, 136.

26. Plekon, *Community as Church*, 91–92.

27. Plekon, *Community as Church*, 171–76. I know of this example through my long friendship with the church's director, Father Justin Mathews.

4

Cathie Caimano

"Free Range" Priests

"FREE RANGE" PRIESTS: OUT OF THE ECCLESIAL BOX

Cathie Caimano calls herself a "free range" priest.[1] How did she get to be "free range"? While she serves St. Paul's Church in Salisbury, North Carolina, doing exactly what clergy are ordained to do—presiding at the Eucharist, preaching—on closer examination, things for her are rather different than in the usual full- or part-time appointment. At St. Paul's, the small community of about thirty does a great deal of the day-to-day ministry. This includes meeting as the parish vestry/council, maintaining the building, paying bills, and the rest of what most parishes require to remain in operation. During the week, they also assume pastoral care tasks such as visiting and bringing communion to the sick and shut-in, as well as responding to other calls for information and assistance from church members and others in the neighborhood.

Caimano is contracted for priestly services by St. Paul's two Sundays a month. This means she does not have a full-time salary, other benefits, or housing. Neither does she participate in vestry meetings and decisions. When not at St. Paul's, she works at other parishes and is involved in several other online and in-person efforts that mentor clergy. Reflecting her situation, at least 20 percent of Episcopal parishes do not have a full-time, paid pastor (to be precise, 20 percent of male clergy and 28 percent of female

1. Caimano, "Free Range Priests."

clergy are part-time); more recent data suggests that this could be more than 40 percent.[2] About half of clergy in mainline churches are paid for full-time work and about 10 percent of all clergy are non-stipendiary, that is, they serve without pay. While some still decry part-time clergy or employment alongside ministry, such as "worker priests" who hold a secular occupation, the reality on the ground in parishes and with actual ordained people witnesses that these types of appointments are necessary. The classical model of a pastor for every congregation, supported by that community, is simply no longer the norm. As Caimano notes in her fascinating, often provocative blog, recent figures from the national Episcopal Church indicate that the number of what she calls "free range" priests is at 14 percent and growing.

In the two decades since Caimano, who prefers to be called Father Cathie, has been ordained, she's been an assistant in an urban parish, rector of a different parish, and canon or assistant to a diocesan bishop. In her book, articles, podcasts, and blog, she shares her discerning vision on ordained ministry and the situation of the local church of the parish today. For me, her views are both realistic and critical. In the various church positions described above, she has experienced the pressures of finances on shrinking congregations and known the personal stress of being looked to for leadership as well as counsel. Like Barbara Brown Taylor, she also knows how easily things can turn and understands how the pastor is often blamed for every difficulty, taking the brunt of congregation members' anxiety and anger.

DO LESS, LOVE MORE:
LESSONS AND ENCOURAGEMENT FOR PASTORS

Equally, Caimano makes no excuses about the reality of God; although the church may be human, she remains clear that God is in charge and always present. In her weekly podcasts, she brilliantly distills the gospel of the past Sunday. Rather than telling us what to do, she is the medium through which Christ's words and actions are conveyed. Again, George Keith's superb line is incarnated in what she offers; she brings God to the people and the people to God.

Spread across the main page of her website, just after her photo and brief introduction, there are three suggestions, each boiled down to two

2. Church Pension Group, "Trends in Ministry," 19:48, 21:13, and 23:41. Cf. Church Pension Group, Research and Data Team, "Trends in Ministry."

words: "Do Less," "Love More," "Embrace Abundance." These are not cute quotes like those people frame and mount on their walls. Nor are they quick fixes, for in each case, there is a great deal to unpack. Accompanying "Do Less" is a photo of her walking on the beach.[3] She succinctly explains what she means: "Stop doing everything. Stop being 'in charge.' Find more peace in your own spiritual life as you reconnect with what's most important." Without exaggeration, those few sentences compact what pages and pages and weeks of classes on clergy self-care communicate. In this manner, at the very outset, Caimano hones in on what became Barbara Brown Taylor's principal affliction, namely the obsession with being in charge, being in control, and thus feeling responsible for everything in the parish. This leads to the fatal mistake of trying to do everything instead of allowing the church to be the life and work of the whole people of God.

The other two suggestions echo and fill out the first. To "love more" is not a sappy urge to be a 24/7 available chaplain to every boo-boo and all the real traumas and events in peoples' lives. What Caimano means is what seminary professors and the best mentors of interns and curates/assistants try to convey: do the truly pastoral things. Be a priest. Allow others to do the mundane yet necessary stuff. This brings me back to the time I heard at an ordination that all newly ordained should receive a toilet brush and plunger in addition to the typical stole, chasuble, and perhaps Bible or service book. The priest who said this was not being a comedian. Rather, he observed that while vestments or a service book might seem more appropriate, the toilet brush and plunger are also tools of the trade. The parish pastor, after all, would be the one on the premises when a toilet overflowed, when the lights were left on, when no one showed up to shovel the steps after a snowstorm. While the pastor should not be expected to be a building custodian, groundskeeper, etc., there is truth in what this experienced priest said and meant. Aside from the physical maintenance of a building, there is a great deal of mopping up and cleaning in ministry.

The idea that clergy ought to be more than what they expected when they were ordained leads into the proposal to "embrace abundance," which Samuel Wells describes in another context. Abundant life is what Jesus told us he came to bring and thus the reason that both ordained ministry and the church exist. Father Cathie repeatedly dares to ask why pastors should not be paid well, which may mean working part-time on contract, with time for another occupation. Is there a contradiction here, between generous

---

3. As her Facebook feed reveals, Caimano is a serious runner.

ministry and care for those who minister? Essentially not, for we all hear the same good news that encourages extravagant love, thus supporting abundant life. Caimano does a great service by emphatically rejecting the expectation of no, or woefully inadequate, compensation. It is a disservice both to the ordained and the rest of the people of God to expect what we ourselves would not accept from our pastors.

In the many articles on her website, Caimano provides a substantial course in the basics of ministry today, that of both the ordained and of the church community.[4] For example, "The Road to Church Change Goes by the Parish Administrator's Desk," a stunning piece, synthesizes a great deal in the title alone. For one thing, the pastor ought not to be the parish administrator—this is a breakthrough for some but both a return to ancient tradition and a more effective division of labor for both the laity and the clergy. The administrator, formerly the "church secretary," likely has been there before the present pastor and will be there after his or her departure. In this manner, there is a sense of real community and legacy at play.

Caimano goes on to identify the fear of change that exists in many parishes, locating it in the parish council, other groups like church school and choir, charitable circles, and, in particular, in the parish office. She shows that it was not just the pandemic lockdown that forced changes on parishes; the digitization of records, bookkeeping, documents, and other shifts that COVID-19 accelerated also threatened administrators. The need to livestream the service as well as meetings, for example, became a major challenge and remains so for some. With the aging of parish memberships, it is not just fear of COVID that has kept people from attending in person. Some are physically unable to do so but desire to participate both in worship as well as other activities such as meetings, classes, and gatherings. My experience has been that parish council meetings have continued online, freeing participants from travel and compelling leaders to be more time-effective. To return to Caimano, she suggests that a rearrangement of parish administrative tasks is necessary, urging greater cooperation between pastor and community. It may be necessary to hire or contract out technical work for which office and council members are not equipped. There may be members with skills who can volunteer, which will also require rethinking the parish division of labor. At root here is the realization that the old line "we've never done it that way before" has become a drag on parish life,

---

4. See https://freerangepriest.org/.

almost a surrender to the past and a rejection of the future as well as a forgetting of all the adaptations and changes that occurred in years past.

Using a phrase that is quite current, Caimano also has a piece, "How 'Quiet Quitting' Changes the Church."[5] This TikTok moment, she explains, is no mere realization of a popular cliché. Rather, Caimano thinks, it is just another way of coming to terms with the mandate to do less and thereby do what one is called to do more effectively. She connects this idea to a favorite author, Rabbi Edwin Freidman, who spoke of "defecting in place." However you describe it, the movement expressed in these two phrases really articulates a commitment to personal transformation. Not unlike the call the church makes at the start of Lent, I would link it to the first words out of Jesus's mouth in Mark's Gospel: "Turn yourselves around, inside out," which used to be translated as "repent" but is far better put as "transform." Both the Greek Gospel expression "*metanoiete*" and the Hebrew behind it, "*t'shuvah*," contain far more than sorrow for the sins one has committed. Rather, the root meaning is to do the hard work of personal change. For Caimano, this precisely is conveyed in refusing to be a "utility infielder," a jack of all trades in the parish, either as the pastor or as the parish administrator. In *Community as Church*, I provide numerous examples of parishes that have reoriented everyday tasks. In some cases, this freed up the pastor to be part-time, concentrating on essential activities such as preaching, presiding at liturgy, teaching, providing pastoral counseling, as well as taking part in parish council deliberations, offering perspectives brought by his or her pastoral formation and experience.

REIMAGING AND REINVENTING MINISTRY

In other articles, Caimano delves into the reinvention of the role of pastor. Rather than settling for a minimal part-time salary or worse, what amounts to supply stipends for Sunday services and necessary pastoral care, is there not a better way, she asks? There most certainly is. She locates the answer at the core of "free range" ministry. As noted in *Community as Church*, the actual elements of the local church, the parish, have changed significantly over the centuries, shifting from small assemblies in private homes to the highly structured organizations of denominations, or church bodies, with national and regional levels and various forms of staffing and funding. In the early medieval time and beyond, staffing included pastors appointed

5. Caimano, "How 'Quiet Quitting.'"

and assigned by a bishop, sometimes with support often at the request of a local landowner, who footed the bill for maintaining the pastor, his or her family, as well as the fabric of the church building. In addition, other wealthier families often made substantial contributions, as commemorated on the memorials, monuments, and plaques inside older churches across Europe and even in America. In a custom that continues to this day, the members of a congregation have selected someone to be their pastor, often with the approval of the bishop or some other regional leader, and supported that person and their family with housing and a salary. They sometimes also made contributions from their own gardens, farms, or land to support the parish glebe, or church farm, following agricultural models that are long gone. Endowments and investments either from outside of the parish or from within now play the same role, maintaining the staffing and the fabric of the parish building.

Nonetheless, this is not the place for more detailed excavations into church history. What Caimano challenges is the universal/ecumenical, accepted pattern that a pastor is a full-time hire by a congregation, works as such, and is compensated adequately. The reality is that fewer and fewer parishes can do this, as shown by substantial data in my earlier book, which I will not repeat here, and reflected in the shrinking size of the average parish. Many cases of congregations who could and have stayed open remain vital forces in their communities, which they can do because of part-time ordained ministry, or essentially what Caimano means by "free range" priests.

Going forward in her vision of ordained ministry, Caimano takes critical aim at the following titles: bivocational, "tent-making," and non-stipendiary ministry, which refer to a minister who earns her or his own living outside of the parish, or who has another source of income. This follows the model of St. Paul's occupation alongside preaching.[6] To these, one could also refer to "ministry alongside secular profession/occupation" and the model in post-WWII Europe of "worker priests" who entered the labor force in factories in solidarity with the working class. I am an example of this category, as I have spent more than forty years with an academic position as my "day job," the primary source of my salary, pension, and health insurance, which compensates me for teaching, research, writing, publication, and scholarly presentations. Caimano's argument is that getting clergy "on the cheap" because they have full-time occupations is not

6. Caimano, "'Tentmaker,' 'Non-Stipendiary,' and 'Bi-Vocational.'"

sustainable either for clergy or parishes. No matter the goodwill intended by such clergy, their contribution of service dismisses the parish of a mutual responsibility and its obligations. She reminds us that the New Testament supports the compensation of ministers, specifying that the laborer deserves his pay and that animals who do important work like pulling carts or driving mills are fed.[7]

Looked at from another vantage point, when a pastor only does so much in and for a congregation, congregation members step up and do ministry tasks that they are absolutely able to do. They can visit the homebound, those in care facilities, and others. Whether financial administration, scheduling, fellowship activities, or education, they can contribute to all areas of parish life where ordination is not necessary but discipleship is.

BRING CHURCH TO THE PEOPLE: A LESSON FOR LAITY

In another article, "Bring Church to People," Caimano offers several ways in which church can come to people who might not come physically themselves. The necessity of online worship, learning, fellowship, and gathering during the pandemic's lockdown period and after has brought technical challenges to many congregations that they have somehow been able to overcome. Thus, now people who cannot attend in-person can pray with the community, learn, be informed, and exchange questions and reflections online. Some do not look favorably on online services, like Tish Harrison Warren, a clergy columnist for the *New York Times* who urged all online church efforts to be simply shut down after the pandemic, in effect forcing people to come together in the same place, which was for him the ideal and most effective experience of church community.[8] This, in my view, is limited thinking and insensitive to the people who simply cannot come to church. In spite of such critics, Caimano, along with the consensus of clergy and church leaders, assumes that online church is here to stay.

This issue reveals another that Caimano also highlights frequently:[9] the resistance to change seemingly embedded in church institutions. Detailing all the ways in which churches have refused change through their history—including denial, refusal to acknowledge change in the world and in the community, romantic adherence to the past, an obsession with

7. 1 Tim 5:18.
8. Warren, "Why Churches Should."
9. See https://freerangepriest.org/.

tradition, and more—could be a book in itself. Rather than dwell on the factors that contribute to such resistance, in typical "free range priest" fashion Caimano accepts that those remaining in congregations must somehow find that resistance is working for them. This is something that my own experience questions, especially in the last couple of parishes where I served. The continued disappearance of members and persistent shrinkage of faith communities to me says that even those who have been coming are not destined to remain. Caimano, however, looks elsewhere in developing her insights. "Preserve what you can," she says. Even smaller parish communities can be powerful, she notes, not only in mutual concern within the congregation but as real leaders and lights in their neighborhoods, towns, and the world around them. Further, she suggests that pastors, especially if on contract or part-time, can be proactive in changing their working arrangement. This can include revising how many Sundays they cover for service, how many hours of pastoral care they provide during the week, whether they will sit in on council and committee meetings, and so on. The resultant changes, she observes, would result in gains for both pastors and the rest of the congregation. The pastor would be able to devote time to writing, consulting, practicing a profession, and, perhaps, part-time care for yet another congregation. The people, as already noted, would discover that they are also ministers in many ways for which ordination is not necessary at all. Put another way, when both the ordained and the people come to accept changes in how they work together as the presence of Christ in the world, living out the gospel in which they believe, there can be new ways of being "church" despite trends toward shrinkage and decline. Pointing to examples of the reinvention and resurrection of congregations through the repurposing of property, the replanting of churches in the larger community, and more was the aim of *Community as Church*.

Caimano continues to make her point by questioning the use of several traditional church words:[10] stewardship, outreach, committee, volunteer, and livestream. Of course, there is nothing inherently wrong in their root meanings, but she notes that each term carries a lot of baggage that should be critically considered. Why should a parish budget be presented in the same way as traditional stewardship campaigns: as a matter of obligation and with a heavy dose of guilt? In the end, when a budget is associated with stewardship, some studies suggest that 20 percent contribute more than the other 80 percent. Dropping this approach would challenge parishes to

10. Caimano, "5 Church Words."

think hard about what they include in their budget, contemplating what could be cut and what could be paid for in other ways. Meanwhile, the word outreach is almost always translated into programs that are often minimal, even embarrassing in their limitations. Could working with another congregation, or with an already existing, functioning not-for-profit, be a more effective way of reaching the goals of outreach committees? Although people tend not to be excited to join parish outreach committees, many remain because no one has asked whether they are still needed or how they can be reinvigorated. More might step up to take responsibility for necessary tasks, along with others they enlist. Outreach possibilities are waiting for many congregations right down the street or across the way, in their neighborhoods and larger communities. These include food banks, soup kitchens, and other projects for feeding those in need. There are thrift shops where recycled clothing, household wares, and more can be purchased at more reasonable prices. A congregation can offer space that is unused during the week to nonprofit groups for a wide range of services, from health clinics to after-school childcare, tutoring, counseling, employment services, and more.[11] Related to this is the constant call for volunteers, which is never something we want to have to do and usually frustrating. If few say they would be willing to take on a task, perhaps the task itself needs reconsideration. Finally, a parish community must come to terms with the great deal that online worship, education, and meetings can do for the community. If a parish lacks the necessary technical skills to implement virtual services, then contracting with those who could provide them may be the way to go. Caimano emphasizes that these five church words simply represent a few of many issues that a congregation sooner or later must confront. If these issues are forced upon a community, there will be denial, evasion, avoidance, and the like. Caimano says what should be obvious: a living community finds ways to move forward when conditions within and outside change.

In other blog posts on her *Free Range Priest* website, Caimano provides other provocative reflections both on the state of the local church and on that of the ordained. She writes that when unable to offer more than what amounts to a stipend for supply, that is, conducting Sunday services, a parish need not contemplate closing its doors. With a contracted two-Sunday presence, Caimano herself keeps more than one small congregation going. She also makes it possible for others to have a priest to celebrate the

---

11. Plekon, *Community as Church*, provides numerous examples of such outreach.

Eucharist, preach, and do pastoral work as needed. Further, she can devote time to writing, consulting, and offering online sessions for clergy and laity wanting to think about new ways of being "church." Strange as the expression may sound, she foresees scriptural legitimation in parishes becoming more entrepreneurial, as both pastors and laypeople find other paths to do the work of the gospel. Surely, a most basic consequence of this is that such reimagination would turn a congregation outward, toward the world, as opposed to when they are turned inward in what my friend and next-town neighbor, Presbyterian pastor David Frost, whom I will discuss in the next section, aptly calls "survival theology," finding whatever way there is to keep going, trying to survive without truly living and working as a community. Pastor of a congregation that dates to the 1770s, Frost was implored to step up when his congregation almost closed. He did so, and almost fifteen years later a small community of committed, vibrant people maintain a powerful presence on the Main Street of their town along NYS Route 311. With parishioners and several community members, he has transformed the formerly unused buildings that belong to the parish—including a former elementary school, local grange hall, and the congregation's educational and meeting hall—into a thriving thrift shop, a food bank, a soup kitchen and community meeting place, as well as a space for a Quaker group and others to meet.

ANOTHER "FREE RANGE PASTOR": DAVID FROST

Frost's leadership as a pastor may be rooted in that he has spent his entire life observing the traditions of ministry. As a PK, the common abbreviation used for "pastor's kid," he grew up with a father who led the Patterson, New York, parish for twenty-five years. Also a longtime community farmer, he provides organic produce at farmstands that now benefit the activities of the parish and feed the hungry. I call him a "flypaper pastor." He is able to attract all kinds of tradespeople to contribute their services around the parish buildings. Further, he connects with all the town networks, the Rotary and Chamber of Commerce as well as the town government and town officials. As the only pastor in town, he *is* the town's pastor. After he made an agreement with a local supermarket to get their surplus food, the parish soup kitchen uses gifted commercial refrigeration and freezer units. He has always invited students to come and learn community farming as well as complete community service requirements in working at the food bank and soup kitchen improvement efforts. All of this is in service of Christ and the people of God, and his recorded sermons offer a sustained rationale for the latticework of relationships he's created and sustains, very much bringing God to the people and the people to God.

I mention Frost because he is, in some ways, another incarnation of Cathie Caimano's "free range" priest or pastor. Though he holds a special mission elder or pastor position in his local presbytery and has a complete theological education, he envisions the work of the church as not just his but the result of cooperation with the parish members. He says all the time that he is there "to equip and support the saints." He receives neither housing nor a standard compensation package from the congregation (which could afford neither). Rather, like Caimano, he cobbles together a living from an honorarium and other income from his agricultural and community work. Both he and Caimano show us that the work of ordained ministry can and must continue for the life of the church and to spread the church's mission through the world. Yet it need not be linked indissolubly to the models of the past. "Free range," among many other things, can mean free to find new paths and ways of service. Others among the pastor-theologians represented in the following chapters will suggest the same.

5

C. Andrew Doyle, David Barnhart, Andrew Root

Rethinking the Place and Ministry of the Ordained

REIMAGING MINISTRY: BISHOPS, PRIESTS, AND DEACONS IN THE TWENTY-FIRST CENTURY

In the last chapter, we discussed how Cathie Caimano shows some concrete ways in which the ministry of the ordained could be reimagined. In this chapter, we continue to focus on ministry-in-practice with the reflections of a bishop, a pastor of house churches, and a theologian. The bishop, C. Andrew Doyle, works in the Episcopal diocese of Texas. He describes his autobiography in six words: "Met Jesus on pilgrimage, still walking." Here, we listen to his probing prediction at the shape that ordained ministry is taking as it heads toward the future.[1] He gives careful attention to the historical path of the ministries of bishop, priest, and deacon. He makes no apologies for respecting the tradition and the institution of the church while, at the same time, challenging any rigid, absolute allegiance to the most familiar patterns of ministry. His aim is to push the church to think outside of its comfortable boundaries and models. From parish experience, he legitimates such provocative reflection in a commitment to active mission rather than preservation or survival strategies.

---

1. Doyle, *Vocātiō*; Schlesinger, "Called to Be More"; Doyle, *Church*.

Like many others in this book, Doyle is well aware of the church's various forms of crisis: decline, the pressure of a secular society, and the estrangement of many due to clergy intolerance and abuse. He knows that there are ever-growing numbers of religious "nones" and "dones" and has no illusions about simply hunkering down in the strength of Scriptures and liturgy, the sacraments, and the canons. Rather, his focus is on the roles of the bishop, presbyter, and deacon, the three forms of ordained ministry that emerged in the first few centuries and became essential elements of the church in the East and West. Paramount to his vision is the structure of these ministries in the church, including their function and forms of compensation. Given current parish and diocesan financial situations, he believes that a return to the ancient pattern of self-supporting ministries is warranted. Yet, he adds that calling for non-stipendiary, self-supporting priests and deacons is not primarily an emergency response to financial shortfalls. In this vision, he sees substantial liberation, a freeing up of numerous structural obligations and restraints. He explains that when ministers are no longer viewed as employees of a diocese or parish, there will be a freeing, or better, a transformation, both for the ordained and the rest of the people of God.

Suffice it to say, this is decidedly not a cost-saving view for Doyle. Compensation, however, is not the only target of his reflection. He also stresses the important function of these ministries, questioning the present requirements for formation. Here, Doyle is in the company of others who also have called for the revision of centuries-old residential seminary programs. Such formation models did not exist until the post-Reformation era. The exceptions were the few candidates trained in universities. Rather, parish-based apprentice under a mentor was the most widespread mode of formation for clergy who would serve parishes. Academic training in cathedral schools or university faculties was for the elite who would later rise to leadership positions. A formation model based on academic distance learning with in-person gatherings and parish-based apprenticeship in pastoral work, he stresses, is a more appropriate model for the twenty-first century. In the Church of England, this pattern has grown considerably, and it is being adopted at a number of locations in the US. For instance, Luther Seminary in St. Paul, Minnesota, has run a MDivX program, as has Bangor Seminary in Maine. Meanwhile, Bexley-Seabury has a "competency-based" mentoring program,[2] and Emory University Candler School of Theology plans to launch a hybrid program in 2023.[3]

In addition to wanting to disentangle clergy from complete compensation by parishes, Doyle urges a de-professionalization of clergy identity, retreating from the pattern that emerged in the first three to four centuries. As we have seen, Afanasiev also discusses this, and both he and Doyle point out the lack of scriptural or substantial theological legitimation for the development of a clergy caste separate from and above the non-ordained. Rather, the origins are cultural, political, and sociological, deriving from the patterns in Roman and later Byzantine imperial organization. In particular, the New Testament describes a diversity of ministries and communities, providing little evidence for what would become the institutionalization of ministry. I believe the New Testament and early-church visions of ministry open up contemporary formation to diverse paths and models, valuing vocation over professionalism.

Doyle should not be understood as a mere iconoclast, intent on removing pieces of tradition as occurred in certain areas of the Reformation. He makes it clear that while he reveres the tradition, he wants to see it as more than a continued presentation of patterns. Historical perspective shows clearly that the exercise of ministry in all three offices has changed considerably, even in the last centuries. The rationale for renewal and change, he stresses, ought to be the mission of the church. In his diocese, throughout the wider Episcopal Church, as well as in other church bodies, there are different forms of parish organization that have been freed from the encumbrances that have canonically governed all parishes. These go by different labels, but one that he often employs is "missional community." The requirements for a parish council and a budget with the finances to compensate a full-time pastor are among the obligations that he recommends modifying to support continued life in and by the community of faith. In this sense, his perspective is really that of the life and work of the whole of the church, hence the title of his book, *Vocātio*, or vocation. It is wrong to focus on clergy reform and renewal without considering the whole of the people of God. All baptized Christians, as he emphasizes, are called to put the gospel into practice.

---

2. Woerman, "Bexley-Seabury Launches."

3. Candler School of Theology, Emory University, "Emory University's Candler School."

BISHOPS, PRIESTS, AND DEACONS: HOW THEY CAN WORK TODAY

Doyle's argument is that the ordained must transcend ecclesiastical structure—whether that of the national church, diocese, or parish—for the sake of the essential mission of the church. The weight of the forms of the past millennium do not outweigh the gospel. While it is hard to justify the continued clericalism in the church, it is, Doyle claims, possible to have the historical offices of ministry without some of the social and cultural baggage of the past. Bishops, priests, and deacons could be real members of their communities, which would be a true gain for the church. They could still equip and sustain the ministry of the baptized by preaching and teaching, presiding and administering the sacraments, offering pastoral care, and leading the community. Though the look this would take on in practice is difficult and risky to project, Doyle believes some broad outlines are possible. If all ministry is local, Doyle writes, then bishops have a more regional scope. As pastors of an area, not just one congregation, bishops could support not just numerous parishes but their priests as well. Such a pattern is quite like the most ancient models of episcopal service; he explains that bishops would become more like pastors than administrators located in diocesan headquarters. They would also be more collegial with presbyters instead of authority figures.

Doyle's view is supported by the important relationships with deacons that bishops held in the early days of the church. Deacons served as a bishop's immediate coworkers, the presbyters eventually based in scattered congregations. The permanent diaconate is still in need of real revival that moves it beyond the stage of presbyteral ordination and comes back to a deacon's historical function in a variety of ministries, from caring for those in need, their primary original role, to assisting bishops and pastors. While the current pastoral range of deacons includes preaching and teaching, assisting in administration of the sacraments, pastoral visitation, as well as administration, further reform is needed to extend their work. Deacons are barred from the anointing of the sick, for example, in the Roman Catholic context, though they baptize, officiate at weddings and funerals, distribute communion, lead the prayers of the people in the eucharistic liturgy, and preach.

In his call for non-stipendiary clergy, Doyle collides with Cathie Caimano's insistence that clergy need to be compensated for their service. Doyle is well aware of the ancient, scriptural basis for this, citing a number of New Testament passages defending clergy compensation.[4] But, there is also a legacy of pastors who earn their own living, as we see through St. Paul, who claims that pastors are worthy of support but also writes of his profession in the leather and fabric trades.[5] In many parishes, the ability to support a pastor long ago ended, and the most that is possible is an honorarium not unlike the one paid to supply priests. Perhaps my own experience as a long-time non-stipendiary who serves as a priest with a secular profession convinces me that this is a workable model. I would pair it up with Doyle's conviction that pastors will serve better as members of their congregations, not as a class of professionals with whom they are externally contracted. Having to manage a job and a household like the rest of a community of faith is an important experience for shaping ordained ministry going forward.

The third office in ministry is that of the presbyters. In early church communities, presbyters were a council of advisors to the bishop as well as the elders or heads of congregations. Eventually, they became the functional pastors of those communities, which were distanced from the congregation of the bishop. More local or "country" assistant bishops (*chorepiskopoi*) disappeared. Since priests are synonymous with parish service, Doyle sees no need to contest this now centuries-long established role. In effect, presbyters are the pastors of local communities; there they preach, preside at liturgy, and encourage the people of God to put the gospel into action in everyday life, as they do themselves. The liturgical renewal of the past decades has witnessed not just the concelebration of liturgy by all but the call of all to be the body of Christ in the world. As we have seen, laity are already engaged in work both within the parish and in the larger neighborhood. With presbyters and deacons pursuing professions and jobs alongside their ministries, there is now a stronger shared sense of mission and witness.

As argued at length in *Community as Church*, the model of the parish that has been in use since the early Middle Ages is no longer viable. Many church people cannot comprehend this, assuming that this model is the only that God imagined since it was established in the first days of the church. Nothing could be further from accurate. There is nothing theologically binding, nothing sacred, about what made sense in the agricultural small town or the urban world of the Roman and Byzantine empires. The political system in place during much of Christian history no longer exists;

4. 1 Cor 9:9–14; Phil 4:16–19; Acts 10:7; Luke 6:2.

5. 2 Thess 3:7–10; Acts 18:1–3; Acts 20:33–35.

neither do many other situations. In addition, our life expectancy is longer. As described in previous chapters, the result of the lack of change has been the shrinkage of many parishes, as seen in the Church of England diocese of Chelmsford, which made a decision to cut sixty full-time, paid clergy positions.[6] This has happened in many other places too, including here in the US, where parishes continue to contract. Hence the importance of Caimano's "free range" priests and Doyle's idea about self-employed clergy, not to mention the yoking together of parishes so that one priest might cover multiple churches. While large congregations with multiple pastors will remain, these have always been exceptions.

Whether differentiated as bishops, presbyters, and deacons or simply considered pastors, the ordained have ministries specific to their position and local setting. It is not just Doyle who sees parishes as "missional" communities in the future, freed from many of the canonical obligations of the past. Put differently, congregations theologically need not be the local franchise of a denomination, like a McDonald's or 7-Eleven. Local congregations are, in effect, returning to their original identities as gatherings of believers for worship, fellowship, and works of love. Each is not a new parish plant but a community in mission, an assembly gathered for witness and service in the larger local community. This model makes sense in the twenty-first century even if it did not in the fourth, eleventh, or, for that matter, the nineteenth or early twentieth. Perhaps in time, the path of establishing full communion among historic church bodies will increase. The buildings that presently house various denominations might be united in word, sacrament, and work. The ordained ministries of presbyters and deacons, as well as bishops, could be recognized by what were once independent church bodies. Competition among denominations might become a thing of the past. Already, this is happening among some Lutheran, Presbyterian, Episcopalian, and Reformed Church parishes. It would be the coming to reality of the ecumenical movement of so many decades, now for the life of the body of Christ and the life of the world.

The rooting of the ordained in congregations is a good thing. In his study, John Jillions brilliantly sustains that this is, in effect, traditional, showing Paul's passionate concern for the "building up" of the community, the body of Christ.[7] There are no first- or second-class citizens in the church, just those who bear the cross and strive for the justice and love

---

6. Williams, "Chelmsford Set to Cut 60," 5.

7. Jillions, *Divine Guidance*.

of the kingdom of God in the world. Some are pastors, others evangelists, teachers, and so on. All the church does is realized by the community as one, together, and, as Afanasiev repeatedly reminds us, this is maintained in the Acts of the Apostles. It remains the task of all who minister, both the ordained and the rest.[8]

DAVE BARNHART: FORMS OF MINISTRY AND CONGREGATION THAT ARE NOT SO NEW

Staying with practical aspects of the ministry of the ordained, we turn to Dave Barnhart, a United Methodist pastor with years of parish experience in the planting of mission congregations and a Duke Divinity School doctorate in homiletics and ethics. In recent years, Barnhart has distanced himself from denominational programs of congregational expansion. Rather than spreading what he calls the typical "white steeple" new parishes of his church body, he has returned to the very earliest model of parish life, that of house churches. He is chief pastor of a network of house churches called the parish of St. Junia, named for one of Paul's colleagues in ministry who, with her husband, Andronicus, led a house church in the first century CE.[9] He describes this work in a series of posts in *Ministry Matters.*[10]

The type of small, house-based congregations that Barnhart leads were the parishes of the early years of the Christian movement. The apostle Paul names them, describing some of their activities along with their serious conflict. He also writes to some of them in locations such as Thessalonika, Corinth, Philippi, Galatia, and Rome. He identifies leaders and members of these congregations as his coworkers, including Junia and Andronicus, Lydia and Phoebe, Prisca and Aquila, and Nympha, among others.

Not surprising, religious "nones" and "dones," as well as other non-churched people, have been the target populations of denominational mission efforts. Although house churches are very different social and spiritual realities, such "white steeple" strategies have still operated with the idea

8. For another vision of how the threefold ministries might look, see Croft, *Ministry in Three Dimensions.*

9. See Saint Junia United Methodist Church's Facebook page at https://www.facebook.com/SaintJunia/. See also Worthy, "Pastor David Barnhart"; Barnhart, "Travel, Faith, and the Environment."

10. Barnhart, "Methodist House Churches." See Barnhart's ongoing posts in *Ministry Matters* at https://www.ministrymatters.com.

of church planting and growth as measured by the number of members and, of course, their contributions and activities. In some mission-planting programs, specific numbers of "bodies and bucks" are required to move to the stage where a pastor is assigned.

Barnhart does not argue with the suitability or preferability of house churches. Unlike mission plants, they have few if any startup costs; there is no rent for a meeting space, no salary for a pastor, and no goals for membership growth. Intimate and small, the absence or loss of a person or a family is monumental. They can also be very welcoming; a small group can facilitate powerful bonds and sharing at levels deeper than in a typical parish. However, like all small groups, they do experience challenges with dynamics. While intense in interaction and relationship, their psychological and social demands make little room for avoiding conflict. House churches also have a tendency to be allergic to additional members, fearing that they might upset patterns of interaction. The norm, as a result, has been to spin off another house gathering when the church begins growing. While classic church plants emphasize events and programs that attract new members, recruitment, and retention, house churches have no need for strategies to increase membership. In addition, when the life cycle of a house church is complete, it can discontinue without the drama and the complications of an established congregation.

Barnhart offers many other lessons learned from the experiences of the St. Junia network. Without descending too extensively into detail, a few are worth noting. One is the absolute centrality and importance of the service of worship. This is what house churches gather to do: to hear the word, break the bread and share the cup, pray, and learn. The home setting encourages hospitality and is supported by simplicity and generosity. Everyone who comes is crucial, and those who do not are missed. While there is a much higher level of commitment, there is also no performance preaching. Rather, the leader is responsible to reflect on the readings while those gathered react and share their takes. This type of interaction also occurs during the prayers in the liturgy. In addition, there is usually a strong inter-generational character, likely because of the appeal of house churches to families with kids. Sunday school takes on more casual but intensely interactive forms. As a result of the dynamics inherent to these institutions, formation in the faith comes not just from lessons but from participation, sharing in prayers, communion, and everything else the house church says and does.

At a house church, the living out of the liturgy during the week, or the enactment of faith, is not a congregational project with a parish logo on it. Rather, members find niches and corners for their service. Although the question of "viable congregational size" diminishes, maintaining a building, supporting a contracted pastor, and all the other machinery of a typical congregation are not done away with but assume simpler, smaller forms. In all of these ways, house churches, as Barnhart convincingly argues, show that "bigger" is not better.

HOUSE CHURCHES AND PASTORS

As shown in the above section, house churches have aspects particular to their size and character and are not quick fixes for denominational decline. Barnhart observes that they have their own rhythm, a way of growing and dividing, and even of attrition, quite unlike typical parishes. The spinning off of another house gathering is quite intense spiritually and emotionally. Careful inspection of Jesus's ministry and the community of his disciples in the Gospels, particularly the apostolic letters and Acts of the Apostles, is most useful in discerning how to continue to make these assemblages viable not as a recreation of the first-century house church but in the complicated, often divided and discouraging world of the twenty-first century.

While Barnhart does not devote extensive attention to it, what happens to the ministry of pastors in the St. Junia network is tantalizing. The Methodist tradition is a highly structured, rule- and committee-governed ecclesial reality. Yet its history contains some surprising elements that at least in principle support ministry in house church contexts. In the eighteenth century, John Wesley remained a priest of the Church of England, and the liturgy of *The Book of Common Prayer* formed his vision for Methodist worship and church order. For Wesley, the bishop remains essential, as do the elder and the office of deacon. In time, there was much missional adaptation of ecclesial components to Methodism. Meanwhile, Will Willimon's approach to the ordained and their ministry makes clear the continuity of tradition and adaptation of mission to different times and settings. It is obvious that house churches cannot simply send a member off to seminary or even to the years-long hybrid, mentor-focused formation systems in use now. If there are precedents that are instructive, these would be given by the lay preachers who emerged in Methodism's earliest days, local leaders who would preside and preach in gatherings or classes that met in homes. Likewise, today house church pastors can emerge from such gatherings. They can be mentored by a supervising pastor or overseer, as Barnhart is for St. Junia's.

The development of indigenous clergy in some mission contexts is useful here. I refer not so much to the location of European or North American seminaries but rather to community-recognized lay leaders who were then mentored by presbyters and in turn functioned within their own communities. This was an earlier pattern among Eastern Orthodox communities in Alaska. Provisional elders or lay pastors in Methodist and Presbyterian contexts would be other examples of ministerial adaptation. I find it perplexing that ordination is withheld, requiring a more classic formation and certification, something with really no precedent historically before the Reformation. With alternative, nonresidential, and hybrid formation programs being used both here and abroad, could not the same happen, with further modifications, for leaders of house churches?

Last, Barnhart cites the importance of mutual pastoral care among members of house churches, which Cathie Caimano also underscores as necessary for priests in parishes today. Rather than a replacement for the care of pastors, the idea is that pastors help members learn to exercise their own vocations as the priesthood of all the baptized. In the mutual care of each other that it entails, this highlights something that has always been present in congregations. Barnhart then goes on to devote attention to how the size of house churches makes interpersonal dynamic and conflicts more crucial than in larger congregations. As mentioned earlier, destructive behavior is much more a threat in small group settings. While there will always be stronger and weaker personalities, those who dominate and those who are recessive, there is a greater need in these congregations for boundaries and strategies for dealing with disruptive personalities and behavior. Barnhart draws on psychologist John Gottman and others on these matters.[11] Suffice it to say, there are no magical solutions, only the facilitation of the pastoral care of members for each other. Clearly, the lines between private matters and those that impact on the group are different. Sickness, employment loss, marital and family conflict, and financial challenges are all more immediate and evident than in even a smaller typical congregation in which there is more "room" to retreat or conceal details. Likewise, disagreement is more immediate and intense, requiring members to tolerate differences more than in the typical parish context. There is simply more that is visible,

11. Barnhart, "Methodist House Churches."

audible, and shared among eight to twelve people in a private home. The challenges of the first century CE remain instructive to these contemporary interpersonal challenges. As Afanasiev observes, each house—whether of Junia and Andronicus, Prisca and Aquila, or others—was truly the church in all its fullness, "the church of God in Christ," but only in communion with other churches in other households. There was in the first century CE, of necessity, the stability of a communion of the many local churches with each other.[12]

Church bodies or denominations continue to have trouble when they do not see their own particular patterns and theologies replicated. Hence, they often cannot see "church" or "ordained ministry" unless it looks like what is typically "Orthodox," "Catholic," or, for that matter, "Methodist," "Episcopal," "Lutheran," or "Presbyterian." House churches highlight just how trapped we can become by our ideas of history and tradition, as well as how dynamically tradition can be lived in very different settings.

While Barnhart offers a great deal more on the intricacies that house churches offer to typical congregations, he also underscores what many others in this book say about the ordained and their ministry. It might seem that the ordained are tied to the typical parish model and have no place in house churches. Yet pastoral ministry, while something that all members can do, remains crucial in the life of every community of faith. It is not a vestige of another time and sensibility any more than the figure of Rabbi Jesus and the disciples who led churches established in the houses of Phoebe, Lydia, and the rest.

ANDREW ROOT: PASTOR IN A SECULAR AGE

Another voice that should be heard is that of Andrew Root, who teaches at Luther Seminary, in St. Paul, Minnesota, where formation for ordained ministry includes the already mentioned, mostly nonresidential mentor and parish-based program that recently ran for three years. He has produced a veritable shelf of very challenging books, taking on topics including faith formation, the pastor and the congregation in the secular age, how congregations face decline, and what happens after innovation has tried to "save" the local church. It is courageous, some might say a bit crazy, to discuss so much that has to do with God in a time when people increasingly have little use for religion. Root's work is in constant conversation with several

---

12. Wooden, "Eucharistic Ecclesiology"; Wooden, "Limits of the Church."

contemporary social scientists and theologians, including Charles Taylor, who describes the penetration of our lives, and thus also of the church, by secular culture.[13] In particular, Root examines how the secular age in which we live, according to Taylor, shapes how we are formed in the faith and how we then put that faith into practice.

In Root's examination of the role of the pastor in this context of secularism, it is the apostle Paul's conversion experience on Damascus Road and in the Damascus Church that serves as a model of what ministry looks like in its most ancient enactment. It could be argued that one should look at other figures and in other places in the New Testament, starting with the apostolic letters, then the Gospels, in addition to Paul. To be sure, Root does take these into consideration. Yet, for him the Pauline case is significant. It is a profound personal transformation, the change in name from Saul an indication of the radical movement from oppressor to preacher and witness. There is also the kenotic dimension, a self-emptying of the former persecutor and the taking on of a vocation as messenger, as pastor. Root's perspective here is radical. The call to ordained service and subsequent formation and preparation for a life of ministry should be as demanding and extreme as Paul's conversion experience.

Root's attitude toward the concept of a congregation is just as radical. Throughout his books he criticizes and summarily rejects the desperate strategies of denominations, often extreme in their belief that *only* innovation and change can revive and grow parishes whose pastoral ministry tend to be committed to ecclesial tinkering often derived from corporate marketing schemes. He leans on sociologist Helmut Rosa's concept of "resonance" as an apt stance that pastors and congregations can, and indeed must, take over against the relentless intensity and pressure from within the institutional church to constantly bring about change and new programs. It is as if everything from the past, distant or recent, is taboo, a turnoff to prospective joiners. From hairstyles to eyeglasses, clothes, music, and language, we find amazing "decay rates" in our world, today almost instantly becoming "so yesterday." Root forces us to see the abnormality and the counterproductive quality of this culture, in particular for congregations and their pastors. He sees the wisdom in a contemplative waiting, a quiet openness to God and to each other.

Over and over, Root insists that authentic sources are always there in the tradition, rooted in the Scriptures, sacraments, prayer, and fellowship.

13. Taylor, *Secular Age.*

The dramatic Damascus experience contains these—the encounter with the risen Christ, baptism, healing, and then the lead of the Spirit into apostolic ministry. Paul will argue that this is the path of death and resurrection, the cross and new life, the path for everyone who seeks to follow Christ and for the community of disciples, the church. This is the path for both congregations and their pastors, not the importing of trendy marketing strategies for growth.

LOOKING TO PASTORS FROM THE PAST

A most valuable element of Root's examination of ministry is his historical overview of pastoral figures. He does this by highlighting pastors whose lives and work exemplify the periods in which they served: Augustine, Thomas Becket, Jonathan Edwards, Henry Ward Beecher, Harry Emerson Fosdick, and Rick Warren. Through these six individuals, he looks at two thousand years. The pastors he selects are not chosen because they are necessarily the finest, holiest ministers or even the most notable preachers or administrators. Rather, his aim is to see how historical and cultural factors affect the church and those who serve in ordained ministry.

Given Root's caveats, I think it might have been better to expand the selection, since some extremely important pastors are left out. Although those he examines do embody their historical periods, he overlooks some of the other paradigmatic figures, including those noted through our chapters here, such as Irenaeus of Lyons; Ambrose, Bonhoeffer and Basil the Great; Luther and John Wesley; Billy Graham, Martin Luther King Jr., and Desmond Tutu. Nonetheless, through his selections we see how Augustine contends with the ancient period's situation in which Christianity evolves into a major tradition in the Roman Empire. Becket, meanwhile, represents the medieval world, an enchanted realm of saints, angels, as well as devils where church is the core of culture and the state. The other turns in church history he highlights are familiar. The Reformation's claims of the profound decadence of the Western Church and its motivation for biblical reform, which he also overviews, have, in recent years, been challenged by Eamon Duffy and Diarmaid MacCulloch.[14]

In effect, the historical path of ministry Root describes leads through the medieval period to the Renaissance and Reformation and down to

---

14. Duffy, *Stripping of the Altars*; Duffy, *People's Tragedy*; Duffy, *Reformation Divided*; MacCulloch, *Reformation*; MacCulloch, *All Things Made New*.

the early modern era. It is a history of continuing separation of religion from life, both public and private. That is, it is a history of the emergence of the individual and the appearance of modern nation states through colonial exploration and expansion, revolutions both in Europe and North America, and the appearance of new political arrangements. All the developments we know appear in this timeline—industrialization; slavery and its precipitation of civil war and abolition; immigration; and the rise of national alliances, political movements, and ensuing wars. While the overview provides the backdrop for the dominance of the secular world and culture and all this means for the church and for ministry, Root does not overlook moments of resistance and revival. Still, echoing Taylor, Root repeatedly stresses the loss of faith in our time. We can no longer believe in anything beyond the empirical and experiential. Somehow absent is the emergence of the profound cultural, economic, political, and religious divisions of the twenty-first century, admittedly many of these with their origins in earlier decades.

Although for me Root's vision cries out for the inclusion of others, the figures he holds forward do indeed tell us much about ministry across the church's history. Among other things, Augustine creates a sense of church and the world that later will become a view of two kingdoms. Becket stands against the king and pays with his life, a martyrdom that will inspire pilgrimage and veneration for centuries, reminding us of the centrality of the cross in the life of all Christians, in particular the ordained. He also embodies the conflict that will always exist between the church and the world. Edwards, meanwhile, tries to revive God's transcendence and the fragility of humanity even in a time of the ascent of reason and rational political action. Beecher speaks out against the monstrosity of slavery and racism, as Fosdick raises up the plight of the dispossessed: the workers and immigrants upon whom capitalism preys. Through his selection, I think Root wants us to recognize the diversity of challenges ordained ministry has faced in the past and will continue to confront in our time. Moreover, he points out how each pastor encounters specific situations in past centuries with the same toolbox of prayer, word, sacrament, and dependence on the Spirit.

GOD AS MINISTER

Lutheran pastor-theologian Robert Jenson figures significantly in Root's focus on the core of ministry, as does Barth.[15] In a surprising turn, however, he argues that we must again recognize ministry as "the central shape of divine action itself." God is the exemplar par excellence of ministry, the God of Exodus and Resurrection. This shift clarifies why the particular cultural, political, and social expressions of faith from periods now past and gone need not weigh upon us unduly. These, he explains, are neither to be restored nor jettisoned. Further, although the pastoral figures he presents offer models of ministry appropriate to their times, there is no point in trying to become an Augustine, Becket, Edwards, Beecher, Fosdick, or Warren. Nonetheless, we should listen to them and note their efforts, since ministry, for them as well as us today, is doing what God does. The model Root highlights is that of God as minister.

Root's discerning criticism of the particular trends and strategies of our time—the urge to innovate, to keep producing, building, growing, and changing as if spiritual authenticity would result from such efforts—becomes evident in later books. His distinctive take becomes clear as he reveals why the religious "nones" and "dones" find institutional religion so useless. As he takes us back to the Hebrew Bible and New Testament, he highlights how the experience of God by the people documented in the Scriptures encompasses imperial power, murder, rape, torture, and every other atrocity repeated around us, whether in Afghanistan, Ukraine, Yemen, or elsewhere. He emphasizes that the cruelty of human beings—their indifference to suffering, pain, and hunger—for some reason does not sound as loudly as the sermon on the mount or some of the psalms. But it is all there, in the word of God, both a record of what God wants to say to us and what we ourselves do, despite that word. This is precisely what those called to ordained ministry are supposed to be confronting as they remind their congregations that there is repulsive human evil as well as immense good.

While God has many names or descriptions throughout history—king, shepherd, lover, hunter, farmer, nurturing mother, forgiving father, and mountain, to mention just a few—Root, as noted, directs us toward God as "minister." If this sounds strange at first, it makes sense when we push our vision wider. God is the spouse betrayed who yet searches after the unfaithful one. God is the maker of all who is closer than our own

---

15. Jenson, *Systematic Theology*, vols. 1 and 2.

heartbeat and breath. God is the king and the servant of all. God is the messenger who keeps returning, no matter the abuse endured. God is the healer ignored but resolute in continuing to pursue the wandering child. To see God as the model for the all too human pastors we know—the one who serves and ministers—is both reassuring and troubling. This vision is what lies behind the skepticism and sharp critique of the strategies and methods associated with "church growth"—innovation, change, attracting new members, and increasing resources—that Root raises in the books that follow his study of pastors. If nothing else, his radical image of the Divine Minister raises serious questions about the ways in which large churches employ celebrity-modeled pastors to attract and retain members.

Particularly relevant to our interests here is, in effect, how Root's model of God as minister shapes those who seek to serve God and the people. For Root, what is most important is a pastor's presence, attention, and listening, as pastors are the presence of God and God's messengers. This is accomplished in leading the liturgy, guiding prayer, listening to readings with the assembly, trying to convey what God has to say in those readings, gathering up all the concerns and intercessions of the community, and asking and offering forgiveness from God. Then there is the presiding at the Eucharist, where the minister shares the bread and cup, the washing of baptism, the anointing of the sick, the blessing of marriages, and the commending of the dying and the dead to God with those gathered. Once again, George Keith's refrain is echoed here. Throughout the church's history down through the periods represented by the pastoral figures Roots selects, these sacramental, incarnational actions have been the principal work of pastoral ministry. Today, for many, these divine and human actions are not known, not wanted, not valued, perhaps clouded by negative aspects of pastoral identity and behavior. Nonetheless, they still remain powerful gestures in which bread, wine, oil, touch, and words connect heaven and earth, unifying the divine with the human. They remain powerful even in a secular age, where only what is immanent and verifiable seems true.

In other books, Root retains this view of pastoral ministry, insisting that it be based in prayer and contemplation of the Scriptures rather than in programs for growth or projects for combatting congregational decline and loss of faith. He constructs several case histories, stories of parishes in impossible situations, seemingly destined to close. The answer to their crises, he indicates, is not a brilliant new pastor with radical ideas for change. Rather, their real crisis is loss of faith, or of the ability to do what they have always done, and their path is therefore to wait for the Spirit, continuing with prayer, worship, study, fellowship, and service to those in need. In these holy actions is their future. Authentic pastoral discernment knows this and offers no more, no less. In one recent publication, Root employs the symbolic device of a watchword, explaining that to come upon one is to rediscover the identity of the community and of each member, an identity in and with Christ.

In spite of the institutional apparatus—from the diocese or conference to the larger church body—the church is essential in Root's perspective. The people of God need somewhere to assemble, whether in someone's home, a former public space or basilica, urban cathedrals, or parish churches consecrated to God and offering continuing signs of God's presence with their crosses and steeples, their fonts, altars, pulpits, and icons. As Danish bishop and hymnwriter N. S. F. Grundtvig's writes, the building is an earthly accommodation for the heavenly guest. The people of God are the house built of living stones The church is the household of faith because they are the household of ministry, the site where Christ's ministry is experienced in word, sacrament, fellowship, service, and study. God has gathered people into this household, taken strangers and made them a community. The occupants are ordained in baptism and sustained through prayer, the Scriptures, and the Eucharist. Among them are those who are called and set apart by the Spirit and the laying on of hands to be pastors, priests, and ministers. Together, they act with and in the neighborhood and the larger world around them. Because this community and its pastors have received the ministry of Jesus, they are a community of gratitude, of giving and rest, rest meaning not an absence of action but its goal—the justice and peace of God's kingdom. Community is church. Church is community.

6

Sam Wells

Ministry with the Church, Abundant Life

CHURCH IN THE CENTER OF LIFE

As with some of the others in this book, Samuel Wells also appeared in *Community as Church*, where we learned that alongside his academic training in Oxford, Edinburgh, and Durham, he has spent years in parish ministry, particularly in urban settings. He is presently vicar of St. Martin-in-the-Fields, a large, historic downtown parish on Trafalgar Square in London. Before that he was a visiting professor and dean of chapel at Duke Divinity School. In the UK, he also served socially and economically disadvantaged parishes in impoverished parts of Newcastle, Cambridge, and Norwich. His books poignantly reflect this pastoral service, highlighting numerous narratives of suffering and discouraged people from his parishes and their neighborhoods. His publications are both serious scholarship and vivid accounts of ministry in everyday life.[1] Along with Sarah Coakley, Jessica Martin, and others, he was also a member of the Littlemore Group, whose gatherings and essays produced several powerful books about priestly work and life in the twenty-first-century UK. In this volume, we are drawing on several contributions by members of this group.

Wells has, over the years, pushed many strong perspectives on the church and ministry. He insists that the church must return to be the center

1. Wells, *Learning to Dream Again*; Wells, *Nazareth Manifesto*; Wells, *Incarnational Ministry*; Wells, *Incarnational Mission*; Wells, *Future That's Bigger*; Wells and Quash, *Introducing Christian Ethics*.

of social life in cities and towns. Acquiescing to a marginal position because of decline in members and attendance is unacceptable. So too is turning inward, rejecting the outside world and disdaining the lives of others with the desire to maintain biblical rigor. This retreatism is the sectarian impulse, not the response of a church. The followers of Jesus should be aiming to be at the heart, not the periphery, of the social life of our time.

For centuries, the church held such a central position with respect to its role as a principal patron of literature and the arts. In Protestant culture of the US, this role is not as evident as it is throughout Europe, where even in thoroughly Protestant countries like England and parts of Germany the artistic influence of great churches emanates through the paintings of frescoes and altarpieces and the glorious music of Palestrina, Vivaldi, Bach, and Handel. As they were often the very space where painting and sculpture adorned the liturgy and music and where drama was performed, European churches have been the home of the arts. Today, choral Evensong remains a major attraction of cathedrals all over the UK. In "It's about Abundant Life, Not Hell-Avoidance," Wells wonders why the church should not return to this cultural and social entrepreneurship that characterized the past.[2] Even more importantly, he argues, the church could also engage in social entrepreneurship.

As we have seen, *Community as Church* contains many examples of church spaces used for feeding people, providing counseling and medical services, and even housing. Wells highlights several parishes where the church has been refitted for daily use, such as St. Peter's in Peterchurch of the Hereford diocese and St. James in the West Hampstead neighborhood of London.[3] St. Peter's hosts a community nursery school, spaces for local craftspeople, and a café. Furthermore, at The Hub at St. Peter's, there are art exhibitions, community meals and dances, classes in yoga and Pilates, in addition to the other activities. In this manner, a space that has been sacred since the thirteenth century continues to thrive as a many-splendored community center, or hub, as its name indicates.

Wells describes St. Peter's, including each member in the parish, as "with God on the edge," which, he explains, is where Jesus spent most of his time: on the margins, with those who live at the edge of poverty, desperate, forgotten, and looked down upon. In an essay about the use of imagination and storytelling not only for children but for adults, he makes a similar

2. Wells, "It's about Abundant Life."
3. See its website at https://www.hubcommunity.org.

point. In parishes in very disadvantaged areas, the experience approximates the first-century Palestinian world of the Gospels themselves. The same vivid details evoked in Jesus's parables can be brought to life using methods of narration and response with roots in the Montessori schools and what some religious educators call "godly play."[4]

By now it should be clear why we are listening to Wells. He sees the church at the heart of life. In addition, there is a great deal to be gotten from his analysis of the prepositions we use in talking and thinking about either the ministry of the ordained or the mission of the whole church. Prepositions say a whole lot more than we ordinarily think. Being or working "with," rather than doing things "for" or "to," those in need creates a harmonious, cooperative environment. This, according to Wells, is the "incarnational" way. Insisting that how we describe our relationships shapes how we engage with others, Wells says that mission is always incarnational; it is the continuation of the work of God with us, God in the flesh, Jesus. The ministry of the ordained, in this manner, is inextricably linked to the mission of the church, global as well as local. You cannot have the mission of the whole people of God without the ministry of their pastors. The ordained, then, continue the incarnation in their ministry just like the rest of the community. This is what it is to be the body of Christ.

MINISTRY WITH THE CHURCH AND THE WORLD

As discussed above, ministry and mission are not brought "to," or even done "for," the world, according to Wells. He insists that both ministry and mission are being and working "with" the world, not bringing the world what *we*, the pastors or people of the church, think it is deprived of or needs. This, I think, gets to the heart of Wells's vision of the ministry of the ordained, as well as that of the rest of the community of the people of God, the church. The model is, in effect, Jesus's ministry with others, as the Gospels portray.

Unlike a top-down, clericalist vision of the ministry of the ordained, for Wells ministry is a communal servant endeavor. If an apostolic father like Ignatius of Antioch could say that nothing should be done without the bishop, then perhaps with Cyprian, nothing should be done without the pastors and the rest of the community. This is where Nicholas Afanasiev derives his eucharistic ecclesiology in which the power of love overrules the

4. Wells, "Imagination," 65–84.

power of law. The ordained start out as members of the community, where they are identified and by whom they are called to ministry. Because they are "with" those being served, the ministry of the ordained and of the rest of the baptized is a relationship of sister and brother; they are not benefactors or the enlightened, privileged. The ministry of the ordained is communal in another sense as well; it is rooted in solidarity, both with those in the ecclesial community and with those in the world beyond.

Wells reminds us that in so many areas—education, social services, health care, the protection of the environment, and the development of investments and jobs—we routinely think of ourselves as the sole agents of change, those we seek to serve as the passive recipients, the less-than-able targets of generosity, uplift, and betterment. Two of his books expound very clearly on what he sees as the "incarnational" model of ministry. In *Incarnational Ministry*, he offers a sustained meditation on the different dimensions of "being with"— being with God, being with oneself, being with child (that is, pregnant), and being with all sorts of other people including the called, troubled, hurt, afflicted, challenged, and dying. In each of these encounters, Wells has us regard the connection from different perspectives such as presence, attention, mystery, delight, participation, partnership, enjoyment, and glory. These are both different, personal, individual modalities of interaction as well as collective or communal. In this manner, "incarnational" ministry provides a walk through all stages of life, all the points of passage from birth to death, from joy and commitment to depression, distress, and isolation. If I were teaching or supervising seminary interns, I would make this required reading, though Wells intends it for all Christians. All, as the word "incarnational" indicates, are "prophets, priests and kings"; the church, in essence, is "a chosen race, a royal priesthood, a holy nation, God's own people."[5]

Wells's reflections are important not because they offer a "recipe" or "how to do it" guide to faith and life. Rather, he refers to his own journey, acknowledging those from whom he himself has learned, including the biblical figures of Mary and Martha, Lazarus's sisters and Jesus's friends; writers Thomas Traherne and George Eliot; and two public figures from Durham, North Carolina, African American domestic worker Ann Atwater and former Ku Klux Klan leader C. P. Ellis. In effect, the voices to which he has us listen are diverse and riveting, and his book is a powerful and

---

5. 1 Pet 2:9.

provocative call to reassess what we believe and how we live. It is his earlier *Nazareth Manifesto* made more specific.

In addition, *Incarnational Mission* offers powerful accounts of pastoral interactions, both Wells's own and those he has culled from wider reporting and reading. He draws on John Betjeman as well as Dostoevsky, George Eliot, Augustine, Karl Barth, and Charles Wesley, very eclectic voices to be sure. Though rooted in Anglican tradition, he is always ecumenical, open to all traditions and the broader world. In effect, to go beyond the ministry in the church, he turns to the mission or outreach of not just pastors but of all Christians to the entire world.

For me, Wells's emphasis implies that ordained ministry has no future as parochial, as afraid to venture out past the boundaries of a body, denomination, or, for that matter, faith tradition. Serving in a small, remote desert town has impressed on me that being ecumenical needs to be natural, simply how we operate. Whether Episcopal, Methodist, Lutheran, Catholic, or Latter Day Saints, we are all children and servants of one God, disciples of the same Christ. We are there with all people, those who identify with a congregation or tradition and those who do not. This is made clear when we assist those in great need, as occurred during the pandemic. I speak here from my experience in the Borrego Ministers' Association, the ecumenical group of laity and clergy in the small desert town of Borrego Springs, California, that I mentioned earlier.[6] Still today, though the pandemic has softened, those who come with serious financial needs know they are going to be heard and answered by laity and clergy, people of faith and compassion. Their own faith identification is not important. Their needs and those of their household are.

While Wells insists that mission is the call upon all members of the people of God to serve, it necessarily incorporates the ministry of the ordained. The dimensions of mission that he specifies include presence, attention, mystery, delight, participation, partnership, enjoyment, and glory. These are ways in which we relate to others, expressing ourselves and what we believe. Wells knows that these dimensions are not exhaustive and that some overlap. When describing glory, for example, he compels us to reflect upon how often we experience this in engagement with others. He invites us to see how the Spirit breaks into our interactions, how grace erupts upon us. He reminds us that God ought never be excluded from our relationships with those around us. For me, his effort is consistently incarnational, an

---

6. See https://borregoministersassociation.org.

echo of the saying of Irenaeus that the glory of God is a human being fully alive.[7]

As he moves through the other dimensions, Wells underscores that when we are present with another, when we listen carefully and attend to the ones before us, we ourselves become "sacraments." When we stand before the other, God is standing with them. Meanwhile, delight and enjoyment are dimensions of mission already incorporated into preaching and church school through storytelling, as "godly play." Mystery reminds us that we see only partially, dimly, and our careful theological statements and canons ultimately fail in capturing the splendor of God, the wonder of the kingdom and nourishing community that is church. In all of these dimensions, Wells insists that to be "with" means to be present and aware that the other is present to us. It means listening, awareness, and resisting the urge to turn every neighbor and situation into a "problem" to be solved. Rather, he reminds us to appreciate that they are also a mystery, a wonder. Delight, he explains, is allowing oneself to be surprised, to discover something new and different as well as to enjoy the person or situation for their own sake. The "with" of being with is most clearly evident in modes of engagement that are participatory and partnering rather than professional dominance. Glory is praise, thanksgiving, and joy all at once. It is experiencing God as all in all, in Christ.

MINISTRY IS IN AND WITH THE WORLD

Wells fits these dimensions of being into an inventory of persons and situations we encounter all the time. He wants us to consider the sheer diversity of those with whom we relate and work. At one end of the spectrum are government agencies, large organizations, and corporations. On the other, he describes various kinds of people—the lapsed; seekers; those of no faith; those of other faiths; those hostile to faith traditions or to various ethnic, racial, and religious communities; as well as neighbors who work and live in proximity to us. Through the diversity he describes, he stresses the complexity of our world. Although we are one in humanity with those around us, we are so different. As already stated, Wells also emphasizes our being with a variety of people who have been excluded by oppression; disadvantage; another form of affliction; or a physical, emotional, or social challenge. The temptation to take a superior position, even out of concern and a desire to

---

7. St. Irenaeus of Lyons, *Against Heresies*, 4.20.7.

help, must be evaluated as removing us from solidarity with the excluded. Rather, Wells's vision of ministry consistently connects the church with the world around it, with those living and working in area streets, apartments, houses, schools, and shops. There is no retreating into the church building as a kind of escape from the diverse, noisy, messy, conflicted world. Rather, the church exists to be "with" this world, to share the bread of life and cup of salvation, to extend liturgical action into the life of the larger community.

The consequence of this for the ordained is clear but not necessarily accepted. The pastor of a parish is compensated, or used to be, for the "cure" or care of the souls therein. The priest is there not only for the active members, those who pay his "freight," as it were. Historically, the priest was in the service of every person living within the boundaries of the parish, whether they came to church or not. Still today, a priest can be active in community groups such as Rotary, Chamber of Commerce, and other not-for-profits. Sometimes, as in the case of the Borrego Ministers Association, clergy create a new ecumenical organization to meet the specific needs of that community. There are others, including the Welcome Ministry of El Cajon.[8] We see now more clearly than ever that neither parish nor pastor exist just for themselves. Rather, as John's gospel puts it, they are here "for the life of the world."[9]

MINISTRY, CHURCH, AND ABUNDANT LIFE

As we have seen, and as noted in my earlier book, Wells has something powerful to say about ordained ministry as well as about the purpose of church in the community. In effect, he thinks about the local church of the parish as a priest of the Church of England. Across the UK, there are hundreds of historically designated church buildings, some with Saxon or Norman parts, many with later medieval sections. They are not all needed anymore, given that cars have made travel to church quicker. Also, there are often several churches within a very limited distance, sometimes in the same village. Some have been officially declared "redundant" and are used only for specific events like a wedding or harvest festival. Others remain integral parts of a parish or benefice that now encompasses several churches. Sensitive to these treasured, sacred spaces, Wells writes about efforts to better use them. He emphasizes that they are not buildings preserved by

8. See its website at https://welcomeministryec.org.

9. John 6:51.

the Church Conservation Trust but parishes "still open for business" even when part of a cluster.

In this manner, Wells homes in on a question that could not be more basic. Why is the church here? What is the church's mission, reason for being, in the twenty-first century? In "It's about Abundant Life, Not Hell-Avoidance," he goes right to the New Testament for a powerful statement on the church's purpose: "Christians don't have to look far for a mission statement for the church—'I came that they may have life, and have it abundantly.'"[10] Wells continues: "Jesus is our model of abundant life; his life, death and resurrection chart the transformation from the scarcity of sin and death to the abundance of healing and resurrection; he longs to bring all humankind into reconciled and flourishing relationship with God, one another, themselves, and all creation. Discipleship describes inhabiting that abundant life. Ministry involves building up the Church to embody that abundant life. Mission names the ways that abundant life is practiced, shared, and discovered in the world at large."[11] For me, the idea that church is for living life in abundance rather than mostly keeping people out of hell, where they'd otherwise go, is a decidedly necessary turn in our theological vision. What else could church be for, in light of Jesus's life and work, his death and resurrection? Down at the bottom of it all, it is a matter of who God is, what our relationship to God entails, and what we make of this.

It was not that long ago that the primary focus of church, and, for that matter, most of Christian faith and practice, was avoiding hell and reaching salvation, its opposite. I can remember vividly the emotional weight that hell and eternal punishment had on me as a child. Heaven, envisioned as a goal or a reward, was always much vaguer. Anyone who had Protestant, Catholic, or Orthodox religious instruction over fifty years ago would have had a similar experience. The imagery was truly ecumenical, though not by intent. I have even heard the echo of that perspective in recent sermons, in which maintaining a "correct" belief, attending services, and contributing to the support of the church are spoken of as if they were an insurance policy for salvation, particularly gracious because it has been provided by God. Surely, the idea of church as a ticket for heaven and an insurance policy for avoiding hell is still around and at work. Likewise, some churches emphasize how they differ from and are superior to others. The writers represented here would not spend much time on this type of insular, exclusive

---

10. John 10:10. Cited in Wells, "It's about Abundant Life."

11. Wells, "It's about Abundant Life."

thinking, sometimes to their own intense criticism. I think here of Pope Francis in particular.

As we have seen, while Afanasiev grounds us in the early church's understanding of both church and ordained ministry, Sam Wells tries to keep us on the streets, in the neighborhoods. He reminds us of the transcendent, vertical dimension of the church while also underscoring its interpersonal and communal responsibilities. He thinks church should be in the middle of things, not at a distance. In terms resonant with the Gospels, the gathering of believers and the work of those set apart is all about new and abundant life—with God and with each other.

7

Barbara Brown Taylor

Ministry Difficulties and Failures

REVEALING THE HARDSHIPS OF MINISTRY

The temptation is to call this chapter "ministry miseries," in particular those of one priest, well-known preacher and writer Barbara Brown Taylor. However, that sounds maudlin and heads in the direction of indulging in victimization. Rather, people of integrity and strength have talked about the real difficulties of being pastors. The literature here is rich, discerning, and powerful, including accounts by the theologically provocative former archbishop of Edinburgh, Richard Holloway; the late priest, psychologist and seminary president, Donald Cozzens; Orthodox priest William Mills; and Lutheran pastor Barbara Melosh.[1] And then there is Barbara Brown Taylor. While popular culture delights in the dramas of "spoiled" and fallen priests, Taylor is one of few who focus on the challenges of the life of the ordained.

Pastors are often the chief casualties in the shrinkage and decline of parishes. They get blamed for everything, from blocked toilets to the temperature in the church building and the state of parish finances. Most often, the issues covered in surveys and studies are severe challenges to their psychological, physical, and spiritual health. While found throughout the population, "burnout," chronic depression, anxiety and panic attacks, struggles with eating, substance addiction, and self-medication figure as

---

1. Holloway, *Leaving Alexandria*; Cozzens, *Notes from the Underground*; Mills, *Losing My Religion*; Melosh, *Loving and Leaving.*

major issues for priests. Clergy families are not immune to the challenges and problems manifest in their congregations and in society as a whole. There are financial worries as well as stresses from relationships and congregation expectations. As a result of such hardship, within the last decade or longer, surveys have revealed that a third or more of clergy opt out of congregational service or ministry itself within five years of ordination. For more than twenty years, I served at a parish that regularly had seminarians assigned for a year's internship. Following former interns, while an admittedly small sample, nonetheless evidenced the ending of marriages and all the issues just mentioned.

Barbara Brown Taylor's *Leaving Church*, one of the most riveting clergy memoirs in recent years, is part of her series of powerful reflections on spiritual life.[2] First brought to my attention years ago by one of my former interns and students, William Mills, himself the author of a moving account of his ministry, the memoir, along with the rest of Taylor's work, figures importantly in my own.[3] There is a paschal quality to it, a narrative of hope and loss, of leaving and finding, a kind of dying as well as resurrection.[4] After decades in parish ministry as an Episcopal priest, Taylor spent almost the same amount of time as a professor of comparative religion at Piedmont College, the focus of another of her books, *Holy Envy*.[5] In *Leaving Church*, she offers an unflinching account of leaving a parish that she helped grow and flourish. Full of conflict and complications, it is a story difficult to quickly summarize. As the others represented in this book would agree, she shows that the ordained are fallible, often defective, and unsuccessful. In spite of their spiritual formation, they remain human beings. While making no attempt to minimize her shortcomings and failures in ministry, Taylor reveals how she becomes a witness to the mystery of God. Using very ordinary tools, she manages to do what God needs to be done. Although her account is indeed one of loss, as her story continues, it is clear that it is also a narrative of finding what God wanted her to be and to do. She thus leaves us a tale of dying and rising, of strength in weakness.

---

2. Taylor, *Leaving Church*; Taylor, *Altar*; Taylor, *Learning to Walk*; Taylor, *Holy Envy*.

3. Plekon, *Hidden Holiness*; Plekon, *Saints as They Really Are*; Plekon, *Uncommon Prayer*; Plekon et al., *Church Has Left*; Plekon, *World as Sacrament*.

4. *Time* included Barbara Brown Taylor as one of their 100 most influential people in America for the year 2014. See Dias, "Barbara Brown Taylor."

5. Taylor, *Holy Envy*.

Rather than summarize Taylor's substantial account of her life before seminary and ordination, I urge readers to go to *Leaving Church* themselves. Although elsewhere I have written about it, along with Taylor's other books, at some length, for present purposes I will note only a few details pertinent to ordained ministry. Some of us in ordained ministry cannot recall a time in life when we did not want to live out this calling. I count myself among those and remember pretending I was presiding at mass as a child. Not surprisingly, being drawn early in life usually leads to serving as an acolyte or as a reader. Back in the day, as was my case, one could do secondary school in a "minor" or "junior" seminary, a church name for a prep school. This early path for teenagers, however, is long gone. Joan Chittister's memoir is powerful in recounting this path, as is Richard Holloway's, and I too attempted a similar description.[6]

Unlike mine, Barbara Brown Taylor's route to ordination was not so clear, as she comes from a non-churchgoing family. Still, her passion for the priesthood, the liturgy, and pastoral work ignited quickly when she was an undergraduate. She went to seminary right after graduation and then realized diaconal and priestly ordinations before going on to do very challenging work on the staff of a large urban church. It was there, however, where the first signs of trouble appeared to her. Completely immersed in her work to the point of having little time for anything else and to the extent of experiencing serious symptoms of stress, she and her spouse, Ed, decided to move to a more rural area.

After making plans for building a house with gardens and horses, Taylor and Ed almost miraculously stumbled upon a small-town parish seeking a new rector: Grace-Calvary Church in Clarkesville, Georgia. The rest became history. The first woman priest at this small parish, she soon attracted more and more members. An extra service became necessary, then another, then an assistant priest and thoughts of enlarging the building. The good work that Taylor did there emanates through her loving descriptions of the parish. Clergy reading this part of her memoir will nod knowingly as she refers to the splashing of the pages of the prayerbook during baptisms, the holy noise of little kids, the beauty of visiting the ill at home or in hospital, the joy of breaking the eucharistic bread and sharing it with the cup, the encouragement of the burial liturgy, and much more, in particular the deep friendships built up with people in the parish:

6. Plekon, *Saints as They Really Are*, 104–49; Plekon, *World as Sacrament*, 1–13, 233–52; Plekon, *Uncommon Prayer*, 95–119, 168–221.

In years to come, when people would ask me what I missed about parish ministry, baptisms and funerals would be high on the list— that and the children who hung on my legs after the service was over, clinging to my knees when I shook their parents' hands at the door. Because they were not old enough to serve on committees or wrangle over the order of worship, the children often had a better grasp of what church was all about than the rest of us did. When one four-year-old rode by the church with his mother and her out-of-town friend, he interrupted them by tapping on the window. "That," he announced to the friend, "is where God gives us the bread." Because he was right about that, the congregation grew. God gave us the bread and we gave it to one another. Then we carried it into the community, dishing up soup at the soup-kitchen, handing out food at the food pantry, setting the table for mothers and their children at the women's shelter.[7]

Taylor's account records the joys of a community regularly gathering at the table. Together, pastor and people pass through the church year from Advent and Christmas creche through Lent, Holy Week, Easter, Pentecost, and then all over again. Meanwhile, baptism, weddings, and funerals mark the lives that move forward in the parish. Taylor is eloquent is capturing this wonderful, shared life of churchgoers.

In spite of the joy she experienced at Grace-Calvary, however, Taylor again became overwhelmed by exhaustion and came to believe she was on duty 24/7. Dread, she describes, became her first response to church council meetings, even to preparing sermons. Sleep became elusive, and her back problems returned. Again, there was no time with her husband. Whatever fire the Spirit once burned in her became distant and inaccessible. Though on the outside she was still bustling about in pastoral caregiving, on the inside she was drying up. The liturgy and the Scriptures felt like they required so many words, which emerged from her not false or hateful but hollow. She had nothing left for her spouse or for herself.[8]

Even worse, Taylor writes that she began to feel the dampening of confidence that tends to happen when a pastor stays long enough in a congregation. She began to hear self-doubt that many eventually experience, which the congregation tends to notice. The type of situation she describes often begins when people get bored with a pastor. What was once

---

7. Taylor, *Leaving Church*, 97–98. Though I have used this quote elsewhere, it's well worth another citation.

8. Taylor, *Leaving Church*, 98–99.

effervescence and eloquence dissipates, and folks also start to find fault with other aspects of a pastor's work. Participation in higher level church and greater community activities tends to be interpreted as ignoring the needs of congregation members. Although the entire parish does not feel the same, the few who start complaining and whispering are notable. In Taylor's case, this added to her own depression and propelled her toward burnout, making the situation nearly catastrophic.

Complicating matters, when all this unraveled for Taylor there were cultural conflicts in the greater church context. As stated, Taylor was the first woman priest in Clarkesville, and she had to help resolve issues surrounding LGBTQ people in the church and larger society, and questions of marriage and ordination. As continues today, abortion, climate change, the status of immigrants, and more were also tense topics with unknown futures. While it is clear that none of these issues can ever be resolved by a single pastor, Taylor's account reminds us that for many parishioners such dividing issues are often brought home to roost with the local priest. I too have seen members both leave quietly and voice their displeasure publicly about a pastor's politics in sermons and activities. Today, clergy routinely note being targeted with the wrong political and cultural perspectives when they make their "great resignation." For Taylor, this all simply became too much. "Having tried as hard as I knew how to seek and serve Christ in all persons, I knew for sure that I could not do it. I was not even sure that I wanted to do it anymore. . . . Feeding people was no longer feeding me."[9]

MINISTRY SEEN LARGER

Although the stress of this situation led Taylor to leave Grace-Calvary, she did not leave everything. At a goodbye gathering, she was tossed, fully clothed, into a swimming pool, an event that in retrospect she describes as a kind of baptismal plunge, a dying and rising. As the incident symbolizes, from her descent into doubt, depression, and discouragement, there would be a resurrection. In the process of leaving, she came to terms with and subsequently wrote about the ways religion can become toxic, suffocating, and escapist.[10] As a result, she came into touch with her core humanity: "I saw that my humanity was all I had left to work with. I saw in fact that it was all I ever had to work with, though it had never seemed enough. There

9. Taylor, *Leaving Church*, 113.

10. Taylor, *Leaving Church*, 150, 168.

was no mastering divinity. My vocation was to love God and my neighbor, and that was something I could do anywhere, with anyone, with or without a (clerical) collar. My priesthood was not what I did but who I was. In this new light, nothing was wasted. All that had gone before was blessing, and all yet to come was more."[11]

Still, Taylor acknowledges that leaving also brought with it a loss of identity and activity. Gone were the vesting, preaching, and presiding each Sunday, the being at the center of a community where she felt needed and of real use to people. At first, as other long-term pastors who have left a congregation or retired have experienced, the deeper loss of identity that had been associated with work was a profound shock, something over which to grieve. But, as clergy often find in retirement and as Taylor implies in the citation given at the end of the former paragraph, she was able to discover new forms of being a priest simply as a believer. Piedmont College offered her a faculty position in comparative religion, and she felt an entirely new vocation as a teacher and mentor. She remained there for pretty much as long as she was engaged in active ordained ministry, teaching, listening to students, and trying to advise them until her academic retirement; she reflects upon these years in *Holy Envy*.

One last piece of Taylor's writing deserves attention here, the sequel, as it were, to *Leaving Church*, and, if one counts them in this way, the middle book in a trilogy, which is how I considered *Leaving Church* and the two books that followed it until Taylor published *Holy Envy*, a fourth book that also seems to fit into the series. In several ways, this "sequel," *An Altar in the World*, offers an important statement. While it does show us where Taylor's path took her after leaving Grace-Calvary Church, and is in this sense also a personal journal, more importantly for our purpose here, it also examines the ministry of the ordained and the ordained themselves through discerning and provocative observations. Taylor notes that in her years of ordained ministry, she had come to regard the world principally through her pastoral vocation. Put another way, she did not take in the world as it is, in all its messiness and beauty, but rather saw it as a target for the work of the church, both her own pastoral efforts and the service of the rest of the members of her parish. Although there is nothing inherently bad or wrong in this, looking outward only from within the walls of the church, or perhaps its stained-glass windows, results in a limited vision that is not unlike how the political leader—or, for that matter, a corporate head, head

11. Taylor, *Leaving Church*, 209.

of marketing, or any other professional—regards the world. The world, in effect, shrinks; it is experienced primarily as a market for sales, an arena for financial development and economic growth, the path toward re-election, or, as medical professionals saw throughout the pandemic, a hospital with endless patients.

By coming to terms with these limitations, after leaving Grace-Calvary Taylor did not at all experience a rejection of church or ministry. Rather, she felt a profound rediscovery—at once theological but also psychological and cultural—of reality, of the importance of what is worldly. Many aspects of this had to be avoided or handled ever so delicately in church—money, sex, gender and identity issues, political conflict, racism, and, in short, so much of the daily experience that both defines and divides us. In teaching undergraduates, she was able to work with a population that is increasingly not churched and often experience religion as judgmental and hypocritical. I incorporated a lot of material on the distancing of people from the church—religious "nones" and "dones"—and reflections on what has led them there in *Community as Church*. A citation of Taylor's that I quoted there deserves use once more: "Somewhere along the line we bought—or were sold—the idea that God is chiefly interested in religion. We believed that God's home was the church, that God's people knew who they were, and that the world was a barren place full of lost souls in need of all the help they could get. . . . The problem is, many of the people in need of saving are in churches, and at least part of what they need saving from is the idea that God sees the world the same way as they do."[12]

AN ALTAR AND MINISTRY IN THE WORLD

Though no longer at the altar or pulpit regularly, Taylor is in ways an even more discerning pastor in her reflections on the worldliness of faith she rediscovered beyond church. To be clear, she is not an opponent of church as a center for gathering around the sacraments and Scripture or organizing both fellowship and service. Taylor does not single out liturgy, creeds, vestments, sacred images, or church teachings in her critique. Rather, to use another expression that I have employed, she wants us to see the world as sacrament.

Taylor sees numerous ways in which such a vision is a return to the Scriptures and the liturgy, the primary sources of theology. In the former,

12. Taylor, *Altar*, 5–7.

God cannot be contained, whether in the tent/tabernacle, the Jerusalem Temple, or any house church or basilica. The sacraments, in effect, are an exchange between the divine and the human, the material and the spiritual. They connect people to God and God to people through water, bread, wine, oil, touch, human gestures, and words. The church buildings that house these events will always reflect the beauty of the kingdom of heaven, the radiant light of Christ, through their expanses and the images within, but the earliest such spaces were truly public, with people coming and going, even during services, engaging in all kinds of activities that were as worldly as they were spiritual. From the mystery plays of the medieval period to church councils and installations of political leaders, these activities were, like the liturgy, actions in which God and humanity interacted. The world, Taylor insists, is therefore not other than, not separate from, the church.

Rather, church and the world, at least from the Scriptures' point of view, are both God's space; they are interconnected. After all, how many New Testament parables and metaphors stem from agriculture, fishing, bread baking, and herding animals? Throughout the Scriptures, both in the Hebrew Bible and the New Testament, we inhabit a world created by God and we are asked by God to follow a teaching, a way that is life and leads us toward light. Within this path there are rulers, many of whom are monsters. There are vengeance killings and other violent events perpetrated by religious people in defense of their traditions against those whom, because of their own faith, appear as threats. There is infidelity and there are traitors. However, there is also love and passion between lovers and spouses. There are faithful friends. If the Scriptures are thought of as a book of life, then it is the whole of life contained therein, the proverbial good, the bad, and the ugly as well as the beautiful.

Taylor is very much the pastor in her rediscovery of the interaction between the world and the church. Although a reader might expect someone who has left parish ministry to think differently, experienced pastors know that we allow ourselves to make church a refuge or escape to our own peril. As Sam Wells implies, the world has turned from the church because the church has turned from the world. Thus, we not only receive from Taylor a moving account of her own journey as an ordained minister, including moments that are really high and very low, but we are also gifted with an embrace of the world and a holistic vision of Christian life through her discernment about an approach that many saints recognized and supported in the past. She captures the drift of all she says with precision here:

"I can set a little altar, in the world or in my heart. . . . Human beings may separate things into as many piles as we wish—separating spirit from flesh, sacred from secular, church from world. But we should not be surprised when God does not recognize the distinctions we make between the two. Earth is so thick with divine possibility that it is a wonder we can walk anywhere without cracking our shins on altars."[13]

MINISTRY IS MESSY, MINISTERS A MESS

Taylor suggests that ministry is not lost but rather opened, even liberated, by experiencing and relating to God in everyday activities. The realization that priesthood is ultimately not tied to a parish; diocese; church body; or the classic activities of liturgy, preaching, teaching, and visiting is another aspect of ministry her suggestions reveal. This often-elusive idea has sometimes been captured where we least expect it in TV dramatizations of clergy. Sarah Coakley, a serious scholar and priest, notes that the popular, hilarious, and sometimes loathed series, BBC One's *The Vicar of Dibley*, was actually brilliant in portraying a pastor's relationship and ties to all of the people in a community. In the series, Dibley gets its first woman priest in the Rev. Geraldine Granger, played by Dawn French, a boisterous, sometimes zany, compassionate character. Vicar Geraldine needs affirmation, companionship, and intimacy. She is human all over the place, and this, above all, is what gradually cements her bond with the people of the community. The over-the-top comedy spans over thirty episodes, and though it sometimes renders stereotypes of clergy and parish council members, playing with personality eccentricities and a parish institution expected to run as efficiently as the postal or health services, it also offers a consistent celebration of the sacred and beautiful in the ordinary.

I think a more recent series from BBC Two, *Rev*, which is based on the memoir of inner-city priest Richard Coles and features Tom Hollander as the Rev. Adam Smallbone, vicar of a declining urban parish in Hackney, East London, may be among the best depictions of the challenges of ministry in the twenty-first century. Father Adam confronts not only the conniving of his immediate superior, an archdeacon, but also his bishop's indifference. His congregation is shrinking, the neighborhood is not supportive, his wife is frustrated, and the decaying church building is targeted for sale by the diocese. In the midst of these problems, Adam comes face-to-face with his

13. Taylor, *Altar*, 15.

own humanity through his weakness and discouragement. Amid his failure to bring back the parish, we see, at the end, a glimpse of the cross/death and the resurrection. Through his journey, the show echoes much of what Taylor shares in her writing; seeing a priest's defects and lack of success in ministry neither devalues the calling nor rejects ministry's power for good.

In effect, Taylor's aim, especially in the books after *Leaving Church*, is to share her own reinventing of her vocation. It is a powerful realization that making a meal, baking bread, weeding a garden, hosting or attending a dinner party, enjoying intimacy with a spouse, and the deep joy of friendship are all are parts of a liturgy of life, moments at "an altar in the world." As she explains: "No work is too small to play a part in the work of creation."[14] Taylor goes on to suggest several practices to stretch liturgy out to all areas of one's life. She includes the most basic of activities: waking up to God, paying attention, wearing skin, and walking on the earth. She goes on to incorporate getting lost, encountering others, living with a purpose, and saying no. Still other practices are carrying water, feeling pain, being present to God, and pronouncing blessings. If there is truth in that pastors care for all of us and all of creation, then the holistic quality of the practices she recommends make sense. I would underscore that many of them are intensely physical, something with which institutional religion has been most uncomfortable. "Wearing skin," for example, precisely means becoming comfortable in and with one's own skin. Although I doubt I would meditate naked before a mirror, the image symbolizes the importance of feeling everything, portraying the sacredness of our senses. It conveys the human need to touch and be touched. Still after the pandemic, we miss the type of physical exchange conveyed by the kiss of peace at the liturgy. Touch, of course, has always been in other aspects of church, whether through the imposition of hands at baptism and ordination, the anointing with oil in the sacrament of the sick, or the joining of the hands of those being wed. Taylor also alludes to the Buddhist practice of walking meditation, which describes the importance of every moment of each step we take. She goes on to talk about being lost in the dark in the woods, a preview of another of her books that carefully examines darkness, another element religions tend to avoid. In effect, the power of the natural world and its impact on Taylor's experience runs through several of her books, starting with *Leaving Church*. She describes staring at the stars with her father as a child or spending the night alone with her dog in a dark cabin. She shows

14. Taylor, *Altar*, 115.

what it is to be, as Alexander Schmemann puts it, a priest experiencing the world with love and offering it to the One who made it.[15]

In addition, Taylor's reflection on the experience of pain is excruciatingly graphic in several specific incidents in her works. Echoing a line from the book of Job, in *An Altar in the World* she observes that pain makes us theologians or at least forces us to come to terms with time and death. The toll that it takes on sleep, our appetite, and, in essence, everything in and about us, however, makes it a terrible teacher.[16] She elaborates that suffering also consists of not being able to feel or relieve the pain of another.[17] Finally, though it may seem all-encompassing, she reminds us that pain does not exhaust our experience of living in the world. Countless instances of healing are also part of our lives.

Throughout her writings, Taylor lifts up community as the essence of church; it is, she insists, what church celebrates and nurtures even if it is also often the site of suspicion, division, fear, and hate. Is this not what a priest, a pastor, is ordained to do? George Keith made precisely this point in his sermon, as we heard earlier. In addition, what John Chrysostom and others saw as the "sacrament" of the sister or brother, the neighbor, is a crucial spiritual practice and a mode of ministry. These writers remind us that although all that makes us what we are can seem to divide us, in the end, it is also what unites us.

Perhaps the best way of conveying the world as a sacrament is by acknowledging, as Taylor does, our corporeal humanity. Bodies, she highlights, are shared by everyone. "My body is what connects me to all of these other people. Wearing my skin is not a solitary practice but one that brings me into communion with all these other embodied souls."[18] Throughout the Scriptures, God constantly keeps coming among us, "moving into the neighborhood," as Eugene Peterson puts it, by coming through matter in the form of words, messengers, food and drink, and bodies. Incarnation may be most obviously represented in Jesus of Nazareth—who connected with his friends by healing touch, prophetic words, and in fellowship through bread, fish, and wine—but a lot of other incarnation went on before and

---

15. Cited in Taylor, *Altar*, 10.

16. Taylor, *Altar*, 164.

17. Taylor, *Altar*, 160.

18. Taylor, *Altar*, 41–42.

continues after him. Taylor insists, "Our bodies remain God's best way of getting to us."[19]

Listening to Barbara Brown Taylor, as we have seen in this chapter, makes for a profound lesson about our focus, ordained ministry, along with the great deal more that she offers. It is important to remember that despite what *Leaving Church* might suggest at first, her account is hardly just one of "ministry miseries." Although she allows us to see some of the toxic properties both of ordained ministry and of the parish through the stress and depression she experienced to church demands,[20] later, as she discusses, she employs her considerable gifts as a preacher and pastor to significantly grow a small-town parish. Her equally superb gifts as a writer allow her to bring her experiences in ministry to us, both the joys and beauty as well as the ugly realities of life in a community of faith. Through these, we also come to see how ministry and the life of faith can be resurrected, reimagined, and refocused on the world outside the walls of the church.

In the books since *Leaving Church*, Taylor does not reject parish ministry but shows how faith is alive and at work everywhere in the world, not just within the confines of church. Numerous other discerning writers like Richard Rohr, Sam Wells, Sara Miles, Darcey Steinke, and Marilynne Robinson, among others, have argued the same.[21] What we receive from Taylor is the "other side" of the story of congregations in our time, one that is seldom studied or narrated, namely the experiences of pastors in the midst of decline and efforts to revive. It is an incarnational narrative of death and resurrection.

---

19. Taylor, *Altar*, 41–42.

20. It seems important to highlight that she experienced these hardships even though she went through the formation program at Yale Divinity School, one of the oldest and most prestigious, and had further training in her church body.

21. Rohr, *Falling Upward*; Rohr, *Immortal Diamond*; Wells, *Incarnational Ministry*; Wells, *Incarnational Mission*; Miles, *Take This Bread*; Miles, *Jesus Freak*; Miles, *City of God*; Steinke, *Easter Everywhere*; Robinson, *Gilead*; Robinson, *Home*; Robinson, *Lila*.

8

Nadia Bolz-Weber

Pastor on the Edge

LIVING AND WORKING ON THE MARGINS

Lutheran pastor Nadia Bolz-Weber is known both for her tattoos and her preaching, as well as her writing and creative work in pastoral ministry. Most often she appears in a clerical collar and with a lot of ink, of which she is proud. It is not easy to do her justice in describing her work. Her autobiographical *Pastrix* is honest in its portrayal of her roots in and flight from rigid evangelical Christianity.[1] The turbulence of her early life, which echoes her friend Sara Miles's similar account, *Take This Bread*, comes across in her forthright details of her addiction, relationships with some very hard people, movement into recovery, and decision to embrace the seminary and ordained ministry.

Upon ordination, Bolz-Weber specifies, she did not desire a call to an ordinary parish. Taking a leap of faith with a tiny group of eight others, she decided to establish a parish that borrowed space from other churches and became the antithesis of virtually every other parish in her Lutheran synod or Episcopal diocese. The church called itself "A House for All Saints and Sinners." Usually referred to as HFASS and facetiously pronounced "half-ass," it was radically open to everyone. In particular, Nadia and the parish

---

1. Although there is much to learn from her account, Bolz-Weber's often very contrary, aggressive attitudes are exasperating. An entire chapter in *Pastrix*, "The Wrong Kind of Different," is an extreme account of her in-your-face vision and behavior. It got me going, and not in a positive way.

offered a haven to the LGBTQ community, people in gender transition, people in recovery, people of color, and others outside the margins. Not your average middle-class parish, it included all those not often welcome in mainstream congregations and even condemned in some church bodies. Though traditionalists in doctrine and liturgy—Bolz-Weber and the parish clung to the ancient liturgy, the Creed, and the sacraments, celebrating the Eucharist every Sunday and feast day—they were radical in communal openness and pastoral outreach, especially to those usually marginalized, excluded, or rejected by the church. Their approach was also undergirded by Bolz-Weber's often cantankerous, always provocative preaching and theology.

After a decade, Nadia decided the time had come for to her move on from HFASS and allow the congregation to develop further with another pastor. She bid farewell on July 8, 2018, and her associate, Episcopal priest Reagan Humber, took over as pastor.[2] On August 20, 2021, Bishop Jim Gonia of the ELCA Rock Mountain Synod installed her as their first pastor of public witness.[3] He noted in his homily that decades earlier, the Presbyterian Church in America had similarly installed the Rev. Fred Rogers for ministry in the public sector for the learning and development of children. Bolz-Weber had never made that connection and loved the idea that two pastors of such different personalities were both to be public ministers and theologians. Though one can only wonder about Fred's take on her most intense and provocative Lutheran personality, I myself think he'd have powerfully embraced her and her commitment to serving God and God's people in very different ways than those of a traditional pastor.

Bolz-Weber's public ministry is self-funded. She is now what Caimano would call a "free range priest." Also a freelance writer, as a speaker and pastor in the public sphere she supports herself as would any other writer or artist in the same circumstances. What is different about her is that the church recognizes her atypical work as authentic pastoral ministry. Perhaps of all the voices we listen to in this book, hers is the one that most definitively breaks the mold of clergy identity and work.

2. Julig, "Headed for a Larger Stage." Humber came to HFASS from St. Gregory of Nyssa Church in San Francisco, home of Sara Miles who, along with sharing Bolz-Weber's turbulent type of upbringing, has similarly documented her parish's doctrinal and liturgical traditionalism and radical openness. See Miles, *Take This Bread*; Miles, *City of God*.

3. Miller, "Nadia Bolz-Weber Installed."

Bolz-Weber's publications include a number of books, two of which inform what we hear in this chapter. Her online presence includes a podcast from *PRX* and *The Moth*, "The Confessional," in which people confess their worst moments, and she offers a personalized blessing in return. The subtitle of her online newsletter, *The Corners*,[4] is "Grace for Fuck-Ups. Prayer for the Impious. A Space for Spiritual Misfits." Repeatedly in her writings, Bolz-Weber specifies that her work has focused on grace and compassion, a message she offers because she herself continuously needs to hear it. She also characterizes her style of pastoral leadership as "screw it, I'll go first," because she is not embarrassed to share her own failings, enabling others to feel they can share theirs.

Bolz-Weber is based in Denver, and her call to public ministry is ecumenical. In addition to the ELCA Rocky Mountain bishop and synod, other sponsors include St. John's Episcopal Cathedral in Denver, where she regularly preaches, and Montview Boulevard Presbyterian Church, a congregation in Denver that hosted her 2021 installation service.[5] There is also New Beginnings, an ELCA worshipping community inside the Denver Women's Correctional Facility, where Bolz-Weber regularly conducts services. Her sermon at St. John's Cathedral in Denver presented the new prison ministry to a wider audience, and Nadia also consistently shares her work in guest preaching and in the online venues mentioned.[6]

RANTING AND RIGHTEOUS, A PASTOR FOR SAINTS AND SINNERS

I suspect that Bolz-Weber might agree that a good way to get to know her is through a rant she shares in a chapter 17 of *Pastrix*.[7] The chapter describes the sudden fame she experienced after giving an Easter sermon in 2011 before an audience of approximately 10,000 at Red Rocks amphitheater; afterward, she returned to her parish to all kinds of folks wanting to visit and worship with her. In the chapter, she ridicules them for wearing clothing brands like Dockers, describing them as soulless suburban liberals who probably eat at Applebee's. She views such conformist though respectable people as invading her congregation of proud deviants and misfits. At first

---

4. See https://thecorners.substack.com.

5. Saint John's Cathedral, "Choral Eucharist May 21 2023."

6. Bolz-Weber, "Enjoy Your Forgiveness."

7. Bolz-Weber, *Pastrix*, 178–87.

read, this chapter is very troubling. Personally, I found myself scowling at her for trotting out of her beyond messy life, full of lousy choices and the apparent manipulation and abuse of people; I wanted to slap her out of her fixation. But she does that herself! In *Accidental Saints: Finding God in All the Wrong People*, she takes on a similarly sneering tone.[8] However, once again, this is precisely where the most striking aspect of her personality emerges. In the midst of her rage, Bolz-Weber hears Ezek 36:26 speaking directly to her, describing God turning a heart of stone into a heart of flesh. Her rant comes to a halt. Her clarity returns, a real gift of God. As she consistently says when she describes moments when her defects and failures have shifted into successes and accomplishments, she realizes that it is not Nadia but God who is acting. She then reflects on how a pastor friend confirms for her that her rage is misplaced and wrong. Why should her congregation of self-styled "misfits" be privileged over white bread, middle-class folks who come to visit? Why assume they are there to gawk? As Nadia's beloved Martin Luther would have said, put the best possible construction on the intentions of those coming to visit HFASS.

Like all of us, Bolz-Weber cannot help being anyone except who she is. She is loud, whether in her tattoos, her jewelry and makeup; her emotions; or her speaking out for those who are too often rejected and marginalized, not just by cultural conservatives but also by their supposed fellow Christians. Nadia has used her loud voice to speak up for so many "saints and sinners"—the very name of her old congregation. One of these is the community of those attacked for their sexual identity, an issue that has divided major church bodies in America and elsewhere perhaps more than any other. At present, it is splitting the United Methodist Church. Meanwhile, it has already broken up the Episcopal Church, the ELCA, and the Presbyterian Church in America, and it is an ongoing point of division in the Catholic Church. Other "culture war" issues include abortion, the role of women in the church, the status of divorced people, the situation of refugees and migrants, and even recently vaccines. As Bolz-Weber knows, it is these and not dogmatic or even doctrinal matters that are separating the followers of Jesus. By welcoming those alienated by these issues back into the church, she helps to heal the church from deeply divisory conflicts.

Like Bolz-Weber, Pope Francis, whose thinking on ministry will be the focus of a later chapter, has also sided with the marginalized. However, the ongoing struggle between the church and these conflict-ridden issues

8. Bolz-Weber, *Accidental Saints*.

has led even him to be attacked by some as a threat to the church's tradition and the very substance of the faith. In spite of this tension, both he and Bolz-Weber are consistent in their solidarity with those who are rejected and condemned. Bolz-Weber's particular embrace of those who cannot conform to middle-class standards and culture is evident in all of her books, which, as we have seen, address marginalization head on. To give another example, *Shameless* is aimed at Christianity's futile obsession with sex.[9] Bolz-Weber sees the church's traditional disdain and repulsion for the body and sexuality as toxic and in need of being burned down. An act of "holy resistance" to the prudery and moralism that persists in the church, the book refutes the idea that these visions are faithful to what God has commanded and put forward in the Scriptures.

CONFRONTATION AND CONSOLATION

Whether in *Shameless*, *Accidental Saints*, or the more autobiographical *Pastrix*, as a narrator, Bolz-Weber remains present in every scene of the drama portrayed as the life of a significantly nonconformist pastor. There is little if any theoretical or conceptual framing of what ordained ministry is in her writing. Rather, there is a running commentary on what she encounters, and this is where she embeds her remarkable insights. With all the self-revelation she presents, it is clear that she is always conscious that she is a person in progress, one in whom God continues to be at work. She says this in particular as she reflects on persons of faith, the holy ones we revere, in *Accidental Saints*:

> I realize God may have gotten something beautiful done through me despite the fact that I am an asshole,
> and when I am confronted by the mercy of the gospel so much that I cannot hate my enemies,
> and when I am unable to judge the sin of someone else (which, let's be honest, I *love* to do) because my own crap is too much in the way,
> and when I have to bear witness to another human being's suffering despite my desire to be left alone, and when I am forgiven by someone even though I don't deserve it and my forgiver does this because he, too, is trapped by the gospel,

---

9. Bolz-Weber, *Shameless*.

and when traumatic things happen in the world and I have no-
where to place them or make sense of them but what I *do* have is a
group of people who gather with me every week, people who will
mourn and pray with me over the devastation of something like a
school shooting,
and when I end up changed by loving someone I'd never choose
out of a catalog but whom God sends my way to teach me about
God's love.[10]

This passage could be a fairly accurate summary of Nadia's take on ministry,
since it is also Nadia's take on life in Christ and in the community of Christ.
The idea of being "confronted by the mercy of the gospel," in addition to
being "trapped by the gospel," underscores the irresistible force of the call
by the Spirit to live the gospel and to serve the Lord and the Lord's people.
There is a Lutheran ring to this down-to-earth description of the experience
of ministry, to the inescapable grasp of grace that, though neither deserved
nor earned, is freely given. Despite weakness and failure, her work comes
back to the central idea of forgiveness.

This work of Christ in a person, as Bolz-Weber indicates, looks remarkably like what a pastor is called to do, not because of inner strength, talent,
or virtue but by and through the power of the Spirit that turns a pastor
into a performer of Christ's work. She makes it clear that her ministry, and
that of all pastors, is centered in Christ, in the word of God. This emanates
through the proclamation of the Scriptures, the washing of baptism, and,
most particularly, in the Eucharist that conveys the sharing of the body and
blood of Christ, which allows the whole people of God to become that body
in and with and for the world.[11] In *Accidental Saints*, Bolz-Weber quotes
one of the members of HFASS who summarize this take on ministry: "Our
'ministry' is Word and Sacrament—everything else flows from that. We see
a need, we fill it. We fuck up, we say sorry. We ask for grace and prayers
when we need them (a lot). Jesus shows up for us through each other. We
eat, we pray, we sing, we fall, we get up, repeat. Not that complicated."[12] She
then goes on to reiterate it in her own inimitable words:

> So often in the church, being a pastor or a "spiritual leader" means
> being the example of "godly living." A pastor is supposed to be the
> person who is really good at this Christianity stuff—the person

10. Bolz-Weber, *Accidental Saints*, 8–9.
11. Bolz-Weber, *Accidental Saints*, 10.
12. Bolz-Weber, *Accidental Saints*, 10.

others can look to as an example of righteousness. But as much as being the person who is the best Christian, who "follows Jesus" the most closely can feel a little seductive, it's simply never been who I am or who my parishioners need me to be. I'm not running after Jesus. Jesus is running my ass down. Yeah, I am a leader, but I'm leading them onto the street to get hit by the speeding bus of confession and absolution, sin and sainthood, death and resurrection—that is, the gospel of Jesus Christ. I'm a leader, but only by saying, "Oh screw it, I'll go first."[13]

PARADOXES OF PASTORING

As seen, Bolz-Weber turns out to be far more perceptive in her understanding of ministry than what seems likely through the brash tone of some of her statements. Another example of her acuity comes forth in her reflections on the pastoral care of a bishop during his wife's terminal illness and death and then as the officiant at her funeral. Somewhat surprisingly, Nadia observes the satisfaction that comes from helping another, noting the creeping feeling of self-importance that accompanies having done something good, assisting another in need. Still, she implies, as Sam Wells articulates in another context, the real embodiment of Christ is in those who are hungry, homeless, mourning, tossed aside, and loathed. The only right preposition for ministry is *with*, not for or to. As the title of a chapter in *Accidental Saints* puts it, "You are not 'the blessing.'" Rather, Bolz-Weber emphasizes, the sister or brother in need before you is. Recognizing this reorients the pastor, nudging her or him back to the example of Jesus in the Gospels.[14]

This notion echoes the take on ministry given by others in this book, underscoring the presumably obvious understanding that ministry is not about the minister but about the one with whom a pastor is working. When ministry centers around self-reference and importance, Pope Francis, for instance, sees gross egoism, a selfishness that is rooted in some sense of divine power and privilege. This can derive energy from an exaggerated idea of professional competence, or again, a mistaking of one's discernment for God's compassion, which ministers should channel. It also manifests in extreme loyalty to a church leader or bishop, blind adherence to the body

13. Bolz-Weber, *Accidental Saints*, 28–29.

14. Bolz-Weber, *Accidental Saints*, 46–48.

of rules governing church activity, and captivity to canons and ecclesiastical structure. Although ministry can become the enactment of corporate culture, as these church leaders remind us, in the Gospels it is about compassion and care. It embodies the compassion exemplified by people like Dorothy Day, telling us not to look past the actual sister and brother in front of us but to rather accept them as the person we should be helping.

Like Day, Bolz-Weber is acutely aware of the sobering reality that our attempts to love and serve are never completely pure, never perfect, never totally effective.[15] We can never fully know, understand, or force the human being who has been called to ministry to act as we would hope. While burying someone who had taken his life—someone she did not know, who was not a part of her parish community—Bolz-Weber made the following points. First, she reflected on how pastors are routinely called to "bury the dead," one of the principal "works of love." Even when doing so for those they have known and loved for years, she subtly observed, for all of their good intentions, eloquence, and the beauty of the scriptural readings and liturgy, there remains a gap. They cannot bridge the chasm between themselves, the living, and the dead. No pastor can make more palatable suffering and pain—that of grief and of wondering if they could have reached out more or, in this case, have been better connected with this young man in his despair. This unexpectedly led Bolz-Weber to realize how very earthy, even disreputable, Jesus's own associations appeared to some, as we see in the book of Matthew: "Look, a glutton and a drunkard, a friend of tax collectors and sinners."[16] For a nonconformist pastor like her, and in the eyes of many others, it remains a mystery how Christianity has become so acceptable, domesticated, diluted, and even at times repulsive.

As a pastor for those outside of acceptable borders, Bolz-Weber is able to extend the power of ministry to those ridiculed and condemned by many who assure themselves of their evangelical faith. Though risky, she takes a stance in her sermons and comments even when she approximates areas often avoided by priests: the "political," the "liberal," or the more recent "woke." Still, as she says, there will always be those for whom a priest is not "traditional" enough and others for whom they are not open and liberal enough.

With all of the division in America, or, for that matter, the world, it would be easy to say that this conflict is a particular malady of our time.

---

15. Bolz-Weber, *Accidental Saints*, 106–10.

16. Matt 11:18–19.

But another cursory look back at the Gospels reiterates how contested Jesus was throughout his ministry and from different groups within his own community of faith. No pastor can escape this, Nadia reassures us. Emphasizing her acceptance of all groups is her sagacious plea to keep the figure of Herod, the monster who ordered the massacre of the innocents in Bethlehem as well as other atrocities, in the Christmas narrative.[17] Though her immediate motivation may seem disarming, she roots her request in a scathing indictment of the romanticization of Christmas through imagery of baby and cozy family scenes portrayed through cultural products like the run of endless Hallmark films that mark the season.

When Bolz-Weber speaks of innocents, she now includes the victims of Sandy Hook and countless other mass shootings at schools and other venues, where hate has been enabled by the access to assault weapons. It is clear, she indicates, that God has not cleaned up or disinfected the world into which God was born as a child, where hostility also ran rampant. In the context of the brutal imperial state and its military in which Jesus was born, crucifixions became more frequent; Jesus's own was dwarfed by the death of 500 Jews a day in late July during the First Jewish Revolt in 70 CE, as Tom Holland and Simon Sebag describe in their respective studies.[18] Even with imagery of the crucified Christ prominent in churches over the centuries—though removed by some Reformation groups—the horror has been numbed, in early centuries deliberately. By lifting up the innocents of Sandy Hook and elsewhere, however, Bolz-Weber reminds us that this ugly aspect of humanity is often at the heart of God's coming among us. Since early on, by choosing to work with others to build a parish community out of people who would not be welcome in many places, she has shown her abiding sensitivity; she is a pastor for even the most incorrigible and difficult sheep.

Bolz-Weber's writing is particularly pertinent within the current social climate of the church. As parishes decline and shrink, and as clergy start to opt out of parish ministry for less turbulent work, what used to be predictable, safe ministry is now anything but this. I recently heard of a diocese in which most parish openings were being filled with term calls where a priest is appointed for a set number of years; while these contracts are renewable, they retain flexibility for both pastor and congregation. With the financial status of so many parishes becoming more uncertain, this type

17. Bolz-Weber, *Accidental Saints*, 74–79.
18. Holland, *Dominion*; Montefiore, *Jerusalem*.

of more tentative approach appears to have merit; it is not a surrender to changes that will continue to unfold, such as the long-term effects of the pandemic lockdown that closed many congregations for a year or more.

Since Bolz-Weber's call was to be a pastor-at-large, specifically a pastor of public witness who moves toward the type of term calls or appointments just noted, she herself knew when it was time for her to leave HFASS and commit the community to a new pastor. Her type of ministry would be heartily endorsed by Cathie Caimano's model of the "free range priest," where, as we have seen, priests serve part-time and ply their professions alongside parish work. C. Andrew Doyle's and Dave Barnhart's revisioning of pastoral ministry echoes this greater flexibility and freedom, which in some ways hearkens back to the first few centuries of church history, before the church became state-aligned, or later, when it was the spiritual monitor of culture.

Bolz-Weber offers too many riveting narratives to be included here. In particular, her thoughts on the celebrations of Holy Week, Good Friday, and the Easter Vigil are especially moving. She describes, for instance, the "new" paschal candle made from the melted down remains of earlier ones each year at HFASS, so that bits and pieces of past Easters appear for yet another Resurrection feast, a sign of death and new life for all those gathering in the dark to greet the light of Christ, the risen one.[19] Her reminiscence of taking a Good Friday liturgy, which is essential to the paschal mystery, to a litter-strewn lot near where a mother who killed her children then committed suicide stresses her ability to vividly locate the crucified Christ in the midst of tragedy and suffering.[20] However, also aware that life is not unremitting heartbreak and pain, she includes many less serious moments. Many ordained can relate to her tale of promising to officiate at a wedding without looking to her calendar of commitments and noticing that she had previously agreed to speak in Australia. Only after also agreeing to the wedding did she discover that she would be thousands of miles away and unable to be there. The couple, she recalls, assured Bolz-Weber that they loved and forgave her, understanding her frailty and lack of attention to detail. Although she experienced mountains of guilt, remorse, self-torment, and more, the act of forgiveness resounds in so many of her narratives, emphasizing the deep and seemingly limitless mercy that extends from the

19. Bolz-Weber, *Accidental Saints*, 11, 145–53.
20. Bolz-Weber, *Accidental Saints*, 137–43.

couple to be married to countless others, including, in particular, God.[21] While self-importance, self-righteousness, and guilt make even this boundless grace at times sting, particularly when we become consumed by how we have let others down, Bolz-Weber reminds us to feel the prick of the needle of what Thomas Merton describes in another context as the great "mercy within mercy within mercy."[22] Quite the opposite of the tendency to turn inward, this always emphasizes God and the sister and brother who are our neighbors.

In this manner, reading Bolz-Weber's account of her years writing, preaching, and teaching, particularly at HFASS, forces us out from the beautiful and safe spaces found in our sanctuaries, particularly in stable, energetic parishes that are signs of life in a time when the church is in eclipse. It is impossible not to notice that the parish that is the world of her books, HFASS, was by its very makeup constantly not far from falling apart. Located in space leased from other parishes, it began with eight people on a Sunday but had grown to over a hundred when Bolz-Weber left. Her writing implies the question: What parish is there that is not precarious?[23] The itinerant band of disciples following Jesus all over Galilee, Judea, and Samaria, she reminds us, was the original.

No matter how ragtag the finances and the flock, Bolz-Weber makes a great case for the work of ministry to be always possible and needed. When a pastor's time in a specific place comes to end, the work of ministry does not. In effect, Bolz-Weber continues ministry as a pastor-at-large at a women's correctional facility, her bishop having commissioned her to just such public ministry. Her singular personality and way of serving echo in the situation of the distinctive communities she attends. One size, she reminds us, does not fit all. All this said, we have seen much in her words and actions as pastor that we will want to celebrate and take away with us.

---

21. Bolz-Weber, *Accidental Saints*, 173–80.

22. Merton, *Sign of Jonas*, 321–52.

23. In effect, when I look at the profiles of parishes seeking new pastors, I am struck not only by the professional advertising strategies that come into play, in even modest congregations, but also by larger ones with significant endowments, campuses, staff, service schedules, and members.

9

Sarah Coakley and Rowan Williams
Priests as People of Prayer and Place-Keepers

PRAYER IS PRIMARY

In this chapter, we will mostly listen to Sarah Coakley, a teacher and scholar who has also sought out priestly work, though it is worth noting how others in the Littlemore Group that met some years back also had an uncommonly rich vision of what constituted ordained ministry and the life of a priest. From that group, we have already heard from Sam Wells. In both his and Coakley's respective collections of essays, it is prayer that stands at the head of the Littlemore Group's reflections, albeit in very different ways. The centrality of prayer for a priest, they show, is by no means only conceptual, a theological principle. Rather, prayer and what it does to a person figure very powerfully in both of their often-moving experiences of ministry.

In a number of her publications, Coakley has eloquently written of her experience of what happens in prayer, or better, of what has happened to *her* in prayer. She calls prayer "divine propulsion,"[1] which she defines as a crucible in which we are tested by the fire of God's presence.[2] Coakley says that the feelings of utter incompetence, ignorance, or being hopelessly lost are actually the start of God's working in and with us. How could it be otherwise, when, as in the words of the Lord's Prayer, we are called out of our reasoning, our control, our habitual ways of acting, and into a wholly

1. Coakley and Koh, "Prayer as Divine, Part 1"; Coakley and Koh, "Prayer as Divine, Part II."

2. Coakley, "How My Mind."

other and different place—that of the kingdom—where it is God who makes things happen. We should pray as we can, she says, not as we can't. Rather than obstacles, our incompetence and weakness are akin to the road by which God gets to us.

While this principle of weakness as a starting point for a deeper communion holds for all, it is particularly relevant for those called and ordained to serve the people of God. Coakley notes that as a priest, an important experience was her realization of how poor and inadequate her prayer was for the people around her, those who prayed with her at liturgy, those with whom she communed and to whom she listened. I think many pastors can relate here, including me. Many years ago, I came face-to-face with this inadequacy when a parishioner asked me to pray for her mother. Although I listened and assured her of my prayers, I was mortified the next Sunday when she found me at the post-service greeting line and thanked me profusely, praising the power and efficacy of my prayer. Other than the moment of her asking me to pray, I had not thought of her ailing mother at all during the week. As a result of this confrontation, I started a prayer list that I still keep and have copied over many times from a tattered state, which I have written about in *Uncommon Prayer*.[3] Conveying a similar process, Will Willimon's reflections on pastoral ministry emphasize the significance of failure and doubt as one movement of the essence of the paschal mystery—falling and rising.

Further reflecting on the process of ministry, Coakley underscores how weighty a task it is to continually gather up the prayers of the community, pray on their behalf as well as with them, and speak about what God has to say while also listening carefully oneself. That is quite a lot! To do it effectively, one is reminded of the saying carved on the inside of a pulpit centuries ago that indicates that the preacher must first of all hear what is being preached her/himself. That is, the sermon must be a word from God for the preacher if it is to be a word for the listeners. In other words, if our words are going to have any meaning for our listeners, we must first preach to ourselves.

EXPECTATIONS OF PRIESTS

In her reflections on ministry, Coakley insists that the community knows that their pastor is ordained to do things no one else can. This does not

3. Plekon, *Uncommon Prayer*, 95–119.

make the clergy better or more holy, though some believe as much. Coakley rather argues that if attentive, the ordained can become more aware of the ways in which the community is drawn to them. This is not because priests are particularly attractive or brilliant but because, as George Keith said so well, they bring God to the people and the people to God.

Coakley also observes how today, from the parish on up to the diocese, those in ordained ministry are saddled with ever-changing and never-diminishing expectations. These include promoting national or regional programs or emphases and adhering to ever more rigid standards of safeguarding and professional behavior. As if this were not enough, pastors are expected to be successful in their mission to grow congregations and spread the good news. While none of these are really objectionable, the corporate and commercial models employed by bishops and denominational leaders and staff either assume that the clergy have dedicated prayer lives, or worse, that prayer is just not valued in the same way as the urge to keep expanding the project of "church." In this context, Coakley says that pastors would do well to discern what is truly necessary and refers to what Jesus said to Martha about her sister Mary of Bethany. Mary's apparent idleness was the kind of quiet inaction that is silent prayer, in which we present ourselves before God. To do this, as demonstrated by Christians down the ages, opens us up to the whole expanse of our desire. In effect, Coakley goes on to speak of the erotic as a natural component of prayer. Such prayer forces us to experience our smallness, our inability and a great deal of vulnerability. In particular, Coakley sees this type of prayer as crucial for the ordained, who are always vulnerable to the rest of the people of God as well as to the rest of church leadership.

Coakley goes on to contend that as a person of prayer, the pastor comes to all aspects of parish life with more than strategies for growth. In this sense, she echoes Andrew Root, indicating that prayer brings the pastor into God's way of seeing things, a vision that is often not readily apparent, which he or she can then share with the community, returning us to the now familiar theme of bringing God to the people and the people to God. However, in reviewing a document about catching issues before they became serious problems in the parish, I found one item troubling, perhaps because it demonstrated how distant common views of ministry are to this refrain. In a list of issues pertaining to pastors, conflict among parish members and their aggressive, hostile attitudes toward the clergy were listed. I thought to myself, really? Are we in such precarious straits in congregational life that pastors are now somehow responsible for the emotions of their people, for the negativity of their parishioners, even in a time of deep division, suspicion, and hostility among people in our society? On the other hand, do we give too much credit to clergy for apparent success in parishes? We surely blame them, often without justification, for anything that goes wrong, even, as in this case, conflict generated among parishioners.

Coakley has treated the themes mentioned here in several books.[4] Since sexuality is but one part of our identity and desire, the titles are not so baffling. While the intersection of desire, identity, and the practice of prayer and other spiritual disciplines is a given in the Christian tradition, Coakley brings in a procession of important voices to witness to this, from Gregory of Nyssa, Pseudo-Dionysius, Benedict, and the anonymous author of *The Cloud of Unknowing* to John of the Cross, Richard Hooker, and Thomas Merton.

PASTORAL AND PERSONAL EXPERIENCE

Despite her "day job" as a teacher and scholar, Coakley has sought out priestly work over the many years of her academic career, attesting to her profound sense of her calling to ministry. In my own life I have done the same, working in parishes while teaching at the City University of New York's Baruch College. As Coakley surmises, there is a powerful pull toward pastoral work that seems to reside at the heart of a vocation. When I was a graduate student, shortly after completing alternative service as a Vietnam-era conscientious objector, a pastor for whom I worked claimed that he saw this pull in me; I would not be content or feel right, he said, until I realized my call to ordained ministry. Not long after, I took the appropriate steps of speaking to the pastor of the parish we had joined, who sent me to the bishop; forty years later, I know this was most discerning advice.[5]

The locations of Sarah Coakley's pastoral service have ranged from parishes to correctional, therapeutic, and academic institutions in the Boston area, as well as in Oxford and the diocese of Ely in the UK. She was educated at Cambridge and Harvard and taught at Harvard after positions in Lancaster and Oxford. Later, she occupied the Norris-Hulse chair at Cambridge. In retirement she remains associated with several universities.

4. See Coakley, *God, Sexuality and the Self*; Coakley, *New Asceticism*.

5. Plekon, *World as Sacrament*, 1–13, 233–52.

In addition to this academic vocation, Coakley has worked across several fields. She has studied evolution, pain, and a range of issues involving the church and sexuality. These have included the ordination of women as bishops and the place of LGBTQ people in the church. Regarding clerical abuse and the deeper extremes of repression and libertinism, as she identifies them, with respect to sexuality, Coakley has called for the recovery of the Christian tradition on marriage and monasticism, rooting her views not only in the beauty and sanctity of love and sex but equally in the necessity of ascetic practice. As a woman who is a priest, scholar, spouse, and parent, she brings her own life to the tradition in a remarkable way.

To write openly about one's own pastoral ministry, as Coakley does, is unusual for an academic. In a gripping essay, "Prayer as Crucible," she describes in exquisite detail her personal experience in learning to pray. For years she had used *The Book of Common Prayer* in church services, the daily prayer office of psalms, Scripture lessons, and other prayers. In a study of prayer in everyday life, she describes how in her mid-twenties, frustration with traditional forms of prayer led to her trying transcendental meditation as a way of dealing with stress: "The impact was electrifying. I hadn't been going longer than about two months with this simple discipline of 20 minutes of silence in the morning and early evening when what I can only call a seismic shift of seemingly unspeakable proportions began to afflict me. Whatever was going on here was not only 'transcendental' but severely *real.* . . . Yet it was strangely impossible to step off the spiritual roller coaster which was now in full swing."[6] While her focus in the essay was not on ministry, the consequence of what she has to say for pastors is inescapable. For all the demands of parishioners and their needs, not to mention budgets, maintaining buildings, and cooperating with the leaders at other levels of the church, she remembers through meditation that at the heart of priestly service is God. This is what prayer does for a person, no matter their profession, age, or place in the church.

In *Powers and Submissions: Spirituality, Philosophy, and Gender,* Coakley goes on to explain how the sheer experience of being silent with God, though not grounded in theology or theory, led her to realize that a "surrendering of control to God," or an accepting of vulnerability, is essential to prayer.[7] She further credits this breaking open before God to have enabled her to realize what the Pauline image of the body of Christ means.

6. Coakley, "Prayer as Crucible," 33.

7. Coakley, *Powers and Submissions.*

Jesus's actions, given through the accounts of his words and the impact he had on his disciples, not only came to life, she explains, in Palestine in the first century CE but continue to do so in the present. Her realization refers to what the Creed calls the "communion of saints" that forms through the relationships in Christ that we have with those around us and share with the innumerable holy people who have gone before us. Ministry, she reminds us, is about embracing this and this alone—the community that the Spirit gathers, the circle of Christ's friends. Through ordination—the laying on of hands, prayer, and the Spirit's descent—a priest stands in relationship to these sisters and brothers to say the words of Jesus and, with them, repeat his healing actions.[8]

Prayer also showed Coakley that the notion that we can banish "all earthly cares"—or push to the side our bodies, our desires, our memories, our hurts, and our joys—is nonsense. Prayer is initiation into a life with and in God and others. God, she emphasizes, is community, the relationship of Father, Son, and Holy Spirit.[9] As again I can personally attest from my experience in academia, teaching in a university complicates a theological vocation by facilitating a confrontation with all the issues that boil over in our country, including those regarding sexuality, gender identity, embedded racism, and prejudice.[10] In effect, one can argue that every teacher, no matter their level of education, exercises a pastoral ministry when it comes to these issues, not theoretically but in the lives of students and colleagues,[11] as Coakley discusses. As noted, her experience with these and other subversive issues has been further nuanced through her work as a priest in correctional and therapeutic institutions, both in the US and in the UK.[12]

In contrast to the type of meditative prayer that Coakley discusses, the recitation of daily prayer offices that priests have traditionally been obliged to say—and that is canonically demanded in the Catholic and Anglican Churches—is not the type of professional responsibility of concern to Coakley. With Littlemore Group colleagues, including Sam Wells, Jessica Martin, and Rowan Williams, among others, she sees maintaining a daily "rule" of prayer as essential for those in ordained ministry, who witness

8. Coakley, "Prayer as Crucible," 36–37.

9. See Coakley, *God, Sexuality and the Self.*

10. Plekon, *Uncommon Prayer,* 201–21.

11. Coakley and Gavrilyuk, *Spiritual Senses*; Coakley, *New Asceticism.*

12. Coakley, "Meditation Is Subversive," 18–21.

realities that are often overlooked. I think Coakley and others in the Littlemore Group would agree that prayer provides a distinctive perspective on the challenging situations of congregations today. In particular, when considering church decline and shrinkage, those reflecting more deeply tend to look at the strategies that clergy and laity adopt to confront these issues. Much of *Community as Church*, for example, was concerned with forms of congregational resurrection. As discussed in earlier chapters, a number of parishes reassessed their place in the larger community, finding ways to reconnect and replant themselves to become part of the larger life around them. Meanwhile, Caimano's "free range" ministry compels pastors to serve part time and engage in other work. In the midst of these contemporary changes for the church, Coakley and her Littlemore colleagues unambiguously affirm the centrality of prayer. If there is a fundamental reason for ordination and service, it is to be rooted in God and thus able to bring God to the community and the community to God. Although this sounds self-evident, given all the pulls and strains of ministering in decline, it is not.

As these pastors insist, even amid the division in contemporary society that is marked by injustice, prejudice, and indifference to those in need, God's people must keep doing what God does—standing up for the powerless and finding ways to feed faith and commitment—even in smaller, aging congregations. They insist that we remain in union with God through the end of life; as we grow older, as sickness comes, as we lose those we love, and as we approach death ourselves, we still must find ways to relate to the young and the healthy, even if they show indifference to God. This emanates through their striking pictures of those attending funerals, weddings, and baptisms who have little or no experience of church and do not know what to do or say, unaware of the point of these rites of life and death. Clergy know this situation well.

For Coakley, prayer seems to be the image of a life in and with God. If prayer means being both with God and our sisters and brothers, she seems to ask, what are the consequences? Prayer finds its way into everything, not just church on Sundays and feast days but everywhere and every day.[13] It is an icon of the presence of God in all of our life, the breaking down of the dichotomous categories of sacred and profane, divine and human, formal prayer and just living. Thus, Coakley's contribution is that the priest is, above all else, a person of prayer.

13. Coakley, *Uncommon Prayer.*

ROWAN WILLIAMS: PRIESTHOOD AND THE OPEN SPACE, THE OPEN DOOR

What Is Ministry For?

In an epilogue to one of the Littlemore Group's collections of essays, former archbishop of Canterbury and theologian Rowan Williams says some very striking things about pastors and ministry.[14] While intended to close out the pieces on priestly presence in contemporary culture, specifically in the context of the UK, he nevertheless looks beyond the particular features of clergy in the Church of England, a dramatically more secularized society than that of the US. He starts with the scriptural basis of priesthood. Based on what is found in several places in the New Testament, including the letter to the Hebrews, he asks whether one could say that priesthood is no longer necessary even given the context that Christ was the one and only priest and made his sacrifice once and for all. The sacrifices of animals, bread, wine, and incense mandated in the Torah are gone, along with the Jerusalem temple in which they were offered, Williams writes. The legacy of Aaron and the Levitical priests culminate in Christ. To some extent, he says, the Reformation caught this drift in turning away from what priesthood looked like at the end of the medieval period in the West. Yet, he goes on, this by no means is the end of priesthood. Quite the contrary, the Scriptures are again emphatic that the people of God are royal, priestly, and prophetic. The sacrifice of Christ on the cross has not simply abolished everything that came before. Rather, Williams insists, the coming of God into humanity and the subsequent death and resurrection have, as Paul says, demolished the walls and opened up the door between heaven and earth, between God and us, in a manner hitherto unknown. The decisive difference between the priesthood exemplified by Christ and that of today, he insists, is that God entered time and space through Christ, becoming human flesh and blood. Christ, therefore, is the ultimate priest, the High Priest. Though all priests offer sacrifice, the sacrifice of his life, his body, Williams reiterates, brought together heaven and earth, their reconciliation conveyed through the cross and the empty tomb. All the walls, all the distance between God and ourselves, were done away with through him. This facilitated the possibility of the Incarnation, the state when God is with us and becomes one of us.

What more, then, Williams asks, is there for a priest to do? The Reformation, at least some parts of it, concentrated on the "once and for all"

14. Williams, epilogue to *Praying for England*, 171–82.

character of Christ's sacrifice and priesthood. While there were ministers, pastors, preachers, teachers, and counselors, there were no priests. For some the word "priest" no longer had meaning beyond Christ's priesthood. The former Jewish priesthood had disappeared with the temple, and the old Catholic priesthood was to be reformed and reimagined. All this said, in some Reformation churches, such as the Lutheran Churches of Scandinavia as well as the Anglican Church, the title of priest remained. Many church bodies proceeded in this way, avoiding the title, with the office of presbyter/elder perhaps being the closest they could come. Williams emphasizes that such an understanding is damaging and unnecessarily limiting. In trying to reform and renew the ministry, he writes, the Reformation did away with something important. It lost focus on how what Jesus did as priest now falls to his people. They are to hold the door open, maintaining the space in which God continues to be present and act in the world, among us and with us. Further, among the priestly people there are those women and men who have a special task:

> From the Church's point of view, the ordained ministry exists to remind the Church what it is, to tell it daily by the recital of the word and performance of the sacraments that it does not exist by its own resolution and does not define its place for itself and by itself. The ordained ministry is there to speak of the Church's transcendent origin and horizon, to witness to the nature of the space that God clears. It is necessary to the Church because of our innate drawing toward what I earlier called territorial anxiety; it is the servant of the Church's honesty (its repentance, its gratitude). But this means that from the point of view of the society around, the ordained minister, the person who embodies the particular kind of priestliness that is the heart of the Church's calling, shares in the public perception the same important unclarity that hangs around The Church of England's identity; the same vulnerability to dismissive or derisive perception on the one hand, the same vulnerability to endless and shapeless demands on the other. Priesthood . . . is crucially to do with the service of the space cleared by God; with the holding open of a door into a place where a damaged and confused humanity is able to move slowly into the room made available, and understand that it us accompanied and heard by in all its variety and unmanageability and emotional turmoil and spiritual uncertainty . . . it is a priesthood that may be nourished on the soil of your own emotional turmoil and spiritual uncertainty.[15]

15. Williams, epilogue to *Praying for England*, 179.

In the collection of essays by other Littlemore Group clergy that contextualize Williams's comments, the other writers incorporate several themes pertinent to ordained persons and their ministry as ways to focus their own experiences and the bearing these have on what it means to be a priest today. The function conveyed by the overall title, *Praying for England*, is in large part echoed through the individual contributions, which encourage ministers to pray with and for the people in their communities, both those of their parishes and of the greater society as a whole. Some of the themes included are representation, glory, imagination, presence, attention, honesty, and debate, this last by the lay sociologist and theologian Grace Davie, who writes about the state of religion in the country in general as well as the state of the Church of England in particular. The themes are very similar to those Sam Wells draws from his reflections on ministry shared here in a previous chapter. The essays are particularly riveting because the authors take us into the midst of life, often at its most terrible. In "Representation," for instance, Stephen Cherry puts us into the horror of the murder of a teenage girl in his community and the aftermath. Jessica Martin takes us through her everyday life as a university lecturer, priest, spouse, and parent living with the terrifying reality of her young adult daughter's ongoing struggle with addiction, rehab, and recovery. Through her, we confront the question of whether she will recover or die, her family seemingly helpless given her addictive behavior.

Priests Takes Up Space

As seen, Williams writes in the context of very difficult, often no-win circumstances. Both he and the others featured in *Praying for England* are grappling with trying to be priests in a society in which people have increasingly had no experience of the church and no real feeling or use for prayer, the Scriptures, sacraments, faith, and, ultimately, for God. Williams is emphatic that a priest is not just a kind of spiritual sponge, there to soak up all the misery of life, to clean up the mess found everywhere in the world. While such a view of 24/7 or round-the-clock chaplaincy emerges now and again—I have encountered it personally in colleagues who are always on call and have no life outside of their station—Williams presses beyond this real misunderstanding to a deeper reason for the existence of the ordained. He describes this as

[an] irreplaceable action that makes the priest what she or he is. It is the animation of the believing community's thanksgiving, its corporate acknowledgement of where it has been brought, its appropriation for itself in constantly changing circumstances of the fact that a place has been opened for humanity where Jesus stands. What priests do is to secure the opportunity for the priestly people to announce who they are—to themselves, but also to the world around; they are trustees of time and space for worship that can be characterized as the action of the whole of the believing community, not just a group of individuals, whether large or small.[16]

The ancient canons that mandated that priests pray the official daily prayer of the hours, whether or not they were accompanied by others, understood that the priest is always a liturgist, always a person of prayer, not just on Sundays. The priest has the task of continually summoning the community of faith back to the space Christ has opened, so that the society around sees that it remains there, no matter the conditions. This remains the rationale for the church building, whether centuries-old or recent, no matter how many are at services. Even if just one or two people come to pray Morning Prayer or Evening Prayer, the priest continues not because he or she has been imposed by a burden, but because he or she is reaching out to God with and on behalf of everyone else. In addition to this community function, praying is also essential to the individual; it is the very sustenance every pastor or priest needs in order to live.

One last observation Williams offers is that while leadership indeed is part of the priestly role—along with teaching, administration and organizing—it is rooted in something else. The priest has to have learned, he writes, "what it is to inhabit a place and to speak from that place into the community's life," referring to both the church community and the wider community in which it is located.[17] In very practical terms, here I am reminded of what I learned from the very first rector under which I served over thirty years ago, H. Henry Maertens, at Trinity Lutheran Church in Brewster, New York. Maertens said that his experience had taught him that it takes anywhere from three to five years for a pastor to be known and trusted by the people of the parish, and vice versa. The priest, he stressed, needs to know the community and to be able to speak and act with it with trust, without fear. That this does not always happen is a sad reality

16. Williams, epilogue to *Praying for England*, 180.

17. Williams, epilogue to *Praying for England*, 181.

of ordained ministry. Sometimes pastors arrive after significant scrutiny and conversation, and the community finds that the bishop approved of someone completely other than the candidate with whom they had spoken. Equally, sometimes a parish hides its anger, dysfunction, and mess during the call process, presenting a rosy picture of itself as a community, but when the new pastor arrives, he or she soon discovers that they are at war with each other. Still, this new pastor is expected to negotiate a peace treaty or he or she becomes a target of that warfare.

In contrast to these insular parish communities, in another essay Williams emphasizes the importance of church and ministry "taking up space" in the world and keeping this space open for everyone.[18] Such an inclusive vision is what scholars have seen as a hallmark of church against sect. Church, he emphasizes, is in solidarity with women and men in the world, facilitating a being-with that echoes Sam Wells and connects, as George Keith put it, God with the people and the people with God.

Priests Keep Open God's Space

Much like the epilogue Williams wrote for *Praying for England*, Williams wrote an afterword for the collection *For God's Sake*, which features essays that revolve around daily prayer, baptism, Eucharist, marriage, education, and funerals, namely those points in daily life where heaven and earth, God and humanity, connect with the present. The writers included highlight moments in which the priest interacts with people not in a magical way but by conducting rites that produce expected results. As the essays illustrate, there are numerous very human, messy, sometimes comedic, sometimes tragic moments in these "rites of passage," or sacramental encounters, that are magnified by the current secular climate, which features an increasing presence of those who are not at all clear as to what is happening at a wedding or funeral or how they should behave or even dress. These guests, for whom church attendance was not part of their upbringing or exists as a distant memory, illustrate their unfamiliarity with church tradition by making all sorts of requests for music that may have personal relevance but no connection to liturgical action, like popular songs or football numbers. They may be dressed more for clubbing than a religious ceremony, assume they can smoke in church as they do in a tavern, or ask for other things that may have been dear to the deceased or the couple but seem out of place in

18. Williams, afterword to *For God's Sake*, 180.

church. How, in this context, does the priest still make all feel welcome? How does a pastor connect with them given the serious moment in life being celebrated?

Another challenge manifests in the reality faced when one priest cares for several church buildings. How do they move from one service to another, one celebration or community to another? The essays by the Littlemore Group lift up the challenge of trying to be all things to all people in all locations. In particular, Williams argues that pastors are not mere passive custodians of a religious tradition and its rites. However, though by no means "magical," he also adds that clergy have experienced times when conducting one of the above services has allowed something beyond both their planning and control and beyond that of families and event planners. These are moments of encounter, of genuine contact between the people and God, a realization of the church as community, as the body of Christ and not a mere social gathering. All of this takes place against the backdrop of contemporary customs that include destination weddings; weddings officiated by a family member or friend in a backyard or natural setting; and "celebrations of life" with no religious context and sometimes quite distant in time from an actual death instead of funerals. In some places, data suggests that there is a decrease not only in traditional church weddings and funerals but also in baptisms and confirmations. In spite of the changes that the authors in *For God's Sake* describe, Williams emphasizes that there will still be requests for these rites of passage. People who otherwise do not have anything to do with church will nevertheless want a birth or a marriage or a death marked by its services, requesting the ministry of a priest to offer readings, prayers, and words of celebration and consolation. There will be more on this later.

Perhaps because of his pastoral experience, along with his immense learning, Williams is a most discerning writer and minister. A teacher and friend of his once shared that at heart, he is a parish priest, someone who can make you feel as though you've been friends after just a few minutes' conversation. He conveys that intimacy in his essays, which emphasize that priests are not mere passive custodians of a sacred space or reciters of words from *The Book of Common Prayer*. Neither, though, are they to be frantic in the innovations that abound in religion today, that is, enacting more intense, more earnest, more trending activity, which he describes as "dancing faster," to make room for the presence and action of God,[19] a

19. Williams, afterword to *For God's Sake*, 180.

notion reaffirmed by Andrew Root.[20] Although praying the daily office by oneself or with others may seem thankless and unable to produce church growth or change of heart, such holy work as prayer is still efficacious, as was the ongoing presence of Jesus across the Palestinian countryside in the Gospels. Prayer is an act of faith, Williams reminds us. So is priesthood.

Williams's view of the presence of the minister of the gospel as a witness to God's solidarity with us in all aspects of life and death echoes Bonhoeffer, who Williams also quotes: "The church is nothing but that piece of humanity where Christ really has taken form. . . . The church is the human being who has become human, has been judged, and has been awakened to new life in Christ. Therefore, essentially its first concern is not with the so-called religious functions of human beings, but with the existence in the world of whole human beings in all their relationships."[21] In spite of the current reality of shrinkage, Williams thus concludes that the ordained have a place; they should and must remain. In precisely the moment when pastors appear to be useless, as signs of the kingdom they must persist among us.

20. Root, *Church after Innovation*; Root, *Churches after the Crisis*; Root and Bertrand, *When Church Stops Working*.

21. Bonhoeffer, *Ethics*, 97.

10

Henri Nouwen

Ministry in the Name and Model of Jesus

HENRI NOUWEN'S LIFE AND MINISTRY

Over his years as a priest and educator, Henri Nouwen produced many powerful books and essays on spiritual life and ministry. He was chaplain and taught at Notre Dame, Yale, and Harvard. Through his lectures and publications, he maintained an influential presence not only at these schools but in the larger church.[1] He published almost forty books and hundreds of articles. In particular, *Genesee Diary* and *Wounded Healer* remain classic readings in the experience of the spiritual life and, for many, of ministry. His book on the prodigal son remains a remarkable exploration of how this parable captures the heart of Christ's teaching and work and thus provides a model for following Christ in our lives. Along with his theological training, Nouwen did graduate study in psychology, and his insight into the pastoral importance of diagnosis and therapy made him a gifted counselor and teacher. In ways, his ministry was unusual in that he really had little experience as a parish priest; mostly he served as a chaplain.

Nouwen's own complicated personality and life have been explored in depth since his death. Though never publicly acknowledged, he seems to have come to terms with his identity as a gay man. In many ways, he remains a model of ministry at a time when the institutional church is declining and becoming more distant from ordinary people and their lives.

---

1. See Ford, *Wounded Prophet*; Ford, *Lonely Mystic*; O'Laughlin, *God's Beloved*; Higgins and Burns, *Genius Born of Anguish*.

Intensely personal, his ministry flowed from his inner life and struggles, and his books highlight the essential place of prayer, the need for honesty with oneself and others, the centrality of friendship in the community of faith, and forgiveness, among other topics. A turning point in his life came after a period in which he was incapacitated by a profound breakdown following years of intense work in chaplaincy as well as a great deal of lecturing, preaching, and writing. What led to his breakthrough from his perceived loss of purpose and direction was the invitation to become the chaplain at Daybreak, a house for cognitively challenged people and part of L'Arche Movement in Toronto, during the last decade of his life, from 1986–96.[2] Shifting from his role as a university chaplain and instructor to living with mentally challenged people was, he notes, a significant challenge that redefined his identity and work as a priest. At Daybreak, it became clear that he was both a chaplain and a member of the community. Although in some ways it was a step down in status from the positions he had occupied at elite universities, his time there capped his years of examining the actual living out of the gospel. It was the high point in his efforts in priestly ministry.

As his work at Daybreak makes clear, in both Nouwen's writings and in his life one can see the valuable effects of his years of training in psychology. Though he did not complete a doctoral degree, his training put him at a vantage point few clergy have. Not only did he better understand the deeper causes of struggles in people's lives, but he also had a keen sense of his own strengths and weaknesses and their sources. His openness to people seeking and struggling with God ranks him with others considered welcoming to those at some distance from the church. At the same time, his admittedly liberal vision makes him a target of suspicion and criticism from traditionalists in the way that Thomas Merton, Richard Rohr, Dorothy Day, Joan Chittister, and Pope Francis, among others, have been so targeted.

JESUS'S TEMPTATIONS AND PASTORS

Almost thirty-five years ago, Nouwen recognized a crisis for pastors in *In the Name of Jesus*:

> Many priests and ministers today increasingly perceive themselves as having very little impact. They are very busy, but they do not

2. The late Jean Vanier was the creator and motivating force of L'Arche Movement but is now a figure in tragic eclipse after revelations of his inappropriate actions and sexual preying upon women.

see much change. It seems that their efforts are fruitless. They face an ongoing decrease in church attendance and discover that psychologists, psychotherapists, marriage counselors, and doctors are often more trusted than they. One of the most painful realizations for many Christian leaders is that fewer and fewer young people feel attracted to follow in their footsteps. It might seem that nowadays, becoming and being a priest is no longer something worth dedicating your life to. Meanwhile, there is little praise and much criticism in the church today, and who can live for long in such a climate without slipping into some type of depression? The secular world around us is saying in a loud voice, "We can take care of ourselves. We do not need God, the church, or a priest. We are in control. And if we are not, then we have to work harder to get in control. The problem is not lack of faith, but lack of competence. If you are sick, you need a competent doctor; if you are poor, you need competent politicians; if there are technical problems, you need competent engineers; if there are wars, you need competent negotiators. God, the church, and the minister have been used for centuries to fill the gaps of incompetence, but today the gaps are being filled in other ways, and we no longer need spiritual answers to practical questions." In this climate of secularization, Christian leaders feel less and less relevant and more and more marginal. Many begin to wonder why they should stay in the ministry.[3]

Including clergy among those he saw struggling, he urged leaders of the church to anchor themselves in God in order to, to cite George Keith again, bring God to the people and the people to God. Like others in this book, he insists that beyond the real, practical challenges of how to serve the people of God, there is a dimension of the life of ministry that transcends the necessary questions of compensation, deployment, and methods.

Nouwen grounds his reflections in two New Testament passages: Matt 4:1–11, the account of Jesus's temptation in the desert, an incident at the very beginning of Jesus's ministry, and John 21:15–19, which details the moments after the resurrection, at the end of Jesus's earthly work, when Peter is called to be a shepherd. In the first, the confrontation of the tempter with Jesus offers a great deal for leaders of the Christian community to ponder. Nouwen contends that the passage shows Jesus's resistance to what was demanded by the culture of the time and perhaps also to the strategies that the institutional church might have considered effective. Jesus's

---

3. Nouwen, *In the Name of Jesus*, 32–33.

wholehearted commitment to do what the Father sent him to do—to reveal the kingdom both by word and action—is what prevails. He emphasizes that the kingdom is God's presence and action, which is always unconditional love for us. Meanwhile, the tempter demonstrates the lure of relevance, dangling forth the possibility of turning stones into bread to immediately feed hungry people. A temptation that still haunts those who seek to lead in the name of Jesus, the type of relevance portrayed in the passage, Nouwen explains, exemplifies the subtle temptation of achievement, of being able to make things happen to solve or raise consciousness about enormous challenges like hunger, homelessness, and poverty. Is this not still a great temptation for pastors, to be able to accomplish something measurable in bringing the kingdom into the here and now? In saying no to the tempter, Jesus stresses that his power was not to overturn nature. He was not going to intervene miraculously to swiftly undo the Roman occupation, poverty, and more. Rather, he emphatically proclaims that we live by every word that comes from God's mouth. Having seen the desperation of the poor in Latin America, Africa, and elsewhere, Nouwen's discernment in highlighting this passage is striking. Rather than a mere spiritualization of hunger, it stresses that ministry is not magic; the real horror, he indicates, occurs when those who minister start believing this is so.

Having experienced himself the enormity of the challenges faced by clergy, Nouwen recognizes the despair that many ministers have that their efforts are ineffective, will produce little change, and will, in the end, accomplish nothing.[4] The low self-esteem he sees in ministers occurs in a context that is well known today, where congregations have begun to shrink and church bodies decline, where fewer are attracted to ordained ministry and seminaries have begun to close and amalgamate.[5] Noticing the emptiness and lack of meaning in people, not just among the marginalized but also in the well-educated and affluent, he indicates that it is precisely to a world in this condition that the ministry of the ordained, leadership in the name of Jesus, is called.

In contrast to the passage from Matthew, Nouwen locates the way in which God still invites people to ministry in the citation from John. In the passage, the risen Jesus asks Peter, "Do you love me?" three times at the end

---

4. Nouwen, *In the Name of Jesus*, 31.

5. All this was beginning to happen when Nouwen was writing this over thirty years ago! I know, for I was serving as associate pastor of a large parish then.

of his journey.[6] By posing the question after years of teaching and healing, after the rejection by his own followers and his suffering, death, burial, and resurrection, Jesus emphasizes that there is but one way to understand leadership and ministry: not as prestige or even so much as a leverage for change but as a response to "Do you love me?" This is the type of service Jesus exemplified, Nouwen implies, when he raised Lazarus, when he fed thousands in the wilderness, and when he washed the feet of his disciples.

In effect, when ministry is about love, the women and men who are called to it become the heart of God in human hearts. The initiative, Nouwen stresses, is from God; it is not our doing, though most of the time we are unable to see this. However, when we seek to discern whether we are called, the focus tends to shift to us, to our gifts or defects, as the formal process leading toward ordination suggests. Instead of focusing on the larger context, there is a great deal of attention given to a person's spiritual biography, highlighting the influences in one's life and the experiences that seem to have pulled one toward ministry. The focus on the individual is exacerbated by psychological evaluation, background checks, and letters of recommendation, not to mention academic and practical pastoral training and a candidate's personal sense of call. In this context, Nouwen maintains a focus on love, distinguishing the "first love" of God for us from the "second love" that we experience with our family, friends, colleagues, and neighbors. The first is boundless, always faithful, unconditional. Having no parallel, it precedes even our thinking or desire for it. The second, in contrast, is understandably human and thus sometimes lacking or denied, betrayed, or even nonexistent. As many experience, it is accompanied by rejection, indifference, abuse, and hatred. Because the first love is true and faithful, it becomes a force that refashions and restores the second, making up for its failings. Through his focus on it, Nouwen identifies the discipline that opens us to it, that keeps us from professionalizing the life and work of ministry and becoming mired in the need for relevance. Contemplative prayer, in effect, is the shorthand he uses to describe the communion with God that nurtures our appreciation of the first love.[7] What he describes could probably be called a prayer life, a relationship with God.

In his emphasis on love, Nouwen does not avoid the harsh realities of political and cultural conflict nor does he ignore the division over so many issues in the church, which we know all too well. From the place of women,

---

6. Nouwen, *In the Name of Jesus*, 36; John 21:15–18.

7. Nouwen, *In the Name of Jesus*, 42.

LGBTQ people, and the laity in the church (which includes their voice and how they could be of service) to the perennial issues of abortion, contraception, euthanasia, and hatred for the other, among others, we live in a battlefield of cultural wars. In addition, there are the numerous battlefields within the church that stem from a historical division that resists being breached and overcome in ecumenical work. Nouwen observes that the struggle over many of these divisive issues remains mostly at the political and moral levels. Like him, I have found that asking how Jesus would think or act faced with these matters is easily neglected or dismissed as irrelevant. That is what Nouwen means when he says that the matters of controversy and division are not connected to the reality of being in union, or being in love, with God. While the canons of the church—including the theological or doctrinal tradition and the authority of the hierarchy—are routinely viewed as the bases for a position on these divisory issues, he compels us to ask the following: What if these were connected with the radical love enacted by Jesus in the Gospels?

Nouwen returns to the Gospels, using the second temptation of Jesus to throw himself off the pinnacle of the temple and be swept up by angels, to counter the fantasy of those in ministry about being spectacular. He writes, "Jesus refused to be a stunt man. He did not come to walk on hot coals, swallow fire, or put his hand on the lion's mouth to demonstrate that he had something worthwhile to say."[8] Whether we look at the entrepreneurial clergy of megachurches or online ministries with stunning records of growth, staggering book sales, and national profiles or to less splashy heroes of success in mainline denominations, these are models derived from corporate precedents, from the culture of the financial and political worlds, not the Gospels. Probably few aspirants to ministry look for such a future, yet the temptation finds subtle manifestations in what bishops and deans often herald as congregations and pastors worth imitating.

PASTORS NEED PRAYER AND COMMUNITY

Nouwen reminds us that Jesus does react to Peter's responses to the three-fold question: "Do you love me?" It is the answer that tells us what ministry is—"Feed my lambs, look after my sheep, feed my sheep."[9] This is what love looks like, and I do not think it contradicts George Keith's "Bring the

8. Nouwen, *In the Name of Jesus*, 55.

9. John 21:15–17.

people to God and God to the people." Constantly evoking life at Daybreak, Nouwen dismisses the shepherd as the lone ranger, a solitary, Shane-type personality. Daybreak is, as he notes, above all a community and provided him with a powerful experience, leading to his insights both about ministry and the larger church. Besides the sheep, he indicates, shepherding requires other personnel, such as the dogs; the work of service in the name of Jesus is no different.

The communal nature of ministry is reassuring because, at the risk of another cliché, there is strength in numbers. However, not all pastors warm to this, at least in my experience. Some really prefer to operate as lone rangers. To them, the idea of working together with others, collegially, as a team, is threatening. They think that only they know how to shepherd. Yet, Jesus sends his friends and disciples out not one-by-one but in pairs. The rest of Jesus's model of ministry presumes a band of disciples to preach, heal, and to break bread together. It is community, always, everywhere.

In effect, those involved in ministry need each other for prayer, encouragement, correction, and for sheer fellowship. However, the real preaching to and healing and gathering of the community is always the work of Jesus through the power of the Spirit. In this manner, Nouwen sees that ministry is both communal and mutual.[10] His view again echoes Sam Well's insistence that ministry is always *with* those being served. Unlike the therapeutic professions of psychiatry, social work, and other medical fields, ministry does not imply a professional distance.[11] Further, those who minister are also being ministered to, and recognizing this reciprocity is essential. The Lord is the vine, we are the branches. Christ constantly strengthens those who minister, attending to them as the Master, the Servant of all. This is Jesus's "new commandment," given on the night before his passion began and embodied as he washed his disciples' feet and told them to do the same for each other.

In this community that forms around ministry, Nouwen identifies a discipline in addition to contemplative prayer for those who serve. Confession and forgiveness, he indicates, are crucial. Those who are engaged in ministry need to acknowledge their own brokenness and ask the forgiveness of those they serve. Most liturgical orders for the celebration of the Eucharist have within the flow of the liturgy such a rite of confession

---

10. Nouwen, *In the Name of Jesus*, 58.

11. I think in this one hears the vulnerability that so characterized Nouwen's personality and became a significant element in his vision of ministry.

and forgiveness. While many pastors do tend to keep their own lives private, putting some distance between themselves and their people, Nouwen believes this is not always helpful to ministry. Rather, for him vulnerability and personal openness are paramount. Mutual confession and forgiveness establish bonds between pastors and people, he specifies, which could help ameliorate the loneliness often acknowledged in the clergy. This may very well be an instance where Nouwen's own struggles to be open and share himself with others had an important impact on his larger vision of pastoral service and lifestyle. His emphasis on the centrality of reciprocal relationships and the community of the ordained has more recently been echoed in Pope Francis's vision of the life and work of the ordained.

In addition to his emphasis on community, Nouwen discerns that the over-spiritualization of ministry stifles the health and the wholeness—the integrity—of ordained service. Ministry, he explains, can provide a type of escape from unpleasant everyday realities, lifting a pastor off into heaven, the lives and miracles of saints, the realm of the otherworldly. Looked at from another perspective, private life can become divorced from one's ordination promises and the commendation to love and serve. In the time since Nouwen was active, the tragic reality of this separation in the church has been disclosed through revelations of abuse by clergy that had been concealed, denied, and covered up by church leadership. Ironically, Nouwen refers to the life of ministry hidden from view as "carnality" and stipulates that neither a revival of the communal character of ministry nor the disciplines of confession and forgiveness will eliminate it.[12] However, he also argues that secrecy and deception are made much more difficult by openness. He points to AA, ACA, and related twelve-step groups precisely as communities of required honesty, openness, and thus trust and mutual responsibility. If priests are full members of their communities, they will not be set apart by ordination and clerical identity. Rather, in a community like what Nouwen describes, pastors would find safe places and people with whom to be open. This, as Nouwen knew well, has been sorely lacking for many in ministry for whom bishops and fellow ministers are perceived as threats, not peers to be trusted.

Nouwen draws on his experience moving from academia to Daybreak to look at one more aspect of Jesus's encounter with the tempter. After years of study followed by professional work and ministry experience in academic settings, Nouwen thought he had been well trained to be a leader.

---

12. Nouwen, *In the Name of Jesus*, 67–68.

The intense relationships he formed with the members of the Daybreak community obliterated the differential status that he had acquired through learning and experience. Members of the Daybreak community did not have socially conditioned styles of deference, patience, or professional engagement. They spoke as their hearts prompted, often impulsively, forcefully. He gives several vivid examples of a Daybreak friend expressing hurt or bewilderment when he left to give a lecture or paper somewhere else. This experience leads Nouwen to reflect on the temptation of power. The tempter seductively offers Jesus all the kingdoms of the world if he will only submit to the "power" of marketing strategy to grow the church, increasing numbers and dollars, or to the idea that a pastor stands above the people. The tempter's enticement remains seductive today. Applying this biblical anecdote to the present, Nouwen claims that the many alliances of the church with power have contributed to the current states of decline and shrinkage. As noted in *Community as Church*, David Gushee and Jon Pavlovitz, along with Kaya Oakes and Brian MacLaren, have inventoried the reasons so many have become religious "nones" and "dones," distancing themselves from the rituals, teaching, clergy, and other aspects and people associated with organized religion.[13] In effect, the sad list of instances of power mongering by the church is long and all too well known.

Along with the story of the tempter, Nouwen notes that the Scriptures are riddled with examples of individuals who clutch at status and power. This compulsion, he reflects, seems to start with the desire to have the knowledge and wisdom of God independent of God and leads, in many cases, to acts in which there is a type of grasping for control. For example, the disciples want the seats closest to the Lord in the kingdom. Others want fire cast down on their enemies. Nouwen speculates that the urge to feel this type of power emerges when there is a lack of intimacy with God or with a community.

Finally, the encounter of the risen Jesus with Peter concludes with a sobering statement that harkens back to the experience of community Nouwen had at Daybreak. He quotes a biblical passage from John 21:18 where Jesus says, "Very truly I tell you, when you were younger, you used to fasten your own belt and to go wherever you wished. But when you grow old, you will stretch out your hands, and someone else will fasten a belt around you and take you where you do not wish to go."[14] Nouwen came

13. Plekon, *Community as Church*, 37–47.
14. Nouwen, *In the Name of Jesus*, 8–81.

to see his own life following the words Jesus says to Peter in the quote. In retrospect, Nouwen realized that most of his life before Daybreak rolled out according to his plans. The call to be chaplain there came from somewhere and someone else. On closer inspection, he indicates, the call to serve is, in essence, a call to empty oneself, to be downwardly mobile, that is, if it in any way resembles the path of Jesus himself.

PASTORS MUST RESEMBLE JESUS

If the church moves toward the type of community described by Nouwen, future leadership will embrace the powerlessness and humility exemplified by Jesus, the suffering servant. In contrast, clergy currently remain distinguished from the rest of the community. They stand presiding and preaching at the head of the assembly with clerical collars, vestments, and titles that single them out. However, if a pastor relates to the community as a sister or brother, forgoing his or her clerical status, then these items of identity are put into a different perspective. They do not obscure the person beneath them, who remains in an authentic relationship with those around him or her. It is in this type of community that the humanity of the priest comes forth, a crucial act. While Nouwen's description of the emptied out, radically poor pastor is somewhat extreme, like Jesus's parables, it emphatically points to the minister's total dependence on God and total commitment to the sisters and brothers who form the community.

In addition to the practices of contemplative prayer, confession, and forgiveness, Nouwen adds the discipline of sustained theological reflection as also essential to ministry. This is not to be confused with the business of academic theological research manifest through teaching and writing. Rather, what he is urging is something he has pressed for throughout his discussions of ministry. Most often, pastors today go to psychology, sociology, advertising, corporate strategy, and the like for inspiration, perhaps using scriptural references and imagery afterward. Predictably, Nouwen wants ministers to go first to Jesus, to reflect with the mind of Christ. Otherwise, he says, they will at best be pseudo-social scientists, pseudo-therapists, and marketers. His focus on Jesus reiterates that ministry is not ours to drive or the preserve of regulations written in church canons, constitutions, and books of discipline. Although we will always have such rules, the grounding of ministry must be in Jesus. Ministry, he insists, is a pastor doing and saying what Jesus does and says. It moves to the rhythm of the kingdom of

God, something Jesus continually stressed not only through his parables but also through his radical actions. Through this theological reflection, Nouwen combines prayer with action. While it must be a component of the formation that takes place in the training of ordinands, it cannot stop with graduation and ordination. It must continue as one of the several disciplines Nouwen identifies, as we have seen.

Today, ministry is shaped by the desire for relevance, popularity, and power. There is nothing malevolent in this. We cannot help being creatures of our time and culture. Yet, as the two Gospel passages Nouwen uses make clear, these can be subtle temptations. Our need to succeed, trend, and control can overtake the core of what ministry is. For Nouwen, it was his sisters and brothers in the Daybreak community in Toronto who radically transformed his experience of being a priest and showed him that community is church. As he then demonstrated, ministry is also community; it is being a part of, serving, and being needed by community members.

I I

Pope Francis
Shepherds "With the Smell of the Sheep"

THE SECOND VATICAN COUNCIL AND THE
REDISCOVERY OF PRIESTLY MINISTRY

The somewhat surprising election of Jorge Mario Bergoglio in 2013 as Pope Francis I, or Bishop of Rome, as he prefers to be called, reminded some of another unexpected election, that of Giovanni Roncalli as Pope John XXIII in 1958. Now a saint, John XXIII astonished many by his boldness in convoking the Second Vatican Council, an action that continues to provoke criticism decades later. "Good Pope John," as he affectionately became known, wanted to open the doors and windows of the church to the world, an idea inspired from his years serving as a Vatican diplomat in Bulgaria, Turkey, and Greece, decidedly non-Catholic countries. He served also as Vatican representative in Paris after working as a military chaplain in World War I. In many ways, he carried with him not just the experience of his work in foreign service but also his striking ecumenism as well as his savvy for political and social matters in a global context. Having come from a very humble family background, he valued other people, becoming one of the first popes in memory to visit all the parishes of Rome and insist on talking with the people and the clergy in these communities. In addition, he visited children in hospitals and people in correctional facilities.

The many documents that emerged from the Second Vatican Council show that the event rediscovered the church beyond the clergy, hierarchy, and canons. It returned to the ancient and profoundly scriptural understanding of the church as all the people of God, laity as well as clergy. In addition, it reached out to other Christian churches, for the first time recognizing their common faith in Christ and common roots in baptism and communion. Further, it extended the church's care to non-Christian traditions and their communities, leaving a legacy of two great statements or encyclicals: *"Mater et magistra"* and *"Pacem in terris."* The first discusses the church's commitment to contemporary social problems and crises, listening carefully to "the signs of the times."[1] The second affirms the church's anti-war stance, declaring it as a promoter of peace among the nations, an especially timely act of faith during the height of the Cold War.

While many accomplishments of the Second Vatican Council also came from bishops and their theological advisors, it remains inextricably tied to the legacy of John XXIII. His influence remains clear through documents produced by Council theologians and then voted on and accepted as church teaching by the bishops at the Council, including the constitutions revisioning the church itself (*"Lumen gentium"*) and the church's position in the contemporary world (*"Gaudium et spes"*). In addition to these two constitutions, there is a declaration on religious liberty (*"Dignitatis humanae"*), a document on relations with non-Christian traditions (*"Nostra aetate"*), and a decree on ecumenism (*"Unitatis redintegratio"*). As these documents show, John XXIII helped demonstrate that the church was not an entity in itself apart from the world. Rather, the church's very reason for existence was to bring the good news of Christ to the world, to stand against hate and violence, and to support the oppressed.

One of the strongest outcomes of the Second Vatican Council is the decree on priestly life and ministry, *"Presbyterorum ordinis,"* which could be seen as an authentic "return to the sources" on the ministry of the ordained and their lives.[2] It is echoed in another decree on the training of priests, *"Optatam totius."* Rather than a cultic figure who offers the sacrifice of the mass on behalf of the faithful, both decrees affirm that the priest, from the very start, is located within the ministry of the whole of the church, the people of God. The vision of the ordained as ontologically different from the rest of the faithful is deemphasized, almost left behind in favor of ministry, as the very word declares, as service to God and the people. In this manner, both return to the New Testament understanding of ministry as rooted in the ministry of Christ, a ministry of the word in

1. John XXIII, *Humanae Salutis* §4, 387.

2. Paul VI, *"Presbyterorum Ordinis."*

the many meanings of this definition. In effect, the priest's primary task is to proclaim the gospel, the good news of the kingdom of God. This means preaching in liturgical settings and teaching the Scriptures and the rest of the lessons of the church's tradition. It also means witnessing the power of the Spirit and the presence of Christ in innumerable ways in everyday life, as John XXIII did through visiting the sick, the homebound, prisoners, and those in other institutional settings. Finally, it includes aiding the poor, the homeless and hungry, and refugees and exiles from war and oppression. In this manner, the vision of ministry and the church that emerge from the Council reverberate today through the figure of Pope Francis.

A RENEWED VISION OF MINISTRY

If the church is not separate from the world, which God created, loves, and has always desired to reconcile and save, then the ordained servants of the church are likewise always connected to the world. As the Council emphasized, to be worldly is not to be opposed to God; the consistent vision of renewal did not imply leaving tradition behind. Rather, as written in the constitution on the liturgy, "*Sacrosanctam conciliam*," it stressed that the liturgical assembly celebrates together with the bishop, priests, and deacons. The insistence that liturgical services are not the sacred preserve of a clerical caste but the right and the privilege of all the people to celebrate echoes Nicholas Afanasiev, along with others in the liturgical renewal movement. If the central action of the church remains gathering to give thanks, break the bread, and share it with the cup, ministry does not hover above or function outside of a community of faith. Rather, like the identity and calling of each and every Christian, all offices of ministry—from bishop to presbyter and deacon—are rooted in baptism. Through water and the Spirit, every member is consecrated to the vocation of Christ; they are "christened" to be priests, prophets, or speakers of the word, and through these tasks they become the royalty of God's kingdom.

To be clear, the fathers and theologians of Vatican II did not on their own create these visions of the church, ministry, the relationship of the church to other churches and faith traditions, or the church's relationship to the world. The Council was preceded by years of research and writing that in many cases embraced a return to earlier church traditions. This includes the work of theologians like Afanasiev, de Lubac, Bernard Botte, Gregory Dix, Max Thurian, Edward Schillebeeckx, and the often-better-known

Hans Küng and Karl Rahner, who sought to show that the imperialistic, legalistic, and siege mentalities associated with the church were not normative. The charge sometimes made that Vatican II was a simple rejection of historic tradition, that it was pure innovation, does not hold up.

As described, the vision of the ordained that emerged from the Council and that is sustained by Council documents follows an intensely pastoral model in which the differences and separation between clergy and lay gives way to a sense of church as community, fellowship, and cooperation. In spite of the criticism that the Council's view of ministry oriented more toward social justice and engagement with political and cultural issues, the constitution establishes its rooting in the ministry of Christ. Ordained ministry and the fellowship of believers are located within the body of Christ, from where they express their consistent concern for the world—the world of God's making—and emphasis on continual reconciling and healing. Put another way, the Council emphatically confessed the divine dimension of ministry and its purpose with and in the world, which includes all the children of God. In this manner, as expressed by others who have been discussed in this book, ordained ministry continues the plan and work of the Incarnation, striving to make God present in and with humankind.

The important elements of ministry that were emphasized by the Second Council are noted in "*Presbyterorum ordinis*." These include, as mentioned above, the baptismal foundation of the people of God and the ongoing ministry of proclaiming the word of God, which manifests not only in teaching and preaching but in action, by building up the members of the body, supporting them in their daily ministries, and seeking to build bridges of peace in a conflict-riddled world. In effect, the document agrees with the constitution on the liturgy as well as those on the church and the church in the modern world. It is clear that the vision across all these documents is consistent; the church is no longer insular, closed in upon itself, or defined by a dividing line between clergy and laity. Rather, as we have seen, all of these constitutions indicate that the gathering of the people of God around the eucharistic table is central to the ministry of the ordained within this assembly. As the Littlemore Group stressed, the daily prayer of the ordained for the community is both a reminder of their calling and of the calling of all Christians to be people of prayer. Parallel to the appeal for the cooperation of clergy and laity, the document also promotes fellowship among the ordained—of the bishops with the presbyters and deacons. In all parts of the church, it is community that witnesses the Spirit's leading and the presence of the risen Christ. It is well worth noting that Francis explicitly refers to "*Presbyterorum ordinis*" in his talks to pastors, calling it a small "compendium" of the theology of the priesthood.[3]

POPE FRANCIS'S LIFE AND MINISTRY

Pope Francis's ministry has been complex and is beyond detailed inspection here. However, a few aspects stand out and inform what he has to say about the ordained and their work. Though he is increasingly criticized and attacked by theological conservatives, including some bishops as well as other members of the clergy and laity, Francis's life is a mixed journey and his views on and aspirations for the church are many. For instance, he is credited for trying to open eucharistic communion to divorced people, an appeal that has been roundly condemned as a rejection of established doctrine. He has also consistently opposed careerism among the clergy and has taken aim at the continuation of the type of clerical caste criticized by the Second Council, in which the ordained are seen as superior to lay people and justified in distancing themselves from them for fear of secular contamination. Controversy also marked his life among the Jesuits, including his role as superior during the "dirty war" years in Argentina, when priests were harassed, tortured, and imprisoned by the government. Although there has been much debate and counter charges on his particular role in the case of two Jesuits who were submitted to the government for torture and imprisonment, he does not appear to have been involved in turning them in. Rather, working behind the scenes, he sought to protect them.

In addition, throughout his life, Francis has been cast both as a doctrinal conservative as well as a radical liberalizer. He has resisted calls for the ordination of women to the priesthood while appearing to hold open the diaconate and appointing more women to Vatican administrative positions than any previous pope. He has also refused to live in the historic papal apartments, preferring to reside in a guest house, Casa Santa Marta, where he requested simple daily eucharistic celebrations, and he has avoided many of the items of papal vesture used by his predecessors. More recently, knee problems have required him to use a wheelchair and cane, making it impossible for him to preside at some liturgical celebrations. At eighty-six, his age and health loom as issues with respect to his future in office.

3. Pope Francis, *With the Smell*, 184.

Along with Pope Francis's criticism of clericalism, he inaugurated the synodal project of conversations among bishops, clergy, and laity, reflecting his preference for an ancient conciliar or synodal model for the church's deliberation and decision-making. This project may have emerged out of his years of close contact with Eastern Catholic hierarchy and clergy. Once again, however, the promotion of communal rather than top-down authority and decision-making provoked attack, seen as a democratizing or Protestantizing of the Roman Catholic ecclesial tradition with centralization in the papal office and the Vatican administrative bodies. Despite encyclicals lifting up the environment ("*Laudato si*") and the family and marriage ("*Amoris Laetitia*"), he is critiqued both by conservatives and liberals.

Having mostly been appointed to academic positions, particularly those of spiritual direction within Jesuit communities, Francis does not have extensive pastoral experience in parish ministry. In his work as auxiliary bishop and archbishop, however, he has immersed himself in the pastoral. In these roles, he rejected episcopal residences and bureaucratic formality and distance in favor of rubbing elbows with ordinary people and spending time with the priests of his diocese, particularly those working in the poorest neighborhoods. Before he was pope, he lived in modest apartments and took public transportation to his office and to pastoral visitations, decisions echoed in his preference for living at Casa Santa Marta. He often disappeared to hear confessions and maintained a close association with the parishes of his diocese of Rome, doing pastoral work as Rome's bishop. As pope, he has celebrated Holy Thursday by washing the feet of young women and men in youth correctional centers. On April 16, 2016, he visited the Mòria refugee camp on the Greek island of Lesbos with Ecumenical Patriarch Bartholomew and Archbishop Ieronymos of Athens to stand with and support migrants fleeing oppression, poverty, and death, even taking several families back to Rome with him.[4] Although he has sometimes had tense relationships with political leaders—as when he was archbishop of Buenos Aires and openly disagreed with Argentine governmental leaders—as pope he has drawn criticism for his reluctance to outrightly condemn Russian aggression in the invasion of Ukraine. There are many other instances of his quietly breaking out of the traditional papal mode in doing pastoral work.

---

4. Pope Francis et al., "Joint Declaration."

SHEPHERDS SHOULD "SMELL LIKE THE SHEEP"

Although Pope Francis came to parish ministry later in his life, speaking about the ordained and their ministry has been a high priority in his preaching and speaking. One of his most memorable statements came in the homily at a chrism mass on Holy Thursday, March 28, 2013. The consecration of the chrism is the context for the opening, while the work of shepherding is the reference point later on:

> The priest who seldom goes out of himself . . . misses out on the best of our people, on what can stir the depths of his priestly heart. Those who do not go out of themselves, instead of being mediators gradually become intermediaries, managers. We know the difference: the intermediary, the manager, "has already received his reward," and since he doesn't put his own skin and his own heart on the line, he never hears a warm, heartfelt word of thanks. This is precisely the reason for the dissatisfaction of some who end up sad—sad priests—in some sense becoming collectors of antiques or novelties, instead of being shepherds living with "the smell of the sheep." This I ask you: be shepherds with the "smell of the sheep," make it real, as shepherds among your flock, fishers of men. True enough, the so-called crisis of priestly identity threatens us all and adds to the broader cultural crisis; but if we can resist its onslaught, we will be able to put out in the name of the Lord and cast our nets . . . . It is not a bad thing that reality itself forces us to "put out into the deep," where what we are by grace is clearly seen as pure grace, out into the deep of the contemporary world, where the only thing that counts is "unction"—not function—and the nets that overflow with fish are those cast solely in the name of One in whom we have put our trust: Jesus.[5]

Pope Francis's urging of pastors to have "the smell of the sheep" has become one of his most familiar lines. In other sermons and talks, he uses similar expressions. As the word "synod" indicates, pastors must constantly be walking with their people, familiar with their jobs, their anxieties, and their joys. How good it would be, he reflects, if priests not only knew their parishioners by name but maybe even knew their pets' names.[6] In another homily, he describes ministry as a joy that comes from the love of one's

5. Pope Francis, *With the Smell*, 6–7.
6. Pope Francis, *With the Smell*, 34–39.

flock, one's community for the shepherd.[7] He recognizes that at times pastors get tired, become disenchanted, doubt the point of their efforts. He insists that God and the people of God always surround them with love and prayer.

Aware that he is usually speaking to priests who, because of celibacy, have no partner or family of their own, Francis also remains clear about what priests give up. While he makes no pious denials, admitting that this can create a state of real poverty, he points to the community they form with the people of a parish and other priests and friends as authentic sources of belonging and joy.[8] This, he insists, sustains their faithfulness to other people and their work. Likewise, their obedience to God is not drab duty but a joy. Though their experience is at times sad, even cruel, the joy of serving motivates them to enter ministry and remain within it.[9]

THE GOOD SHEPHERD CHRIST IS THE MODEL

Francis frequently underscores the point of ordained ministry as a work of mercy, a labor of love.[10] Through the image of the Good Shepherd, he evokes Christ's healing of and compassion for others, offering a model for ministry. Whatever a pastor has acquired in academic formation, theological learning is necessary to perform the work of love always needed in our world. In another homily, Francis draws on the parable of the merciful father, the prodigal son, to emphasize the mercy at the heart of ministry. The parable exemplifies mercy not as abstract or conceptual but as real compassion experienced in encounter. The father never gives up hope on the son who has left. This same son eventually comes to his senses and humbles himself by returning home and begging forgiveness, which the father has held onto for precisely this moment of return. He evokes an excessive or "absurd love," as Paul Evdokimov describes it, that the other son finds repulsive.[11]

Francis goes on to explain that pastors know what it is to be taken back repeatedly by God. From their pastoral care, they also understand

---

7. Pope Francis, *With the Smell*, 8–14.

8. Pope Francis, *With the Smell*, 51–52.

9. Pope Francis, *With the Smell*, 15–22.

10. Pope Francis, *With the Smell*, 23–29.

11. Evdokimov, *In the World*.

how people return to the Lord.[12] He further notes that when set in God's mercy, the experience of ministry propels pastors to side with those who have no power or who remain excluded, with no place or value in society.[13] Francis particularly demonstrated his affinity for the marginal at the Mòria camp for migrants and refugees mentioned earlier. In effect, he has traveled to many places where his presence has been an act of solidarity with the suffering. He exemplifies that priests are there for those wishing to reconnect with God, facilitating spiritual reconciliation.

In Francis's writings and homilies addressed to priests as well as lay-people, several key elements stand out. Pastors are proclaimers of the gospel, he stresses, the good news of God's love and forgiveness. He repeatedly emphasizes the importance of immersion in the Scriptures, of listening to and praying with the word.[14] In addition, demonstrating his sympathy for the suffering and marginal, Francis asks priests if they weep with and for their people.[15] In a very personal anecdote, he recalls a very elderly priest who was father confessor to many of the clergy in Buenos Aires, Francis himself included. When this man died at ninety-six on Easter, Francis visited his wake and decided to take the cross from the rosary in the dead priest's hands in the coffin. He specifies that he has kept this cross on himself for many years, even as pope, as a reminder of this priest's compassion and care as a confessor.[16] The story reminds me of the remarkable photo of Francis kneeling at one of the confessionals in St. Peter's, going to confession with whatever priest was assigned there. He also spends hours sitting for confession like an ordinary parish priest.

The importance Francis places on the act of confession relates to the way that he acknowledges his own defects, failings, and weaknesses, encouraging pastors to also be honest with themselves and, most particularly, with their people.[17] Rather than focus on clerical advancement, he calls priests to remember that they always have before them the figure of Christ, who emptied himself, continually going after the one lost sheep and

12. Pope Francis, *With the Smell*, 40–49.

13. I would add that despite all the recent decline in church membership that reflects the estrangement of many from communities of faith, the church has consistently sided with the marginalized. Many famous pastors of the twentieth century have courageously done so, including Martin Luther King Jr. and Desmond Tutu.

14. Pope Francis, *With the Smell*, 34–39.

15. Pope Francis, *With the Smell*, 45–46.

16. Pope Francis, *With the Smell*, 47–48.

17. Pope Francis, *With the Smell*, 54–55.

making time for one more person seeking healing. Staying close to Christ and seeking to imitate him is, he insists, essential.[18] If there is a theme that runs through Francis's words on the ordained and their ministry, it would be the constant presence of Christ. The heart of the Good Shepherd is mercy, or "limitless love," as Lev Gillet called God's affection for us.[19] As the other point of reference, pastors have the people. In this manner, the Good Shepherd example is the guide for the pastor to seek out the sheep, including those that follow easily, those who don't, and those who wander off. Francis, in this manner, reminds us that ministry is always a gathering of community. In the community of shepherd and flock, or of pastor and people, is the joy of ministry, ministers, and all the people of God.[20]

The centrality of community compels Francis to urge priests to remember their origins in their families, neighborhoods, schools, and in the people of God. Thinking of Paul's words to Timothy, Francis tells newly ordained pastors to remember their mother, their grandmother, and all those who brought them up and shared Christ with them.[21] In a homily on the roots of a priest preached on November 20, 2015, the fiftieth anniversary of the promulgation of the Council's decrees on the formation and life of priests referred to earlier, "*Optatum Totius*" and "*Presbyterorum ordinis*," he says that the family is a domestic church, the source from which we can all trace our faith.[22]

CHURCH HIERARCHY AND COMMUNITY

Maintaining his focus on community, Francis has also frequently called out arrogant clergy or those who think themselves better than the laity who surround them. There is no place for this kind of careerism and pride among pastors. Emphasizing the importance of empathy over conceit, he cites Ambrose of Milan, noted for his writings on ministry in the fourth century: "Where there is mercy there is the spirit of the Lord and where there is rigidity there are only his ministers."[23] This type of arrogance and rigidity is a danger to everyone, clergy as well as the people of God, yet, as

18. Pope Francis, *With the Smell*, 180–81.

19. Pope Francis, *With the Smell*, 146–47; Gillet, "Love without Limits."

20. Pope Francis, *With the Smell*, 148–51.

21. 2 Tim 1:5.

22. Pope Francis, *With the Smell*, 184–87.

23. Pope Francis, *With the Smell*, 188.

we know, it is common. In both my years in the Carmelite order as a student friar and in the forty years I spent in pastoral ministry, I experienced it frequently.

Including bishops in his emphasis on community, Francis does not spare them from his scrutiny. He knows well what their lives and ministry entail and asks them with a tinge of sarcasm whether they are in any way close to their priests, much less their people. In spite of how busy they are, he implies, they should never be so busy as to not be able to at least call a priest in trouble or in need. To stress his point, he recalls an ancient canonical requirement that a bishop live among the people.[24] He maintains his emphatic argument that rigid personalities—those that are common among fundamentalists and legalists—must be screened out and refused entrance to the formation process in spite of the current climate of conservative backlash against him.[25] There is no room for arguing that traditionalism deserves to be represented in the church; rather, it is a clear danger to be resisted, as it does not follow the example of the Good Shepherd and the flock.

Francis reiterates his firm focus on community in talks given to faculty and seminarians of the theological seminaries in Rome, where he specifies four different kinds of formation necessary for ministry. The first, academic formation, almost goes without saying, since an educated clergy is essential; without it, it is easy to become an ideologue with a limited view of the church and the world. The other types of formation, however, cannot be downplayed. As we have seen, he emphasizes spiritual and community formation. He points to the community as a starting place for clergy to develop healthy, even critical, relationships among each other. He also indicates the importance of honesty to community; to illustrate, he provides an anecdotal account of when one of his secretaries confronted him about errors in judgment he made as bishop, giving him a constructive lesson in truth-telling.[26] Finally, he also describes apostolic formation, which reiterates that the ordained, as Sam Wells stresses, should strive to serve, to be with the people.

Francis goes on to explain that "apostolic" also refers to the reality that the ordained are messengers, heralds of the good news, not the employees of a global conglomerate or corporation. Everything in the church's structure

24. Pope Francis, *With the Smell*, 189.

25. Pope Francis, *With the Smell*, 191–92.

26. Pope Francis, *With the Smell*, 159.

is a means to the end of proclaiming the gospel and facilitating reconciliation—the model of Jesus's ministry.[27] I saw how necessary this remains to ministry once in a clergy meeting, when a pastor asked how Christ figured in a discussion of the need for rigid conformity to a canon or ecclesiastical rule, where some "economy" or consideration of the good of the person involved seemed appropriate. The response was, "Don't bring Christ into it. This does not involve him. This is a matter of obedience to the canons and the bishop. This is about the church. And good order in it." While some of this response is indeed true, the thought that Christ could ever be excluded is astonishing. Yet Francis indicates that often the church hierarchy and clergy do behave in a "business as usual" mode, clearly something he has experienced as a priest, a Jesuit superior, and a bishop.

PRIESTLY LIFE

Some of Francis's observations on the lifestyle of priests are understandable in the context of his age and his own formation over a half century ago but sound somewhat pious and perhaps forced today. For example, is it necessary for a priest to spend time before the altar and tabernacle at night before or instead of watching TV? Other remarks are more discerning, especially those that underscore the need for pastors to have a balanced life with time for work, study, and prayer in addition to physical exercise, socializing, music, and other forms of self-care. Although his commentary is particularly solid and sound given how poor clergy are at self-care and time management, it does ring of the Roman Catholic context and presumes a celibate priesthood, lacking consideration of the spouses and children of clergy ordained in the Eastern Church and Reformation Church.

In a specific commentary on pastors based on Augustine's sermon "*De pastoribus*" ("On Pastors"), Francis offers an extended reflection that he addresses to questions from student pastors. In the fourth century in North Africa, Augustine, who at heart was monastic, nevertheless honed in on two related tendencies of parish pastors that remain deadly. One was the profiteer modality where priests are motivated by money, which is not only the situation of "religion-as-success" pastors but also extends more subtly across the churches. The other he associates with those he calls "prince pastors" who latch on to status, focusing on titles, dress, and positions of prominence both inside and outside of the church. In his

27. Pope Francis, *With the Smell*, 155–58.

sermon, Augustine uses the prophet Ezekiel's commentary on exploitative shepherds to make his point. Offering a further analogy, Francis cites a saying that was common among desert fathers of Augustine's age about vanity being like an onion: if the monastic or the pastor peel away layer after layer until nothing's left, the fathers remark, you still smell like onion! Francis interprets the analogy, explaining that it is very, very difficult to remove vanity from a priest.

In another reflection, Francis seems to think out loud about preaching and mentions Luther's feeling that it was a sacrament as important as the bread and cup offered and shared from the altar. However, he indicates that at times preaching can be, in my words, almost sacrilegious, referring to sermons in which priests ramble on, employing vague or technical references and language for twenty or thirty minutes or longer or even starting in on a diatribe replete with condemnations and warnings about one or another social or moral issue.[28] Such vanity or lack of preparation in sermons is worse than boring; it destroys people's faith and desire to gather to worship, as studies of those who have left the church show.[29] As is Francis's custom, he insists that sermons remain utterly practical and last eight to ten minutes. The argument that the people need to hear a great deal more reflects the vanity of priests who want to lecture. Suffice it to say that even if they were speaking in a university or seminary classroom, good teachers no longer adhere to long lectures, which is known as the "talking head" phenomenon. Halfway into my forty-five years of teaching, I learned this from master educators who, almost echoing Francis, spoke of the communal nature of learning that involves both professor and students.

WORKING WITH THE PEOPLE AND LOVING THEM

Perhaps even more than he has addressed audiences of priests and seminarians, Francis has also spoken to gatherings of bishops. One theme that he tends to focus on in these speeches is the question of whether bishops are truly recognizing and incorporating the laity in the work and governance of the church.[30] He returns to this repeatedly, asking bishops to adopt what he eventually proposes to the whole church, namely a synodical mode of listening, along with a practice he terms "walking together," which connotes

28. Pope Francis, *With the Smell*, 171–72.

29. Oakes, *Nones Are Alright*; Gushee, "Why Is Christianity Declining?"

30. Pope Francis, *With the Smell*, 207–9.

deliberating and deciding in a conciliar, communal manner. In effect, like the pastor, the bishop is never at a distance from the model of all ministry, Christ, the Good Shepherd. Both exist as does Christ, for the "life of the world," for the flock, the people of God. There is never merely a vertical axis, though in the past this could be said to characterize the place and role of clergy.

According to this view, the priest or bishop stands in the place of Christ, which has become complicated for some when the characteristics of the minister have differed from Christ in terms of gender or marriage, among other items. Confronting this dilemma, Francis emphasizes that there can never be a stand-in for Christ, whether seen as the unique high priest or the Good Shepherd. He rejects the traditional concept of the priest as *alter Christus* (another Christ). Rather, he explains, the pastor does the work of Christ; as John Chrysostom writes, he or she is the mouth, the hands, the eyes, as well as the heart of the Lord in service of the Lord's people.[31] Further, Francis has also challenged the idea that the ordained retain sole access to the sacraments, the means of grace; there is no baptism, no Eucharist, no absolution, and no ordination without them. However, as Nicholas Afanasiev argues, those set apart and ordained have been consecrated because they come from among the assembly, and it is the assembly who selects and presents them to the ordaining bishop for the calling down of the Spirit by the laying on of hands and prayer. In both the Old Covenant and the New Covenant of the followers of Jesus, God, put simply, acts in and with the community of the faithful. Although to my knowledge Francis has never cited Afanasiev, his understanding of the church and of ministry as synodical, conciliar, and communal echoes his views.[32]

These views of ministry converge in a letter Francis wrote to the bishops' conference of Argentina, his church and family home. In it, he uses the figure of Jose Gabriel Brachero (1840–1914), a parish priest who was made a saint in 2016 and who models the same type of service that Francis practices.[33] Known as the "gaucho priest," Fr. Jose was an itinerant pastor who traveled enormous distances in his widespread parish, not unlike John Wesley before him. He knew his people and celebrated the Eucharist in their homes, often at a great distance from the parish church. As we have discussed, Francis, known as a *callejero* or "street priest," also refuses to

31. Chrysostom, *On the Priesthood*, 72–73.

32. International Theological Commission, "Synodality in the Life."

33. Pope Francis, *With the Smell*, 210–12.

remain in the church building or his residence, preferring to be constantly traveling to his people, even when sick and disabled toward the end of his life. In this manner, he upholds the same type of fierce dedication to his people that Fr. Jose exemplified.

In calling upon bishops in particular to love their priests and their people,[34] Francis urges them to follow the ordinary, normal protocols of the diocese and the canons in which episcopal ministry becomes more the work of administration than anything else. If priests are to be "bridges" linking the people to God and God to the people, as we have heard, so too are archpastors, the bishops.[35] Again his views converge with Afanasiev's, who notes that while the specific details of the ministry of the ordained— whether those of the bishop, presbyter, or deacon—have developed over time in the church, all ministries are rooted in the same example of Christ as the servant of his followers. In effect, there is no need for "clerical" bishops, priests, or deacons who assert their difference, and perhaps also their power and superiority, from laity.[36]

When Francis visited the US in 2015, he spoke to bishops at St. Matthew's Cathedral in Washington, DC,[37] where he returned to the dominant image in all his writing and speaking of ministry, that of the shepherd. He asked US bishops to do just that: watch over and care for their flock. Rather than preach complicated doctrine, Francis encouraged them to joyfully proclaim that Christ's death and resurrection is for us. He told them to give the people and their priests a "taste of eternity."[38] He also urged them to step back, as did John the Baptist, decreasing their own stature so that that of Christ might increase.[39]

Pope Francis's rich and discerning visions of the ordained and their ministry reflect the humanity of his thinking about pastors—the need for them to "smell like the sheep," to be close to their people, other pastors, and the bishop, so that they themselves experience a sense of fraternity with those around them. From the perspectives of his service in the priesthood as a superior in the Jesuit community, an auxiliary and then archbishop of a major city, and, finally, as the bishop of Rome and symbol of unity in

34. Pope Francis, *With the Smell*, 213–47.

35. Pope Francis, *With the Smell*, 214.

36. Pope Francis, *With the Smell*, 215.

37. Pope Francis, *With the Smell*, 224–34.

38. Pope Francis, *With the Smell*, 225.

39. Pope Francis, *With the Smell*, 216.

the Catholic Church, Francis never loses sight of the vertical dimension of ministry. However, for him, Christ, the Good Shepherd, is always the model, always the One present; in effect, his presence is crucial in the life of each priest in prayer and communion. It is not an exaggeration to see community as a core feature of ministry for him, bringing us back to the insights of Vatican II and the rediscovery of church as the people of God and the ordained as the servants of the Lord and the Lord's people.

12

Will Willimon

Pastors from Many Angles

A MASTER CLASS ON MINISTRY

Will Willimon's pastoral experience is long and unusually extensive. He's been a United Methodist Church (UMC) parish pastor in Georgia, North Carolina, and South Carolina and served as bishop of the North Alabama Conference of the UMC for eight years. He remains a professor of Christian Ministry at the Divinity School at Duke University, where he was a professor and dean of chapel from 1984 to 2004. A prolific author—an understatement, to be sure, with his nearly sixty books and numerous articles and lectures—he is a widely sought-after preacher and lecturer. His accounts of what he has said and done both in the parish and as bishop are deft, almost surgical in precision, describing how he has taken on racism and dealt with clergy who could not fulfill their tasks. Having experienced the at times tumultuous life of the parish, he is anything but an elite academician. In effect, for all of his erudition, he comes across both on video and in print as a down-to-earth, warm individual. Vested and in the pulpit, he might as well be your beloved parish priest or pastor.

Given the vast expanse of his experience and talent, I think a most accurate characterization of Willimon would be pastor-theologian. He is at home in research and teaching but also at the intersections of birth and death, marriage and burial; he proclaims the word and presides at the Eucharist but also ordains and appoints clergy to parish ministries as well as transfers and removes them, as in the Methodist polity. In discussing his ministry, the main source of this chapter is Willimon's book *The Pastor*, which he produced for seminaries. In it, he provides a thorough historical and theological overview of ordained ministry as well as a discerning perspective of how ministry is done in pastoral practice, including preaching, teaching, and liturgical leadership. He sets forward what appear to him to be the essentials of ordained ministry and offers a probing look at what it has become in the twenty-first century.

Willimon emphasizes that ministry is first and foremost an act of God, admitting that this often gets lost both in historical and practical considerations. As the Scriptures describe, he explains, service of the community was first done by God, over and over again. However, the tendency of devout people is usually to put themselves first, as seen in the practice of claiming that we, or our forbearers, established this congregation. Basil the Great, John Chrysostom, Luther, Calvin, and Wesley are thought to have influenced this tradition of associating church with the name and character of the founder. Later came the sense of church as the beholder of the truth, which, Willimon assures us, none of these eminent pastors would ever have suggested. For them all, and for many other distinguished pastors, the church always has been and always will be the "church of God in Christ," echoing St. Paul.[1] In this manner, Willimon emphasizes that God's initiative is to speak to us, to love and care for us—this is what ministry is about. Not even the Aaronic priests in the Torah, he insists, could claim authority because they had been set part. While ministry is often treated as a profession, with exacting standards of formation and screening, it is a vocation, a call from God, to do what God does.

Following this line of thought, Willimon also indicates that ministry is an act of the church, that is, of the whole people of God, not only the action of this or that ordained person. The process of selection and ordination, as we have seen, is accomplished through the discernment, prayer, and support of a community of believers. While all followers of Christ are called in their baptism to ministry, some are identified by the church and God to lead, preach, teach, baptize, preside, and commune the assembly. As Afanasiev so emphatically and clearly presented it, only the community can recognize and approve a person to be ordained. It is not a status passed down within the guild, trade, or hierarchy, though it may often appear to be so. Afanasiev himself, as noted, points to the community's disappearance

---

1. 1 Thess 2:14.

from the process leading to ordination over time, since the days of the early church.

Given his academic formation and his longtime service as bishop, pastor, and professor, Willimon's vision of ordained ministry is often striking and radical. Yet no one would question the examples of past pastors that he offers throughout his writing, including Paul and Augustine, Ambrose and Gregory the Great, and Luther and John Wesley. As we will see in this chapter, he enlists among these historical names more contemporary paradigmatic pastors, such as Walter Brueggemann along with other respected voices like Reinhold Niebuhr, Karl Barth, George Lindbeck, William Placher, Richard Lischer, Robert McAffee Brown, Peter Gomes, and Stanley Hauerwas, to name just a few. He has become a real "who's who" of theological and pastoral wisdom in our time.[2]

PASTORS ARE ROOTED IN THE CHURCH

Willimon makes clear that to be a pastor or priest means to be tied uniquely to the people of God, the church. While pastors or priests can never replace Christ, they have the authority, as well as the obligation, to say and do what he did. Bearers of a tradition handed down over the centuries and symbolized through the stole around their necks, along with the rest of their vestments and clerical collar, they belong to a group of those chosen by Jesus to lead. In effect, ordination documents often state that the ordained stand in an apostolic line, a succession. Just like all of those who went before them and all those who will come after, no single member of the clergy is irreplaceable, personal feelings to the contrary. No matter how long a pastor's tenure, their vestments and collar stand as reminders of those who came before them and those who will come after. The transient nature of the vocation leads Willimon to somewhat wryly assert that ministry is always difficult, both for the priest and for the community the priest serves.[3] What an understatement. What truth.

As described earlier, ordination can only occur if a candidate has been baptized and then elected by the community. The historical roots of ordained ministry are in the call of disciples to be the twelve messengers or apostles. This is broadened to other disciples after the Resurrection and, in particular, Pentecost, when the need to continue the model of Jesus emerges

2. Willimon, *Pastor*, 124–31.

3. Willimon, *Pastor*, 11–26.

in the various calls and laying on of hands and prayer for the Spirit found in the Acts of the Apostles. A few of those described include Matthias, who was selected to take the place of Judas; Saul, who underwent a conversion-formation and was then set apart; the deacons charged with the care of widows, orphans, and others in need; and the traveling messengers and other "coworkers" who assisted or accompanied Paul, such as Barnabas, John Mark, Timothy, Luke, and those who Paul names, like Lydia, Prisca and Aquila, and Andronicus and Junia.

As Raymond Brown and others have noted, different names and arrangements of the ordained are evident in various churches and often include bishops, presbyters or elders, and deacons, who are mentioned in the Scriptures and then later in apostolic-era texts such as the Didache and writing by Ignatius of Antioch and Justin Martyr.[4] The early-third-century apostolic tradition of Hippolytus provides prayers for the ordinations of bishops, presbyters, and deacons, which have become the basis for ordination prayers in use up until the present.[5] The action of the laying on of hands in ordination had already been incorporated through the setting apart of teachers or rabbis.

Like Afanasiev, Willimon underscores ordination as the action of God and of the community: the people of God or the church. Eventually the chief pastor of a region, the bishop, becomes the ordainer of all three offices of ministry; in this manner, the ministries of both presbyters and deacons are connected to the bishop, whose service is a sign of the unity of the church. Willimon makes clear that the sole purpose of ordination is service to Christ and to the church; it is not an honor or promotion from the universal status of Christian and the common priesthood of all the believers. Although ordination is "from above," an action of God that is made clear through the laying on of hands and invocation of the Spirit, it is also "from below," invoked through the church community who identifies, acclaims, and approves the candidate. In this manner, it represents the convergence of the acts of God and of mortals, the women and men following Christ.

Knowing that ordination is the result of the participation of the church with God, Willimon admits that in his years of teaching ordination candidates, he was often plagued by the institutional process by which they were groomed, molded, and turned into acceptable functionaries. In my experience as well as that of those I know well as fellow pastors, the longer

---

4. Brown, *Churches the Apostles Left*.
5. Dix, *Treatise on the Apostolic Tradition*.

one serves in ordained ministry, the pressure to conform to the institution—to scrupulously adhere to canons and other rules, to please the bishop or other leaders—seems to collide with the model of Jesus in the Gospels. As I have heard it put in gatherings of clergy, it often seems better "not to bring Jesus into" what appears to be matters of the bishop, canons, or rules. Order, in this manner, is in perpetual conflict with the Spirit. However, as Willimon attests throughout his study, in practice the path to ordination and beyond, to service in ministry, should remain one of compromise and negotiation. The structures and rules will always be there and will always be lacking, even if they have been reformed and renewed over time. Not even church bodies that claim to rely solely on the Scriptures to the exclusion of early church writers and councils can avoid the always present tendency to habituation and institutionalization that has influenced the historical behavior of the church.

PASTORS OVER TIME

Time and space do not permit an overview here of the careful inspection Willimon makes of ordination over the councils, from Chalcedon in the ancient period to the Third and Fourth Lateran Councils in the early Middle Ages and beyond. In his writing, the emergence of tendencies observed by Afanasiev is clear, such as the consolidation of a clerical class and the further definition of the authority of the ordained, particularly that of the bishop over presbyters and deacons. Ordained ministry, he shows, also becomes a personal state with special characteristics that distinguish the ordained from each other and from the laity. As previously stated, their different dress and titles indicate their particular holiness, conferred by God and the church. These features appear both in the Western and Eastern churches and remain up to the present, though they underwent significant transformation in the sixteenth-century Reformation and Counter Reformation. Luther, for example, recognizes that while all Christians are priests by baptism, those called and ordained as pastors are "priests to the priests," an arrangement that is both divine and human, *iure divino* not just *iure humano*.[6] The principal traditions stemming from the Reformation hold on to something approximating this, recognizing at once the human as well as the divine components of ordained ministers.

---

6. Luther, "Apology of the Augsburg Confession," art. xiii–xv.

As noted earlier, it will be much closer to our own time that the most ancient understanding of the church as a community that comprises the people of God will be returned to, especially at the Second Vatican Council and in the writings that sought to further its reform and renewal. It is only in again affirming the baptismal call of all to be priests, prophets, and the leaders of the kingdom that there has been a specific recognition of the place and the function of the ordained among the whole people of God.

Although Willimon covers many other aspects of ministry, only a few can be noted here. Some of the conflicts he describes, which emerged in the renewal period, remain today. One that seems perennial is the belief that true ministry is more rooted in the personal piety of the individual pastor than anything else, which is pitted against the traditional insistence that the divine is what rules rather than the often idiosyncratic and defective character of the actual pastor. One need only recall the cowardice of ten of the eleven apostles at the time of the crucifixion—described through their fear and lack of belief in the tomb being empty—over against the faithfulness of the women disciples who remained beneath the cross and later went to the tomb to see these defects in those chosen to be ministers.[7]

Willimon's emphasis on the communal quality of ordained ministry also comes forth through the principle that no pastor exists in a vacuum; seeing and hearing one is seeing and hearing all. Furthermore, no single pastor controls the wisdom of the tradition, no matter how gifted. As the Pauline letters attest, pastors have been graced with different skills, including teaching, preaching, administration, and care for those in need. Cyprian of Carthage, for instance, insisted that he never acted as bishop without the counsel of his clergy and the consent of the people.[8] Recalling his own ordination on a summer evening at Broad Street United Methodist Church in Clinton, South Carolina, Willimon shares with us the experience of joining the innumerable procession of pastors before him as the bishop and other elders laid hands on his head and invoked the Spirit to make him a minister of the word and sacraments in and for and with the church of

---

7. According to the classic Catholic vision, ordained ministry is incarnational and sacramental; always fallible, weak human beings are the means by which divine grace is accessible in the church. Pastors thus baptize, preside at the Eucharist, commune the people, preach the word of God, bless marriages, anoint the sick, bury the dead, and more. Just as the Spirit uses language, bread and wine, and water and oil, so too do the human beings who are the pastors.

8. Willimon, *Pastor*, 49. Willimon cites epistle 5.4 of Roberts and Donaldson, *Ante-Nicene Fathers*, 283.

God in Christ. The work of ordained ministers is so integral to the community of the church that even those churches who reject a separate clergy by ordination nevertheless have need of someone to perform it.

Willimon, in this manner, stresses that to be ordained as a priest means to join many other confessors and witness to Christ and his gospel. In a particular note, he reflects on the formation of this community among the earliest Methodist pastors, who rode through and served a circuit of people both in the UK and in the US; given the extreme wear and tear of such ministry, the average life expectancy was about thirty.[9] Countless stories of pastors who died of the same diseases that took their people or who were imprisoned, tortured, or executed for practicing their faith fills the calendar of Methodist commemorations, from Dietrich Bonhoeffer to Martin Luther King Jr.

From the earliest practitioners of ministry such as Paul, Peter, Barnabas, Silas, Priscilla and Aquila, Phoebe, Lydia, and Junia and Andronicus to great figures like John Chrysostom, Gregory of Nyssa, Gregory of Nazienzen, Basil the Great, Augustine, Ambrose, Thomas Becket, and the reformers, Willimon makes a sharp turn from this probing examination of the theology and history of ordained ministry to look at how we regard pastors in the twenty-first century.[10] Among contemporary pastors, he looks at Walter Rauschenbusch, Washington Gladden, Henry Ward Beecher, Reinhold Niebuhr, Billy Graham, Harry Emerson Fosdick, and, more recently, Sloan Coffin, and Desmond Tutu, among others. For Willimon, the ministry of the church changes over time, in response to the needs of the church and the world. At the same time, the principal work of ordained ministry remains constant from Jesus's disciples through us today.

IMAGES OF THE PASTOR

One contemporary category of ministry that can be mentioned and quickly dropped is celebrity pastors. These span from dated figures such as Billy Graham, Robert Schuller, and Oral Roberts to the more recent Rick Warren, T. D. Jakes, Joel Osteen, and numerous others. Ordinary pastors seldom have high-profile fantasies, and those who do have often become infamous. One can think here of Jimmy Swaggart, Jim and Tammy Bakker, Bill Hybels, and several celebrity pastors of the Hillsong churches.

9. Willimon, *Pastor*, 36–38.

10. See also Root, *Pastor in a Secular Age*.

Since there are far more pervasive and influential images of the pastor, as stated, such media stars can be acknowledged and moved past. Another more contemporary image—the pastor as therapist—is probably the most prominent in the last several decades and has been critiqued by Willimon, as well as Stanley Hauerwas and quite a few others. Suffice it to say that none of the writers featured in this book put much stock in this view of ministry, though it is often seductive for the ordained; in a therapeutic culture, what could be more powerful an image than that of a spiritual healer? The rise or "triumph" of the therapeutic, as Philip Rieff called it, indeed reshaped the training for pastoral counseling in the twentieth century.[11] Clinical Pastoral Education, or CPE, became a requirement in the formation process of theological schools, with a minimum number of hours of supervised clinical care necessary for ordination. Although Willimon acknowledges the therapeutic role of the priest and its history—the name for a parish priest, curate, he explains, drives precisely from the "care of souls," a ministry that is rooted in prayer and worship and the Scriptures but which enters into the tangles of human relationships and the personal lives of disciples of the Lord—he asserts that therapy was never the principal or defining element of ministry.[12] While he admits to the necessity of therapeutic training for the ordained, he also notes the need for a recovery of the ancient tradition of pastoral counsel as spiritual direction or accompaniment. Even those trained in CPE, he acknowledges, are not equipped to diagnose or treat serious conditions such as clinical depression, anxiety syndrome, addiction, self-destructive behavior, or schizophrenia. In the ancient tradition of pastoral counseling to which he refers—practiced by figures like Gregory Nazianzen and Ambrose, along with Gregory the Great—stress was placed on careful listening that brought attention to the individual and their condition. Willimon's main point is that the pastor as counselor offers a singular gift to those in need: to represent and offer a connection with Christ. Through patient listening and a discerning response, a pastor can bring to the suffering enduring accompaniment in the Christian way. He stresses that through the pastor, it is God who is listening, God who heals, forgives, and gives new life. The pastor is, in this sense, an essential incarnational agent.

Another contemporary image that is as pervasive as that of therapist is the pastor as manager or administrator. Cathie Caimano's work details

11. Rieff, *Triumph of the Therapeutic*.

12. Willimon, *Pastor*, 168–83.

this role, as does Barbara Brown Taylor's. Again, administration is named as a particular task and gift in ministry in the Pauline letters and elsewhere in the New Testament, such as the description of the selection of deacons in the Acts of the Apostles. Yet like Willimon, contemporary commentators—including Caimano along with Sam Wells—stress that the parish is a communal phenomenon. Asking the priest or pastor to administer the entirety of the congregational project, attract new members, and raise funds, or blaming them for shrinkage and decline, shows the absurdity of such executive reduction of the ministry of the ordained.

Of far older vintage is the image of the pastor as the chief local activist, the community prophet, the voice against social injustice and defender of the marginalized and oppressed. Surely the immense stature of the Rev. Dr. Martin Luther King Jr. and Archbishop Desmond Tutu lifted up this image of the ordained; others, like William Sloan Coffin, Daniel and Philip Berrigan, and, more recently, William Barber and Michael Curry have also contributed to it. Brian McLaren and Richard Rohr, along with Barbara Holmes, have emphasized the urgency of the prophetic voice and action by all believers, the ordained in particular.[13] The priestly and prophetic traditions are not contradictory but have existed in dynamic tension, as exemplified in the Hebrew Scriptures through the New Testament and the history of the church. The priest is often understood as a member of the institutional structure of the tradition, ruled by its laws and supportive of its order, while prophets are very often called through the divine to bring messages that are not welcome by the state or the religious establishment. Plenty of them suffer the witness of blood or martyrdom precisely for such service. This remains true today, where, as a pastor I know once put it, the loudest, angriest complaints come when the very words of Christ from the Gospels are cited in preaching. In the twenty-first century's extreme state of divisiveness and contention, the prophetic role of the ordained is the most dangerous contemporary aspect of ministry.

Another image with a long history that remains central today is that of pastor as preacher and teacher of the word of God. The very model of Jesus's public ministry is largely composed of this essential action. Willimon, however, offers some likely ignored angles in his reflection on it. One is that in our time biblical and theological literacy is not widespread. Who else but the pastor is there, week after week, to attempt to connect the Scriptures to

---

13. See, for example, Curry, *Love Is the Way*; McLaren, *Faith after Doubt*; Rohr, *Universal Christ*; Barber, *Third Reconstruction*.

life? Although others in congregations also are involved in faith education, no one pursues this as distinctively as the one there in front, addressing the community in the name of God. Willimon also underscores the role of "priestly listening" in preaching, a term coined by Leander Keck, who Willimon cites, to describe the act of listening to the text as well as to the words and lives of the community.[14] Preachers do not arrive on Sunday from elsewhere but have been sharing the life of the parish community all the week; they are therefore privy to more of the community's sorrows, joys, and challenges than most. Others featured in this book echo Willimon and Keck in emphasizing the necessity of the priest's prayer life and deep commitment to *lectio divina*; this includes study, intercessory prayer, and, in short, everything that composes a spiritual existence. Where this is lacking, the pastor, the act of ministry, as well as the entire congregation suffer.

The next image—the pastor as servant—is perhaps most emphatic on Maundy or Holy Thursday in Holy Week, when many churches practice Jesus's example of washing the feet of people at the service. However, the ordained remain servants of God and servants of the servants of God all year long; they do not hold this up for acclaim but rather for all to emulate. Yet, Willimon admits that the role of "servant" can also easily be used to cover the exercise of power and authority over others. On the other hand, since the pastor very often has advanced degrees and, by virtue of office, a high status both in the congregation and the wider community, at times there is an apparent disconnect between the ordained "servant-leader" and their professional experience. This disconnect has also been questioned. In spite of these issues, Willimon reminds us of the great legacy of those who deliberately sought the status of the poor, seeing this as the model of Jesus in the Gospels. Whether one thinks of Francis of Assisi or Dorothy Day, service needs no defense as a way of being a disciple and a fitting form of pastoral ministry.

Rounding out Willimon's view of images or models of pastoral ministry today, he speculates on the role of pastor as rebel. Surely the rebel cleric has had a crucial role—think of Daniel Berrigan or Thomas Merton; the witness of Archbishop Romero; seminarian martyr Jonathan Daniels; and Sisters Maura Clarke, Ita Ford, Dorothy Kazel, and their companion, Jean Donovan. As apparent from chapter 8, one could include Nadia Bolz-Weber among this list, along with Brian McLaren. Willimon emphasizes that ordained ministry, like the gospel, is countercultural. This might appear

14. Willimon, *Pastor*, 66.

contradictory, since so much of the history of the church features periods in which state and church work together, sometimes through a "state church," and Christianity defines dominant culture. Closer inspection, however, reveals that such cooperation is often not the case. The "good news" of the kingdom of God, Willimon insists, is always at odds with the structure of an empire, colliding with many components of its economy and culture. In the church, the ponderous divides of master and slave, male and female, and Jew and gentile should be overridden. Echoing Walter Brueggemann, he emphasizes the countercultural position that the pastor is often in to follow the essence of the Scriptures in spite of dominant cultural or political regimes. As exemplified through the prophets of the Hebrew Scriptures on through John the Baptist, Jesus, and Jesus's messengers, the priest often needs to invoke an inversion of the status quo. They can facilitate a call to dramatically transform or even overthrow the established order, much to the scandal and rage of those deeply invested in it.[15] In spite of these models, Willimon is not hesitant to admit that authentic Christian tradition and community may currently be at odds with what passes itself off as true Christianity. I think we can read what he critiques as a type of "Christian nationalism" that excludes people because of their gender, sexual identity, and political and social outlooks. When the enemy becomes the political opponent of conservative politics, how can condemnation, or a declaration of war against them, be reconciled with Jesus's preaching and action? Willimon reminds us that no matter the monarch or bishops who appear to rule, only God is Lord and only Christ is the head of the church. Willimon further argues that those who lead the people of God will always need to exercise a prophetic stance in which the histories and structures of various church bodies must be subject to the scrutiny of the Spirit.

Pastor as Priest and Preacher

The body of the text of *Pastor* consists of Willimon's proceeding through the different aspects of ordained ministry as they have developed in church history. He begins quite deliberately with the role of pastor as priest, the leader of the community in worship. What and how we pray is, he insists, the "primary theology," something great liturgical scholars like Alexander Schmemann, Max Thurian, Gregory Dix, Berhard Botte, Geoffrey Wainwright, and Nicholas Afanasiev, to cite just a few, have argued. To start

15. Willimon, *Pastor*, 110–12, 137–55.

with the ordained as liturgists—the presiders at the eucharistic gathering, as those who also baptize, confirm, announce forgiveness, bless marriages, anoint the sick, and bury the dead—is to get to the heart of the tradition and the community, or *koinonia*. The earliest glimpses we have of the people of God assembling in this manner around a priest are in the New Testament, along with, for example, Justin Martyr's *First Apology*. In these early sources we find the key movements of ministry—to gather the people, listen, intercede for the world, offer to God the sacrifice of thanksgiving, share the eucharistic gifts, and go into the world to become what they have received.

It is telling that the role of "pastor as priest" is the first reflection in Willimon's book; he is clear that liturgy leads in the ministry of the ordained, knowing that this is seemingly in contrast, or even conflict, with the contemporary images we have reviewed of the twenty-first-century pastor. In addition, he writes, those favoring a thorough recasting of worship often replace liturgy with musical performance and message rather than preaching. He does not see much of substance in such wholesale purging of the past.[16] For him, the pastor remains interpreter of Scripture and preacher-servant of the word, bringing God to the people and the people to God. While the pastor should not reduce preaching and teaching to purely academic concern with the cultural, social, and economic and religious contexts of the Scriptures, the pastor nonetheless needs to make clear the meaning of texts and connect them to the lives of the congregation. Put another way, the pastor is the principal teacher. The complex meanings of "the kingdom of heaven"; the many layers of Jesus's parables; and the constant pursuit of the people by God and God's messengers, the prophets, all fall to the pastor. First and foremost, it is their task to interpret and serve the word as the presider at the Sunday service, through the reading and preaching of the Scriptures for that day as well as the prayer and sacramental celebrations surrounding it.

Willimon goes on to stress that all we hear and pray and share in the liturgy has to be put into practice. The gospel, he indicates, is only a text unless it is enacted. This remains essential even when people are shocked and angry to hear that God did not produce their perspectives on society, finances, or government. Many pastors know that repeating the very words of Jesus from the Gospels in their preaching often infuriates those firmly set

---

16. Willimon, *Pastor*, 75–108.

in their own religious and political views. Still, they remain witnesses to the truth of the Scriptures, of what God wants us to hear.[17]

Willimon's observations also imply a critique of the notion that the Scriptures are the writings of "primitive" people and that we have far advanced from their simplistic perspectives, a stance that the pastor will have to face. The pastor will also have to struggle, he writes, with the history of using the Scriptures to justify monarchy, slavery, the oppression of other peoples, the subordination of women, and hatred of those who are different than us in belief or identity. Likewise, the pastor will have to contend with the use of the Scriptures to warrant the exploitation of the natural resources of the planet for profit with no sense of the destruction of the environment and its effects on our lives. As briefly discussed in the previous section on the countercultural role of the priest, the history of the church is littered with great atrocities we can only lament and for which we must ask forgiveness, as John Paul II, Francis, and other church leaders have done. In effect, it is not only in our time that the shepherds of the flock have to contend with fundamentalists who cling to literal meanings of the text, claiming there are no alternatives or further contextual explanations and condemning those who cannot agree with them as outside the faith. Even though our contemporary versions of fanaticism often seem singular, this exact conflict has erupted numerous times in the past two thousand and more years of Christianity.

Willimon has much, much more to say about the pastor as preacher and teacher, both in the text I am drawing upon here and in many other of his publications. Since, for him, the ministry of the ordained cannot be reduced to one task, even a crucial task like preaching, he also stresses the other aspects of pastoral identity and work that we have reviewed. He notes that the liturgy and sacraments remain the first source of care and healing, forgiveness and new life for the people of God. He pulls no punches in calling out what in retrospect can be identified as extreme efforts to reform the liturgy, ministry, and the church. While the Reformation, for example, targeted the medieval (and long before it) arrangement of a hierarchy both in the church and society, more often than not it was merely replaced with another hierarchy, sometimes not all that different than the previous Catholic model. In addition, Eamon Duffy's work has confirmed that the pre-Reformation view of the Christian life and corresponding arrangement of clergy and liturgy were vigorous and even far more effective than the

17. Willimon, *Pastor*, 113–23.

caricatures of corruption, superstition, and decadence claimed by some reformers.[18] This bears on Willimon's insistence that the work of the pastor remains rooted in prayer, worship, and the sacraments and Scriptures over contemporary tendencies, including the professionalization of pastoral care as therapy discussed earlier.

Pastor as Teacher

While much of what Willimon has to say about the pastor as teacher has been touched on already, a bit more is worth noting. His view coincides with that of dean of contemporary students of the parish, Episcopal priest and founder of the Alban Institute, Loren Mead. Mead figures importantly in *Community as Church*, offering his take on the future of the parish. His seminal insight is that the parish has to exist for something other than itself; that is, it needs a reason for being other than its own growth and survival. While in the past, the church was primarily seen as the way to salvation—to heaven—even then it was also a social hub: a place to seek knowledge, help, and counsel, as Sam Wells has argued.[19] Wells clarifies Mead's claim, stressing that the parish—and all that goes on in it, from the baptisms, weddings, and burials to the weekly Eucharist, classes, pastoral care, and even food banks and after-school programs for kids—is about and for abundant life, the life of resurrection. Obviously at the center of this is the parish priest, the pastor.

Willimon leans on George Lindbeck, as well as Mead and Leslie Newbigin, to claim that in our time there is need for Christianity to again be a culture, a way of seeing, hearing, feeling, thinking, and living, a way that forms, or, better, transforms us.[20] This runs counter to the popular sense of "religion" as full of doctrine and ritual, and therefore constrictive and imposing, which has led to the more subjective "spiritual" stance of the twenty-first century. This more popular view of spirituality has been further facilitated by the reality that younger people may have had little if any experience of church and do now know the community of a congregation, liturgy, the Scriptures, preaching, or teaching. The mobility of the contemporary population and the disappearance of multigenerational families, along with the aging of congregations and the absence of those

18. Duffy, *Stripping of the Altars*; Duffy, *People's Tragedy*.

19. Plekon, *Community as Church*, 193–204.

20. Willimon, *Pastor*, 200–214.

forty and younger, makes for a formidable lack of understanding of the faith. In this context, Willimon sees the role of pastor as teacher as increasingly important; indeed, it is a necessity in the twenty-first century. The teaching of the Scriptures and the faith, he indicates, occurs through the Sunday service as well as the seasons of the church year, the rites of passage, and all that accompany them.

Further, Willimon insists that Jesus's teachings have little if anything to do with the battle lines of the "culture wars" so promoted by conservative Christians. The Scriptures, especially the Gospels in the Revised Common Lectionary, sustain his claim. The aim of Jesus, he stresses, is like that of the prophets—to facilitate a return to God and God's ways, the kingdom. It is not the world that is problematic but rather what lies within our hearts and minds. Willimon is surprising, however, in noting with admiration the high level of teaching and study in fundamentalist congregations he visits; in such communities he has found greater attention to scriptural texts, specifically to their meaning in the original languages and their bearing on how Christians should be living. Other churches with rich traditions of liturgy and theology, he specifies, need to avoid diluting how they worship or diverting it to causes without substantially grappling with what the Scriptures have to say.

If Willimon seems to place special emphasis on pastors as preachers and teachers, this carries further into their ministry as evangelists. Though his takeaway is somewhat surprising, he remains faithful to his Wesleyan roots in holding together the Lutheran emphasis on justification—God's saving us—and Calvin's stress on the need for sanctification. Of course, these reformers were but echoing the classic Catholic tradition before them, carried from Paul on down. In particular, in his conversion John Wesley saw that being "saved" or justified had to be accompanied by the constant effort become holy. It is this redeemed holiness that pastors offer to their flocks and the world beyond, Willimon indicates, not just in words but in actions.

Willimon is most eloquent in relating his own Methodist tradition to the broader sweep of Christian tradition, showing Wesley as an inspired priest in a very indifferent time and church, a pastor whose own conversion compelled him to work for the lifelong sanctification of all the people of God. Willimon tries to reveal that real transformation comes through applying the actions of the great pastors of the past to our time and people. Evangelism has nothing to do with "growing" the number of members

and contributions of a congregation, or getting more "bodies and bucks."
Rather, it is showing the gospel and how to live it. Pastors must be prophets,
voicing God's messages to the world.[21]

Pastors as Prophets

While all the people of God are prophets through baptism, through ordination pastors are singled out to be witnesses, often in dangerous and
uncomfortable situations, to what God says to and wants for us. Such
prophetic witness was exemplified by Pastor Trocmè and his congregation
in Le Chambon in the face of the Nazi hunt for Jewish neighbors, along
with Mother Maria Skobtsova and her companions in occupied Paris.[22] For
a southerner like Willimon, the further example of Will Campbell in the
years of the Civil Rights Movement underscores the sure confrontation that
the call to ministry brings to the ordained. Numerous other priests, pastors,
and religious figures have been arrested and jailed in the struggles that have
accompanied the role of prophetic witness, some paying with their lives.

To realize the demands of this role, Willimon asserts that the pastor
must be a person of great character and discipline as a leader.[23] He reiterates
Leslie Newbigin's insistence that pastors are always missionaries, not just
when sent to non-Christian populations.[24] In the context of the present-day
church, we are realizing the truth of this argument; as some congregations
shrink and even close, others hear again the good news of the Resurrection
and reinvent, replant, and revive it to maintain their livelihood.[25] After
centuries of assuming that most had heard the gospel and lived it, the
contemporary church thus comes across as more radical and is more like
the earliest years of the Jesus movement, or the "Way," as the Acts of the
Apostles called the church.

Willimon also insists that pastoral ministry no longer slip into the
accustomed slot of maintaining buildings, budgets, and membership lists
or fixate on average Sunday attendance and the number of pledging units.
Rather, pastoral ministry has for some time been occupied by shrinkage
and decline; this shift cannot all be blamed on the pandemic or, for that

21. Willimon, *Pastor*, 239–53.

22. Hackel, *Pearl of Great Price*.

23. Willimon, *Pastor*, 281–93, 303–39.

24. Willimon, *Pastor*, 263–79.

25. Plekon, *Community as Church*, 133–40.

matter, on liberal political views, as some fervent believers allege. It is delusion to think that some "ungodly" forces have declared war on Christianity. Rather, what was evident in the first century CE as well in the 1200s of Francis of Assisi, the sixteenth century of Luther, or the eighteenth century of John Wesley is again evident today: the church is in decline. Willimon goes on to suggest that the current church also resembles that of pious, mid-nineteenth-century Victorian Christians, who believed their churches were packed even though the census, much to their shock, told otherwise. Similarly, the 1950s was not the church "golden age" as some believe. Willimon knows that clinging to visions of crowded congregations is fantastic, wishful, or magical thinking. At their worst, they confuse cultural and social patterns of behavior with living Christ's good news. Willimon further specifies that packed churches in the first half of the twentieth century did not stop two world wars, were later powerless in the face of racial discrimination, and were seemingly indifferent to poverty. Some of the exemplary pastors evoked by the writers here, however, had the courage to confront the injustices they saw and suffered for their commitment to Christ. These include Bonhoeffer, Martin Luther King Jr., Oscar Romero, Desmond Tutu, and Daniel and Philip Berrigan, among others.

Although most of the ordained will not be jailed, threatened with death, or murdered for providing faithful witness to Christ, as Willimon points out, this does not mean that they are free from pain, cost, and suffering. Some will experience fierce opposition from the people they seek to serve. Every year this seems to push hundreds to leave active ministry in congregations and still others to leave ministry completely because they are burnt out, spent, emptied, or discouraged. In this book, I have not considered studies and surveys of clergy wellbeing, analyses of pastoral attraction and attrition, or different types of formation, many of which are nonresidential yet follow quite ancient models of prolonged mentorships and in-parish training and service. These were examined in *Community as Church*, where it is clear that in spite of the difficulty of current circumstances, people still seek to be trained for ordained ministry and their formation continues to change, in sync with the changes that are occurring in the communities in which they will serve.

Willimon recognizes the church's ongoing need for pastors that have been set apart by the community and the Spirit to perform the work that the people of God need done. Perhaps more so than others featured here, he recognizes the broad sweep of ordained ministry's tasks and the gifts necessary for their accomplishment. Over against the present shrinkage and decline of congregations, he wants to assert the enduring aspects of pastors' service. In this manner, his is both a comprehensive as well as an optimistic vision.

13

The Parish Pastor

The Experience of Ministry, Rites, and Passages

In my lexicon, at least, a priest is someone willing to stand between a God and a people who are longing for one another's love, turning back and forth between them with no hope of tending either as well as each deserves. To be a priest is to serve a God who never stops calling people to do more justice and love more mercy and simultaneously to serve people who nine times out of ten are just looking for a safe place to rest. To be a priest is to know that things are not as they should be and yet to care for them the way they are. To be a priest is to suspect that there is always something more urgent that you should be doing, no matter what you are doing, and to make peace with the fact that the world will never get done. To be a priest is to wonder sometimes if you are missing the boat altogether, by deferring pleasure in what God has made until you have fixed it up so that it will please God more. "When I wake up in the morning," E. B. White once wrote, "I can't decide whether to enjoy the world or improve the world; that makes it difficult to plan the day."

—BARBARA BROWN TAYLOR[1]

---

1. Taylor, *Leaving Church*, 44.

If you know Barbara Brown Taylor's work, her voice is unmistakable. If you don't, it doesn't matter. You are halted in your tracks by her clarity, by how right her words sound, yet also how provocative they are. Although an entire chapter has already focused on Barbara Brown Taylor, the distinctiveness of her tone and force of her message has compelled me to feature her again here, at the end of this book. She shows through her words and example that the work of a priest, a pastor, is never done. There is always more. She also acknowledges that it is hard not to be uneasy or anxious about all the things one cannot accomplish, no matter how much one has done.

This was Barbara Brown Taylor's personal dilemma and undoing, as documented in *Leaving Church*. As her subsequent volumes—*An Altar in the World*, *Learning to Walk in the Darkness*, and *Holy Envy*—attest, however, it is possible to enlarge the boundaries of ordained service past liturgical and ecclesiastical confines, past the borders of traditions of faith and beyond what a tradition seems to favor. Even though Taylor has not served a congregation in years, she truly remains a priest and is often invited to preach as well as to lecture. The long shelf of her publications explains why. She seems to always have more to say, from the early collections of her sermons to the series of personal, fearless explorations of her vocation as an ordained person, the sacred character of the world outside church walls, and the dark side of consciousness and faith. Her writing has also examined diverse faith traditions, including their literature, rites, and communities, as exemplified in her most recent book, *Always a Guest*, a collection of sermons from many different denominational locations and services.[2]

Whether she deliberately intends it or not, Taylor's restless spirit makes her a discerning voice on the ordained and their ministry even beyond her substantial writing about it. This will become clearer momentarily. First it will be useful to see where we have been and, in compact terms, what we have learned here in this extended set of conversations with so many writers. Without laboriously rehearsing the views of the ordained and their ministry, looking back for a moment is worthwhile, as some themes were sounded over and over again.

First, George Keith and Will Willimon affirm that the priest or pastor brings God to the people and the people to God through preaching, the sacraments, teaching, pastoral care, leadership, and gathering the community, a theme that was woven through may of the chapters. This might

2. Taylor, *Always a Guest*.

be the most concise definition of what the ordained are for and what they do. Next, Nicholas Afanasiev and Sam Wells indicate that the ordained are inextricably rooted within the community, not outside or above the people of God, and called by them to service. Cathie Caimano and Barbara Brown Taylor, meanwhile, stress that pastors are necessary members of church but not exhaustive of who the church is and what the church does. For Sarah Coakley and Rowan Williams, the ordained are sacraments or sacramental; they provide points of contact between the divine and the human, the spiritual and the material, and the spiritual and the physical. They are living members of the people of God, not just functionaries of an organization or staff performing important tasks. Pope Francis, Henri Nouwen, Andrew Root, and Will Willimon, meanwhile, emphasize that Christ is the principal model for the ordained and their ministry. They are shepherds following the Good Shepherd. Of course, there are numerous exemplary pastors through the ages that they can also look to as secondary models. Barbara Brown Taylor, Cathie Caimano, and Nadia Bolz-Weber focus on the ordained as women and men. As human ministers of God's love, they are themselves fallible, weak, and capable of overwork. As such, they are sometimes the targets of community frustration, blamed for things beyond their control or making. Their joy and commitment can be intense, as can be their sadness and feelings of failure. Finally, Nadia Bolz-Weber, Sam Wells, Rowan Williams, and Will Willimon indicate that the ordained can and do break through cultural, social, political, and even theological walls to serve those at the margins or outside of traditional churchgoer identities, acceptable modes of behavior, and class and ethnic identifications and groupings. They are a transforming force, as they act with the Spirit's power in the name of Christ.

RITES OF PASSAGE, RITES AND PASSAGES:
PASTORAL EXPERIENCE

Quite a few of the writers cited above deliberately dug into their long experience of serving as pastors. They knew that ordained ministry is fundamentally personal and transformative—of themselves and of those with whom they serve. Through the perspective of the specific minister as a woman or man—formed through her or his family, upbringing, study, and training—others are brought to God and God is brought to them. Ministry employs their perception, discernment, and engagement; it accents their intellectual gifts, their weaknesses, and their quirks. Because it is so individual, ministry is always amazingly diverse. While all priests are ordained to do the same work of preaching, celebrating the sacraments, gathering the community, and reaching out to those in trouble and in need, no two ministers will ever be the same. Although this is an obvious reality, throughout years of service every one of us who is or has been a pastor will hear comparisons made between ourselves and some other beloved minister, or, sometimes, to someone less than loved or valued.

Anthropologist of religion Arnold van Gennep, among others, emphasizes the "rites of passage" of traditions of faith and their communities.[3] These are words and actions, formalized over time, that move people from one stage of life to another and define who they are in those stages. Van Gennep's recognition of the significance of these rituals is essential for both the community and the individual. Sometimes, they are colloquially called moments of "hatching, matching and dispatching." When I was studying in Copenhagen, I recall that a tutor who was a priest in the *Folkekirken*, the "People's Church of Denmark," said that people spoke in slang of *fire hjulne kristne*, literally "four wheel Christians." The wheels refer to being driven to the church for baptism, confirmation, marriage, and burial.

With so much being said about the rise of those with no religious ties or activity, the "nones," and those who deliberately have left and stayed away from church, the "dones," it might seem pointless to dwell on "rites of passage." Data indicates that each year fewer marriages are celebrated in a church by a member of the clergy. Instead, there are more destination weddings and celebrations in event spaces, with a friend authorized to witness the union either by online ordination or local legal recognition. Likewise, the number of baptisms is declining, along with church funerals and memorial services, which have been replaced by "celebrations of life" organized by friends and family of the deceased, often weeks or months after the death with no shred of religious content, per the deceased's wishes. Nonetheless, these moments are still significant in the lives of people, as are services on the great "holy days" of Easter and Christmas. One can fill in analogous feasts for other traditions, such as Diwali, Rosh Hashanah, or Passover. Some holy seasons and days still bear rigor in observance, like Ramadan and Yom Kippur. In my pastoral experience, even that of decades ago, I was often struck by the continued meaningfulness of a ritual,

3. Van Gennep, *Rites of Passage*.

readings, or even the mere presence of a priest for people who were not regular worshippers and were possibly not even believers.

Pastoral Experience: A Complicated Funeral and Burial

There was a funeral home not far from where I first served at Trinity Lutheran Church in Brewster, New York, whose director was a devoted member of a local Methodist parish. He usually reached out to area clergy when a family arranging a funeral and internment said they were not members of a congregation and had no pastor of their own. Once, he asked me to provide the funeral and burial of the matriarch of a rather large, extended family that had been bitterly divided by the woman's divorce from the clan's patriarch. What the funeral director apprised me of were two warring family factions; they were at such odds that the director and some family members decided to arrange for identical but separate funeral and burial services, one set for each part of the family.

When I arrived for the first of the two services, I saw members of the first family parking and congregating outside of the funeral home. As I passed them, I could not help but notice some serious day drinking; they were starting the day with toasts to the deceased. Inside, the director further informed me that both parts of the family likely would have partaken in such toasts and would thereby arrive to the services under the influence of alcohol. The first brief service proceeded without incident, the attendees being told where and when to appear for the burial, which was located at a veterans' cemetery about a half hour's drive away. They were asked to reassemble there, perhaps after some refreshments at the local diner, so that the two factions could avoid meeting each other and the conflict that might ensue. Meanwhile, the other faction arrived at the funeral home and the second service also took place without any problems. I was then told to follow the hearse in my car to the cemetery, where one of the funeral home staff would accompany me to the grave. I did wonder whether the timing of the different services and internments would be successful in preventing confrontation. At the cemetery, a staff member escorted me to the grave and pointed out that there were several sheriff's department vehicles deployed for crowd control. The aim was to park the cars of the two sides of the family on different lanes of the cemetery, sufficiently separated both by arrival time and distance. However, as we moved to the grave it became clear that everyone seemed to be arriving at the same time, parking on upper and lower lanes. Those on the upper lane were already gathering at the grave. I was asked to proceed so as to quickly finish the first internment, which I did. But as I did the final commendation and invited people to place a flower on the casket as they left, members of the other faction began streaming up to the grave site. I saw several sheriff's department officers proceeding toward us as well. At this point, my friend, the funeral director, indicated that it was time for me to go, saying: "Father Michael, I hope you can move fairly quickly to your car." I had my vestments on but was able to walk briskly to where they'd had me park. The director went on, saying he regretted that it was no longer possible to say how the encounter of the two factions might play out. Though I offered, he did not think it safe for me to try to mediate. I agreed that given the amount of drinking they had done to the deceased, such an effort might be pointless. So, one of his assistants and an officer hustled me off; as I looked back as I got into my car, I saw not all but at least several members of the two factions encountering each other.

I share this pastoral incident not because I was heroically able to convince these conflicted folk to be peaceable as they buried their mom. Rather, I could look at this graveside moment as the utter defeat of such a hope. Only the presence of law enforcement, I think, prevented their yelling and fighting. However, when I think back to the readings and the prayers in the funeral and burial services, including the following from the *The Book of Common Prayer*, I realize that despite so many other theological and liturgical differences, they ended up being remarkably ecumenically universal:

> I am Resurrection and I am Life, says the Lord.
> Whoever has faith in me shall have life,
> even though he die.
> And everyone who has life,
> and has committed himself to me in faith,
> shall not die for ever.
> As for me, I know that my Redeemer lives
> and that at the last he will stand upon the earth.
> After my awaking, he will raise me up;
> and in my body I shall see God.
> I myself shall see, and my eyes behold him
> who is my friend and not a stranger.
> For none of us has life in himself,
> and none becomes his own master when he dies.
> For if we have life, we are alive in the Lord,

and if we die, we die in the Lord.
So, then, whether we live or die,
we are the Lord's possession.
Happy from now on
are those who die in the Lord!
So it is, says the Spirit,
for they rest from their labors.
In the midst of life we are in death;
from whom can we seek help?
From you alone, O Lord,
who by our sins are justly angered.
Holy God, Holy and Mighty,
Holy and merciful Savior,
deliver us not into the bitterness of eternal death.
Lord, you know the secrets of our hearts;
shut not your ears to our prayers,
but spare us, O Lord.
Holy God, Holy and Mighty,
Holy and merciful Savior,
deliver us not into the bitterness of eternal death.
O worthy and eternal Judge,
do not let the pains of death
turn us away from you at our last hour.
Holy God, Holy and Mighty,
Holy and merciful Savior,
deliver us not into the bitterness of eternal death.

Add to these Ps 23, the passages from the Gospel of John about the many rooms/mansions in the Father's house, the raising of Lazarus, the promise that whoever eats the bread of life will live forever, the words of the Lord's Prayer/Our Father, and other beautiful litanies and prayers. Although the two factions were on a collision course at the cemetery, they had both heard these sacred words beforehand, in the funeral home. I remain aware of this decades later, having led the same service twice in the course of an hour, just as I have led such a service, either as an actual burial or as a memorial, so many other times over the last forty years, including for my own parents, one of my brothers, and my in-laws. Had the members of this family, fractured as they had become, not been moved by God speaking to them before this funeral and internment? Surely there had been baptisms, weddings, and funerals before, not to mention candle-lit Christmases and lily-bedecked Easters. Looking back at what could have become a real melee years ago, I can hope that something was heard in those services.

This makes me think of all the times I have celebrated a wedding service and occasionally the rite of baptism. Most of the time, these rites of passage—baptism, weddings, and funerals—fell to the rector. As an associate, I did preach at and celebrate or concelebrate the eucharistic liturgy on Sundays and feasts. It feels like some kind of act of blind faith to want to believe that the words not only cut their way into me but into those gathered, who also heard them, every person who put out her or his hands to receive "the body of Christ, the bread of life, the blood of Christ, the cup of salvation." I cannot help but think of those who were there to support the person baptized or wed, of those saying goodbye to a friend or family member and those who greeted each other at a Sunday mass, either during the exchange of peace in the service or at the coffee hour afterward.

PASTORAL EXPERIENCE: OVERCOMING A "BAD SELF"

The life of following Jesus and living out his good news does not halt at the end of either the Sunday service or the "liturgy after the liturgy," the parish coffee hour. As the pastor-theologians we have listened to affirm, faith has to be enacted in the everyday we inhabit. What we experience when gathered as a community on Sunday is as real and demanding of us Tuesday afternoon or Saturday morning, whether we are at home, at work, shopping, or anywhere else we go and anything else we do. This seemingly ordinary faith-in-action is what I have called "hidden holiness."[4] We can see it put into practice in the lives and words of Dorothy Day or Mother Maria Skobtsova, Desmond Tutu or Dietrich Bonhoeffer, or, today, in Bishop William Barber or Sister Helen Prejean.

One more vivid experience I had witnesses to the power for transformation that exists as a gift in the community that is church, specifically in the efforts of the pastors who preach and lead within. In a parish I served, a new member sat next to me at a regular potluck supper and we began to converse. As sometimes happens, the simple act of talking while eating became like the fellowship meals Jesus had nightly with his friends while traveling around Palestine, healing and preaching. All I had to do was listen and I was given a detailed account of a life with many twists and upheavals. Many of the pieces were bound together through reflections on parenthood;

4. Plekon, *Hidden Holiness*.

another unifying strand was her career as a medical professional. Not surprising, church had also been a constant in her life, though she had taken some breaks from regular participation. It did not take me long to learn that she was a lively, intelligent, much experienced professional who was also very happy to have discovered the parish; she was there both for the Sunday Eucharist and to begin to participate in other community activities like this shared supper.

In the better part of the hour and a half we spent eating and talking, I learned far more about her life than I would have in a formal interview, a phenomenon to which most priests can attest. She forewarned me that her fairly extreme right-wing politics were not a place to visit, which I took as a kindness, thinking she'd sensed I was on the opposite end of the political spectrum. She also added that she had learned not to inflict her politics on people, knowing that doing so would break relationships and make further connections difficult. Pastors are always very grateful for such a stance of mutual respect and a desire to keep open friendships and conversation.

Sometime later, at a Sunday coffee hour, I spontaneously invited this new parishioner to volunteer the next day at the parish's monthly hosting of a food bank. This was one of the major parish outreach activities; with a substantial truck delivery of nonperishables as well as produce and proteins, our food source was one of the best in the county. I was not prepared for the response I got—a barrage of anger about freeloaders, ingrates, and shiftless, lazy people who only wanted to take. Given our remote location and the demographics of the town, this description was completely inaccurate. Moreover, it ignored the enduring factors that created food insecurity, both for those whose low-income status was more visible as well as for many others, including seniors, who looked as middle class and respectable as the volunteers themselves. I realized I had not been thoughtful enough; I had not considered what I'd learned about this parishioner's politics and their social implications. I apologized quickly, saying I had not been very thoughtful in inviting her to partake in a day of hard work setting up stations and distributing food followed by breaking down the tables and transporting leftovers to the town resource facility, where they would be distributed in the food bank the next day. Later that day, in the afternoon, I got an email message. It was my parishioner, pleading for my forgiveness for her outburst. She said that it had been her "bad self" erupting, and I should count on her being there as a volunteer the next day. The next day, there she was, absolutely bonding with the other volunteers, some of whom she knew from church, others she knew from town, and still others she was meeting for the first time. The two of us worked a station where we distributed frozen meat and tortillas, where her genuine social gifts were apparent in her ebullient laughter and banter. She could not help but show her joy all through the day, and she then told me what a great thing it was, the food bank, and how wrong she was to reject and criticize it simply on principle, because it was a giveaway to those in need. It occurred to me that what I saw that day through her transformation was the emergence of the deeper identity of someone who had spent years treating patients, offering care, and healing in a long medical career. In subsequent food banks, we continued to work together, gravitating to the same station.

Not long before this interaction, this same fellow parishioner had engaged in a dialogue from the *Book of Common Prayer* at a church service that I will share here.

Bishop	Will you continue in the apostles' teaching and fellowship, in the breaking of bread, and in the prayers?
People	I will, with God's help.
Bishop	Will you persevere in resisting evil, and, whenever you fall into sin, repent and return to the Lord?
People	I will, with God's help.
Bishop	Will you proclaim by word and example the good news of God in Christ?
People	I will, with God's help.
Bishop	Will you seek and serve Christ in all persons, loving your neighbor as yourself?
People	I will, with God's help.
Bishop	Will you strive for justice and peace among all people, and respect the dignity of every human being?
People	I will, with God's help.[5]

After, there was a blessing and exchange of peace to welcome new members into both the parish and the larger church. My fellow food bank volunteer was one of those welcomed and received; she had heard these words and responded, she had been blessed and then greeted by the rest of the congregation that Sunday. As with the words read and prayed at the funeral and internment and at so many other services, I believe that there was a

5. *Book of Common Prayer*, 417.

sacrament present and active in this exchange, one of transformation and ongoing growth in Christ. She had seemed to experience an "epiphany" of change, moving from the rage of a "bad self" to the joy of being and working together with sisters and brothers at the food bank.

I hope you can see the point. There are so many aspects of the small scenes of pastoral ministry both in the example of the parishioner at the food bank as well as in the funeral and internment that invite reflection. Although feeding hungry people may not appear to be very religious or spiritual, even if the food bank starts with a prayer—there are no hymns, readings, or prayers; there is no exchange of the peace or communion with bread and wine—it is liturgy if ever there was liturgy. Liturgy emanates from the thanksgiving expressed on the part of the volunteers and the gratitude explicitly expressed by those receiving the food; it manifests in the sense, at the end of a long, tiring day, of having spent good time with good people, in the rapport among the volunteers, and in the smiles of those coming for food, many of whom are known to those of us volunteering.

This small piece of my pastoral experience enables me to lift up the reality that to be a priest, a pastor, means to not just see conversion and change but to sometimes unknowingly be an agent of such transformation. This does not occur through any intent or special gift but simply because the pastor does what the Good Pastor or Shepherd does—or at least is supposed to!

That the Spirit, acting in what I did as a priest, was heard and experienced is for me an act of faith, hope, and love. Perhaps, in the end, that is what all the writers we have listened to would say. In addition to all I tried to summarize, the ordained and their ministry are agents of faith, hope, and love. From Nicholas Afanasiev to Will Willimon; George Keith to Nadia Bolz-Weber; Barbara Brown Taylor to Sam Wells and Sarah Coakley; Henri Nouwen to Rowan Williams and Pope Francis, and all of my other friends and colleagues in different church bodies and parishes, all of them—whether bishops, pastors, or deacons—have prayed and proclaimed the same words as I have, at the same rites and passage points, Sundays and feasts. All of them have, I think, had to make the same acts of faith, hope, and love, trusting that the Father heard those words, that the Son spoke and acted through them, as did the Holy Spirit, and that the people of God heard this good news. We have all known, in our moments of clarity and grace, that whenever we have recited these words, we echo thousands of other pastors through the last two thousand years into a third millennium.

It does not matter whether there are a handful or a packed church receiving them. We know that the entire communion of saints, all those named and recognized and the millions of others who are not, are present whenever we gather to pray, hear the Scriptures, and share the bread and cup.

In *Community as Church*, I argued that the central motif of the Christian faith is death and resurrection. This is echoed when one enters the community through baptism and confirmation/chrismation. It is proclaimed at the side of one who is ill, whether at home or in a hospital; it is reiterated at the graveside, and it is even stressed when two people are starting a life together. As God knows, people will experience death and resurrection many times. In effect, in the eucharistic liturgy, central to the memory and reenactment are the death, resurrection, ascension, and glorious second coming of the Lord.

Put differently, these words and actions are not just hopeful thrusts into the void or aspirations in a bleak, secular, indifferent landscape. Alexander Schmemann was but one of several contemporary students of liturgy and life to recognize that the world is a sacrament, as is life.[6] These are not just the words of an institution. Their sacramental reality extends far beyond where a more scholastic precision strove to locate it. The Eucharist starts when people awaken and get washed and dressed to gather at church. It continues long after the service, into Monday morning and Friday evening. The idea that merely asserting certain beliefs or maintaining particular ecclesial structures and liturgical rites will stop the decline in church attendance and perhaps even affect "church growth" is unrealistic. Denial of decline and shrinkage is delusion. Refuting this and related claims were the purpose of what I gathered, reported on, and argued in *Community as Church*.

Here, at the conclusion of *Ministry Matters*, I confess that I did wonder whether trying to look at the lives and ministry of the ordained after having looked at the church as community was necessary, worthwhile, or even doable. I had no stomach for reciting once more all the numbers about clergy who had called it quits within five years of ordination, reflecting the rate of priest burnout that is associated with blaming them for shrinkage, decline, and the divided world they have had no role in creating. While I was excited to discuss the return to ancient mentoring and community-focused, service-based liturgy stressed in nonresidential formation programs for ordination, I was not so enthusiastic that many church bodies were still

6. Plekon, "Liturgy of Life"; Plekon, *World as Sacrament*.

stuck on worn out models of ministry education. I was saddened by the rigidity of contemporary institutional religious administrators and their inability to bring canons and statutes to life. I myself had gotten caught in the machinery of adversarial church officials and punitive measures imposed without cause.

However, I have found that returning to a method close to the spirit of *lectio divina*—reading slowly, listening carefully, and reflecting deeply on what some of the real masters of ministry and true teachers of pastoral life and work have said—has for sure been more than rewarding for me personally. These pastor-theologians have reinforced many things in my previous book's exploration of church today. They have also affirmed the larger vision that church is community, showing the crucial roles of those set apart and ordained to serve the people of God.

Bibliography

Acta Synodalia Sacrosancti Concilii Oecumenici Vaticani Secundi. Vatican City: Cura et Studio Archivi Concilii Oecumenici Vaticani II, 1971.

Afanasiev, Nicholas. *The Church of the Holy Spirit.* Edited by Vitaly Permiakov. Notre Dame: University of Notre Dame Press, 2007.

———. *Ecclesiology: Initiation of Laity into Clerical Orders.* St. Sergius Institute course, 1950.

Afanassieff, Marianne. "La genèse de L'Église du Saint-Esprit." In *L'Église du Saint-Esprit,* by Nicolas Afanassieff, 12–23. Paris: Cerf, 1975.

Ambrose of Milan. *On the Duties of the Clergy.* Savage, MN: Lighthouse Christian, 2013.

Arjakovsky, Antoine. *The Way: Religious Thinkers of the Russian Emigration in Paris and Their Journal 1925–1940.* Edited by John A. Jillions and Michael Plekon. Translated by Jerry Ryan. Notre Dame: University of Notre Dame Press, 2013.

Barber, William J. *The Third Reconstruction: How a Moral Movement Is Overcoming the Politics of Division and Fear.* Boston: Beacon, 2016.

Barna Group. "38% of U.S. Pastors Have Thought about Quitting Full-Time Ministry in the Past Year." *Barna,* November 16, 2021. https://www.barna.com/research/pastors-well-being/.

Barnhart, Dave. "Methodist House Churches: An Introduction." *Ministry Matters,* June 8, 2018. https://www.ministrymatters.com/all/entry/9050/methodist-house-churches-an-introduction.

———. "Travel, Faith, and the Environment." *Dave Barnhart* (blog), January 9, 2023. https://davebarnhart.wordpress.com.

Becker, Amy Julia. "Hillsong Was Extraordinary. That Was the Problem." *Religion News Service,* June 2, 2023. https://religionnews.com/2023/06/02/hillsong-was-extraordinary-thats-the-problem/.

Bolz-Weber, Nadia. *Accidental Saints: Finding God in All the Wrong People.* New York: Convergent, 2015.

———. "Enjoy Your Forgiveness: A Sermon on Prisons and Empty Promises." *The Corners* (blog), January 9, 2023. https://thecorners.substack.com/p/enjoy-your-forgiveness.

———. *Pastrix: The Cranky, Beautiful Faith of a Saint & Sinner.* New York: Worthy, 2013.

———. *Shameless: A Sexual Reformation.* New York: Convergent, 2019.

Bonhoeffer, Dietrich. *Ethics.* Minneapolis: Fortress, 2005.

The Book of Common Prayer. New York: Seabury, 1979.

Brown, Raymond. *The Churches the Apostles Left Behind.* Mahwah, NJ: Paulist, 1984.

Bullivant, Stephen. *Nonverts: The Making of Ex-Christian America.* New York: Oxford University Press, 2022.

Caimano, Cathie. "Church Stats to Smile About." *Free Range Priest* (blog), August 17, 2022. https://blog.freerangepriest.org/church-stats-to-smile-about/.

———. "5 Church Words I'm No Longer Using." *Free Range Priest* (blog), May 17, 2022. https://blog.freerangepriest.org/5-church-words/.

———. *Free Range Priest: Ordained Ministry Reimagined in the 21st Century.* Self-published, Lulu.com, 2017.

———. "Free Range Priests Solve Traditional Church Problems." *Faith & Leadership*, March 19, 2019. https://www.faithandleadership.com/catherine-caimano-free-range-priests -solve-traditional-church-problems?utm_source=albanweekly&utm_ medium=content&utm_campaign=faithleadership.

———. "How Quiet Quitting Changes the Church." *Free Range Priest* (blog), August 31, 2022. https://blog.freerangepriest.org/quiet-quitting-church/.

———. "'Tentmaker,' 'Non-Stipendiary,' and 'Bi-Vocational.'" Church Pension Group (blog), June 7, 2022. https://blog.freerangepriest.org/bi-vocational/.

Candler School of Theology, Emory University. "Emory University's Candler School of Theology to Launch Hybrid MDiv in Fall 2023." *Episcopal News Service*, February 28, 2023. https://www.episcopalnewsservice.org/pressreleases/emory-universitys-candler-school-of-theology-to-launch-hybrid-mdiv-in-fall-2023/.

Chrysostom, John. *On the Priesthood.* Crestwood, NY: St. Vladimir's Seminary Press, 1996.

Church Pension Group. "Trends in Ministry: Insights into Episcopal Clergy | Church Pension Group." *YouTube*, July 25, 2022. https://www.youtube.com/ watch?v=wdgUnL7IRHQ.

———. *The 2020 Episcopal Clergy Compensation Report.* New York: Church Pension Group, October 2021.

Church Pension Group, Research and Data Team. "Trends in Ministry: Insights into Episcopal Clergy." https://www.cpg.org/globalassets/documents/publications/ research-2022-trends-in-ministry-webinar-presentation-slides.pdf.

Coakley, Sarah. *God, Sexuality and the Self: An Essay "On the Trinity."* Cambridge: Cambridge University Press, 2013.

———. "How My Mind Has Changed: Prayer as Crucible." *Christian Century*, March 22, 2011. https://www.christiancentury.org/article/2011-03/prayer-crucible.

———. "Meditation Is Subversive." *Christian Century*, June 29, 2004.

———. *The New Asceticism: Sexuality, Gender and the Quest for God.* London: Bloomsbury Continuum, 2015.

———. *Powers and Submissions: Spirituality, Philosophy and Gender.* Oxford: Blackwell, 2002.

———. "Prayer as Crucible." *Christian Century*, March 22, 2011. https://www. christiancentury.org/article/2011-03/prayer-crucible.

———. "Prayer, Place and the Poor." Introduction to *Praying for England*, edited by Samuel Wells and Sarah Coakley, 1–20. London: Continuum, 2008.

Coakley, Sarah, and Paul L. Gavrilyuk, eds. *The Spiritual Senses: Perceiving God in Western Christianity.* Cambridge: Cambridge University Press, 2012.

Coakley, Sarah, and SueJeanne Koh. "Prayer as Divine Propulsion: An Interview with Sarah Coakley, Part I." *The Other Journal*, no. 21 (2012). https://theotherjournal. com/2012/12/20/prayer-as-divine-propulsion-an-interview-with-sarah-coakley/.

————. "Prayer as Divine Propulsion: An Interview with Sarah Coakley, Part II." *The Other Journal*, no. 21 (2012). https://theotherjournal.com/2012/12/20/prayer-as-divine-propulsion-an-interview-with-sarah-coakley-part-ii/.

Cozzens, Donald. *Notes from the Underground: The Spiritual Journal of a Secular Priest.* Maryknoll, NY: Orbis, 2013.

Croft, Steven S. *Ministry in Three Dimensions.* London: Darton, Longman & Todd, 1999.

Curry, Michael. *Love Is the Way: Holding onto Hope in Troubling Times.* New York: Avery/Penguin, 2020.

Dias, Elizabeth. "Barbara Brown Taylor." *Time*, April 23, 2014. https://time.com/70780/.

Dix, Gregory, ed. *The Treatise on the Apostolic Tradition of St. Hippolytus of Rome.* London: SPCK, 1968.

Doyle, C. Andrew. *Church: A Generous Community Amplified for the Future.* Alexandria: Virginia Theological Seminary Press, 2015.

————. *Vocātio: Imaging a Visible Church.* New York: Church Publishing, 2018.

Duffy, Eamon. *A People's Tragedy: Studies in Reformation.* London: Bloomsbury, 2021.

————. *Reformation Divided: Catholics, Protestants and the Conversion of England.* London: Bloomsbury, 2017.

————. *The Stripping of the Altars: Traditional Religion in England.* New Haven: Yale University Press, 1992.

Evdokimov, Paul. *In the World, of the Church: A Paul Evdokimov Reader.* Edited by Michael Plekon. Translated by Alexis Vinogradov. Crestwood, NY: Oakwood/St. Vladimir's Seminary Press, 2001.

Ford, Michael. *Lonely Mystic: A New Portrait of Henry J. M. Nouwen.* Mahwah, NJ: Paulist, 2018.

————. *Wounded Prophet: A Portrait of Henri J. M. Nouwen.* New York: Doubleday/Image, 1999.

Francis, Pope. *With the Smell of the Sheep: The Pope Speaks to Priests, Bishops, and Other Shepherds.* Maryknoll, NY: Orbis, 2017.

Francis, Pope, et al. "Joint Declaration of His Holiness Bartholomew, Archbishop of Athens and All Greece and of His Holiness Pope Francis." https://www.vatican.va/content/francesco/en/speeches/2016/april/documents/papa-francesco_20160416_lesvos-dichiarazione-congiunta.html.

Gallaher, Brandon. "Bulgakov and Intercommunion." *Sobornost* 24, no. 2 (2002) 9–28.

Gillet, Archimandrite Lev. "Love without Limits." https://www.oca.org/reflections/archimandrite-lev-gillet.

Gregory the Great. *The Book of Pastoral Rule.* Crestwood, NY: St. Vladimir's Seminary Press, 2007.

Grose, Jessica. "Christianity's Got a Branding Problem." *New York Times*, May 10, 2023. https://www.nytimes.com/2023/05/10/opinion/christian-religion-brand-nones.html.

————. "The Largest and Fastest Religious Shift in America Is Well Underway." *New York Times*, June 21, 2023. https://www.nytimes.com/2023/06/21/opinion/religion-dechurching.html.

————. "Lots of Americans Are Losing Their Religion. Have You?" *New York Times*, April 19, 2023. https://www.nytimes.com/2023/04/19/opinion/religion-america.html.

————. "What Churches Offer that 'Nones' Still Long For." *New York Times*, June 28, 2023. https://www.nytimes.com/2023/06/28/opinion/religion-affiliation-community.html?searchResultPosition=2.

———. "Why Do People Lose Their Religion? More than 7,000 Readers Shared Their Stories." *New York Times*, June 7, 2023. https://www.nytimes.com/2023/06/07/opinion/religion-nones.html.

Gross, Edie. "The Great Resignation: Are Pastors Resigning, Redefining or Re-Evaluating?" *Faith and Leadership*, July 26, 2022. https://faithandleadership.com/the-great-resignation-are-pastors-resigning-redefining-or-reevaluating.

Gushee, David P. "Why Is Christianity Declining?" *Religious News Service*, September 6, 2016. http://religionnews.com/2016/09/06/why-is-christianity-declining/.

Hackel, Sergei. *Pearl of Great Price: The Life of Mother Maria Skobtsova 1891–1945*. Crestwood, NY: St. Vladimir's Seminary Press, 1981.

Harvard Institute for Religion Research. "Navigating the Pandemic: A First Look at Congregational Responses." https://www.covidreligionresearch.org/research/national-survey-research/navigating-the-pandemic-a-first-look/.

Hicks, Sally. "Michael Plekon: Stories Tell You about the Struggle to Keep Being the Church." *Faith & Leadership*, November 26, 2021. https://faithandleadership.com/michael-plekon-stories-tell-you-about-the-struggle-keep-being-the-church.

Higgins, Michael W., and Kevin Burns. *Genius Born of Anguish: The Life and Legacy of Henri Nouwen*. Mahwah, NJ: Paulist, 2012.

Holland, Tom. *Dominion: How the Christian Revolution Remade the World*. New York: Basic, 2019.

Holloway, Richard. *Leaving Alexandria: A Memoir of Faith and Doubt*. Edinburgh: Canongate, 2012.

International Theological Commission. "Synodality in the Life and Mission of the Church." https://www.vatican.va/roman_curia/congregations/cfaith/cti_documents/rc_cti_20180302_sinodalita_en.html.

Jenson, Robert W. *Systematic Theology*. Vol. 1, *The Triune God*. New York: Oxford University Press, 2001.

———. *Systematic Theology*. Vol. 2, *The Works of God*. New York: Oxford University Press, 2001.

Jillions, John A. *Divine Guidance: Lessons for Today from the World of Early Christianity*. New York: Oxford University Press, 2020.

John XXIII, Pope. "Humanae Salutis §4." In *The Encyclicals and Other Messages of Pope John XXIII*, translated by Austin Vaughn, 387. Acta Apostolicae Sedis 6. Vatican City, 1962.

Julig, Carina. "Headed for a Larger Stage, Nadia Bolz-Weber Leaves Her 'House' in Order." *Religion News Service*, August 5, 2018. https://religionnews.com/2018/08/05/headed-for-a-larger-stage-nadia-bolz-weber-leaves-her-house-in-order-2/.

Luther, Martin. "Apology of the Augsburg Confession." In *The Book of Concord*, edited by Robert Kolb and Timothy J. Wengert, 220–30. Minneapolis: Fortress, 2000.

MacCulloch, Diarmaid. *All Things Made New: The Reformation and Its Legacy*. New York: Oxford University Press, 2017.

———. *The Reformation: A History*. New York: Viking, 2004.

McLaren, Brian. *Faith after Doubt: Why Your Beliefs Stopped Working and What to Do about It*. New York: St. Martin's, 2021.

Melosh, Barbara. *Loving and Leaving a Church: A Pastor's Journey*. Louisville: Westminster John Knox, 2018.

Merton, Thomas. *The Sign of Jonas*. New York: Image, 1956.

Miles, Sara. *City of God: Faith in the Streets*. New York: Jericho, 2014.

———. *Jesus Freak: Feeding Healing Raising the Dead.* San Francisco: Jossey-Bass, 2010.

———. *Take This Bread: A Radical Conversion.* New York: Ballantine, 2007.

Miller, Emily McFarlan. "Nadia Bolz-Weber Installed as ELCA's First Pastor of Public Witness." *Episcopal News Service*, August 24, 2021. https://www.episcopalnewsservice. org/2021/08/24/nadia-bolz-weber-installed-as-elcas-first-pastor-of-public-witness/.

Miller, Emily McFarlan, and Adele Banks. "#Pandemic Pastoring Reports a New Era in Ministry." *Religion News Service*, September 1, 2022. https://religionnews.com/2022 /09/01/pandemicpastoring-report-documents-a-new-era-in-ministry/.

Mills, William. *Losing My Religion: A Memoir of Faith and Finding.* Eugene, OR: Resource, 2019.

Montefiore, Simon Sebag. *Jerusalem: The Biography.* New York: Random House, 2011.

Neuman, Scott. "The Faithful See Both Crisis and Opportunity as Churches Close across the Country." *Oregon Public Broadcasting*, May 17, 2023. https://www.opb.org/article /2023/05/17/the-faithful-see-both-crisis-and-opportunity-as-churches-close-across-the-country/.

Nichols, Aidan. *Theology in the Russian Diaspora: Church, Fathers, Eucharist in Nikolai Afanas'ev, 1893–1966.* Cambridge: University of Cambridge Press, 1989.

Nouwen, Henri. *In the Name of Jesus: Reflections on Christian Leadership.* Chestnut Ridge, NY: Crossroad, 1989.

Oakes, Kaya. *The Nones Are Alright: A New Generation of Believers, Seekers, and Those in Between.* Maryknoll, NY: Orbis, 2015.

O'Laughlin, Michael. *God's Beloved: A Spiritual Biography of Henri Nouwen.* Maryknoll, NY: Orbis, 2004.

Paul VI, Pope. "*Presbyterorum Ordinis*: Decree on the Ministry and Life of Priests." Promulgated on December 7, 1965. https://www.vatican.va/archive/hist_councils/ ii_vatican_council/documents/vat-ii_decree_19651207_presbyterorum-ordinis_ en.html.

Peterson, Eugene H. *The Message: The Bible in Contemporary Language.* Colorado Springs: NavPress, 2005.

Plekon, Michael. *Community as Church, Church as Community.* Eugene, OR: Cascade, 2021.

———. *Hidden Holiness.* Notre Dame: University of Notre Dame Press, 2009.

———. "Holy Tables, Living Icons: How a Serbian Orthodox Congregation in Kansas City Offers Hospitality beyond Liturgy." *Christian Century*, September 22, 2021. https:// www.christiancentury.org/article/features/how-serbian-orthodox-congregation -kansas-city-offers-hospitality-beyond-liturgy.

———. "The Liturgy of Life: Alexander Schmemann." *Religions* 7, no. 11 (2016) 127. https://doi.org/10.3390/rel7110127.

———. *Saints as They Really Are: Voices of Holiness in Our Time.* Notre Dame: University of Notre Dame Press, 2012.

———, ed. *Tradition Alive: On the Church and the Christian Life in Our Time, Readings from the Eastern Church.* Lanham, MD: Rowman & Littlefield, 2003.

———. *Uncommon Prayer: Prayer in Everyday Experience.* Notre Dame: University of Notre Dame Press, 2016.

———. *The World as Sacrament: An Ecumenical Path toward a Worldly Spirituality.* Collegeville, MN: Liturgical, 2017.

Plekon, Michael, et al., eds. *The Church Has Left the Building: Faith, Parish, and Ministry in the Twenty-First Century.* Eugene, OR: Cascade, 2016.

Post, Kathryn. "Churches Become Art Hubs as Space-Sharing Website Offers Congregations Off-Hours Revenue." *Episcopal News Service*, August 11, 2022. https://www.episcopalnewsservice.org/2022/08/11/churches-become-art-hubs-as-space-sharing-brings-congregations-off-hours-revenue/.

Rieff, Philip. *The Triumph of the Therapeutic: Uses of Faith after Freud*. Chicago: University of Chicago Press, 1987.

Roberts, Alexander, and James Donaldson, eds. *The Ante-Nicene Fathers*. Vol. 5, *The Fathers of the Third Century*. New York: Scribner, 1907.

Robinson, Marilynne. *Gilead: A Novel*. New York: Farrar, Straus & Giroux, 2004.

———. *Home: A Novel*. New York: Farrar, Straus & Giroux, 2008.

———. *Lila: A Novel*. New York: Farrar, Straus & Giroux, 2014.

Rohr, Richard. *Falling Upward: A Spirituality for the Two Halves of Life*. San Francisco: Jossey-Bass, 2013.

———. *Immortal Diamond: The Search for Our True Self*. San Francisco: Jossey-Bass, 2013.

———. *The Universal Christ: How a Forgotten Reality Can Change Everything We See, Hope for, and Believe*. New York: Convergent, 2021.

Root, Andrew. *Church after Innovation: Questioning Our Obsession with Work, Creativity, and Entrepreneurship*. Grand Rapids: Baker Academic, 2022.

———. *Churches after the Crisis of Decline: A Hopeful, Practical Ecclesiology for a Secular Age*. Grand Rapids: Baker Academic, 2022.

———. *Faith Formation in a Secular Age: Responding to the Church's Obsession with Youthfulness*. Ministry in a Secular Age 1. Grand Rapids: Baker Academic, 2017.

———. *Pastor in a Secular Age: Ministry to People Who No Longer Need a God*. Grand Rapids: Baker Academic, 2019.

Root, Andrew, and Blair D. Bertrand. *When Church Stops Working: A Future for Your Congregation Beyond More Money, Programs, and Innovation*. Grand Rapids: Brazos, 2023.

Saint John's Cathedral. "Choral Eucharist May 21 2023." *Vimeo*, May 21, 2023. https://vimeo.com/828787008?utm_source=substack&utm_medium=email.

Schlesinger, Eugene. "Called to Be More." Review of *Vocātio: Imaging a Visible Church*, by C. Andrew Doyle. *The Living Church*, March 1, 2019. https://livingchurch.org/2019/03/01/called-to-be-more/.

Shapiro, Tim, and Kara Faris. *Divergent Church: The Bright Promise of Alternative Faith Communities*. Nashville: Abingdon, 2017.

St. Augustine. "Sermon 272." https://stanselminstitute.org/files/Augustine,%20Sermon%2020272.pdf.

Steinke, Darcey. *Easter Everywhere: A Memoir*. New York: Bloomsbury, 2007.

St. Irenaeus of Lyons. *Against Heresies* [*Adversus Haereses*]. Rev. ed. Edited by Alexander Roberts and James Donaldson. Jackson, MI: Ex Fontibus, 2017.

Taylor, Barbara Brown. *An Altar in the World: A Geography of Faith*. New York: HarperOne, 2010.

———. *Always a Guest: Speaking of Faith Far from Home*. Louisville: Westminster John Knox, 2020.

———. *Holy Envy: Finding God in the Faith of Others*. New York: HarperOne, 2019.

———. *Learning to Walk in the Dark*. New York: HarperOne, 2014.

———. *Leaving Church: A Memoir of Faith*. New York: HarperOne, 2006.

Taylor, Charles. *A Secular Age*. Cambridge, MA: Belknap, 2007.

Van Gennep, Arnold. *Rites of Passage.* 2nd ed. Chicago: University of Chicago Press, 2019.

Warren, Tish Harrison. "Why Churches Should Drop Their Online Services." *New York Times*, January 30, 2022. https://www.nytimes.com/2022/01/30/opinion/church-online-services-covid.html?searchResultPosition=67.

Wells, Samuel. *A Future That's Bigger than the Past: Catalysing Kingdom Communities.* London: Canterbury, 2019.

———. "Imagination." In *Praying for England: Priestly Presence in Contemporary Culture*, edited by Samuel Wells and Sarah Coakley, 65–84. London: Continuum, 2008.

———. *Incarnational Ministry: Being with the Church.* Grand Rapids: Eerdmans, 2017.

———. *Incarnational Mission: Being with the World.* Grand Rapids: Eerdmans, 2018.

———. "It's about Abundant Life, Not Hell-Avoidance." *Church Times*, October 6, 2017. https://www.churchtimes.co.uk/articles/2017/6-october/comment/opinion/it-s-about-abundant-life-not-hell-avoidance.

———. *Learning to Dream Again: Rediscovering the Heart of God.* Grand Rapids: Eerdmans, 2013.

———. *A Nazareth Manifesto: Being with God.* Chichester, UK: Wiley Blackwell, 2015.

Wells, Samuel, and Ben Quash. *Introducing Christian Ethics.* Chichester, UK: Wiley Blackwell, 2010.

Williams, Hattie. "Chelmsford Set to Cut 60 Stipendiary Posts." *Church Times*, June 12, 2020. https://www.churchtimes.co.uk/media/5669489/8204_12-june-2020_nvrte.pdf.

Williams, Rowan. Afterword to *For God's Sake: Reimagining Priesthood and Prayer in a Changing Church*, edited by Jessica Martin and Sarah Coakley, 178–82. Norfolk, UK: Canterbury, 2007.

———. Epilogue to *Praying for England: Priestly Presence in Contemporary Culture*, edited by Samuel Wells and Sarah Coakley, 171–82. London: Continuum, 2008.

Willimon, William H. *Pastor: The Theology and Practice of Ordained Ministry.* Rev. ed. Nashville: Abingdon, 2016.

Woerman, Melodie. "Bexley-Seabury Launches Competency Based Theological Education Program to Prepare Leaders to Minister in Context." *Episcopal News Service*, March 3, 2023. https://www.episcopalnewsservice.org/2023/03/03/bexley-seabury-launches-competency-based-theological-education-program-to-prepare-leaders-to-minister-in-context/.

Wooden, Anastacia. "Eucharistic Ecclesiology of Nicolas Afanasiev and Its Ecumenical Significance: A New Perspective." *Journal of Ecumenical Studies* 45 (2010) 543–60.

———. "The Limits of the Church: The Ecclesiological Project of Nicolas Afanasiev." PhD diss., Catholic University of America, 2018.

———. *Recovering the Eucharistic Ecclesiology of the Early Church: An Introduction to Nicolas Afanasiev.* Washington, DC: Catholic University of America Press, forthcoming.

Worthy, Ariel. "Pastor Dave Barnhart on What Love Looks Like in Public." *Birmingham Times*, October 11, 2018. http://www.birminghamtimes.com/2018/10/pastor-david-barnhart-on-what-love-looks-like-in-public/.